Also available:

Aronsson: *The Development of Sustainable Tourism*
Bray and Raitz: *Flight to the Sun*
Clift and Carter (eds): *Tourism and Sex*
Foley and Lennon: *Dark Tourism*
Godfrey and Clarke: *The Tourism Development Handbook*
Hudson: *Snow Business*
Julyan: *Sales and Service for the Wine Professional*
Law: *Urban Tourism*
Leask and Yeoman (eds): *Heritage Visitor Attractions*
Lee-Ross (ed.): *HRM in Tourism and Hospitality*
Tribe *et al.*: *Environmental Management for Rural Tourism and Recreation*
Van der Wagen and Davies: *Supervision and Leadership in Tourism and Hospitality*
Wright: *The Management of Service Operations*

Tourism in Latin America

Les Lumsdon and Jonathan Swift

CONTINUUM
London and New York

Continuum

The Tower Building, 11 York Road, London SE1 7NX

370 Lexington Avenue, New York, NY 10017-6503

www.continuumbooks.com

First published 2001

British Library Cataloguing-in-Publication Data

A catalogue record for this book is available from the British Library.

ISBN 0-8264-5147-0 (hb)
        0-8264-5148-9 (pb)

Typeset by BookEns Ltd, Royston, Herts
Printed and bound in Great Britain by The Cromwell Press, Trowbridge, Wilts.

Contents

Figures

Tables

Acknowledgements

The authors wish to thank the many Latin American tourism departments and numerous tour operators who have given generously of their time to discuss tourism development in Latin America. These discussions have been invaluable to the authors in the shaping of this book.

Introduction

The book sets out to explore the tourism offering of Latin America and to look at the future potential of this vast continent. Whilst it is not intended to be a geographical study, nor an anthropological survey, political overview, or cultural analysis, it draws on a wide range of interdisciplinary research in order to provide an overview of Latin America.

The book presents an integrated approach to tourism in Latin America. It has three major aims:

1 to offer an introductory, but nevertheless comprehensive text about a region which is developing tourism for a global market.
2 to introduce the core principles which underpin the business of tourism and to apply them to tourism in Latin America.
3 to discuss the major issues and particularly the impacts of tourism in the countries of Latin America.

As the authors suggest in the first part of the book, Latin America has an exceptional natural resource, and to this end, most governments seek to exploit tourism as a form of economic development. There are, of course, considerable social and environmental impacts. To this end, the book focuses on an analysis of the tourism offering, the governmental and non-governmental sector involvement in the tourism industry and the markets which generate visitors.

The text is divided into three main parts:

1 An Overview of Latin America, which includes a brief geographical and historical description of the region, in addition to an evaluation of the economic contribution of tourism to the economy.
2 The Tourism Offering, which analyses the main components of tourism in Latin America. This sectoral analysis comprises an evaluation of public/private sector involvement in tourism development, plus a discussion of the key offerings – beach tourism, nature-based tourism, cultural and urban tourism.

3 Issues in Tourism Development. This section examines the key impacts which arise as a consequence of the tourism system in Latin America and assesses their level of significance in relation to the wider social, environmental and economic issues facing the various Latin American countries.

Thus, the book is a study of tourism from the point of view of business and is primarily designed to meet the needs of students of tourism and hospitality. It should, however, also be of use to those studying the geography of tourism, international business (especially if it includes developing countries), and Hispanic or Latin American Studies. It seeks to present tourism in Latin America in a holistic manner, for only by embracing different perspectives can the reader even begin to understand the complexity of the region and the myriad of problems and possibilities faced by the nations that comprise the region known as Latin America.

It is also important to appreciate that this is an introductory text, which offers an insight into the processes and structures that comprise the tourism system throughout Latin America. Wherever possible, a range of detailed and advanced literature has been provided to enable the reader to explore particular issues or topics in greater depth.

PART 1

Latin America: An Overview

CHAPTER 1

Introduction to Latin America

WHAT IS LATIN AMERICA?

Introduction

The term 'Latin America' is often used by tourism suppliers to denote a particular destination; however, a review of the literature reveals some degree of uncertainty as to its precise meaning. Some definitions include all those countries to the south of the Rio Grande (USA), whilst others incorporate Mexico in North America. A number of sources divide South America from the remainder, whilst others group Central America and the Caribbean together. Others base their grouping on language, referring to 'Spanish America', or 'Hispanic America' which includes Brazil.

Latin America is perhaps best referred to as a politico-cultural, rather than a geographical division: it encompasses all those independent states situated in the Americas that have historical-cultural links with Spain or Portugal. It is this historical-cultural background that distinguishes these nations from others in the American land mass.

As Niedergang points out, Latin American nations are more easily defined on the basis of their historical, political, cultural, economic and social characteristics (1971, p. 7). Thus, Guyana (ex-British) and Surinam (ex-Dutch) are excluded as they have followed very different patterns of socio-cultural development from those of their immediate Venezuelan and Brazilian neighbours. French Guyana is also excluded from this analysis of Latin America, as it is still officially classified as a French overseas territory. Belize is excluded because, historically, it was a British colonial territory.

Unlike the Central American and South American land masses, which were colonized principally by the Spanish and Portuguese, the Caribbean has been subjected to far wider historical-cultural influences. Many of the islands were colonial possessions of either Great Britain (Jamaica), France

(Guadeloupe) or the Netherlands (Netherlands Antilles). Others, such as Puerto Rico, have come under the control of the USA. There are really only two Caribbean islands that fall into the authors' definition of Latin American: Cuba and the Dominican Republic. Niedergang (1971) included Haiti in his definition, but the island is excluded in the present analysis owing to its historical connections with France and the fact that it is relatively insignificant in terms of both actual and potential tourism offering. Figure 1.1 shows Latin American nations in Central America and the Caribbean, whilst Figure 1.2 shows those Latin American nations situated in South America.

These are the countries that, in the present study, comprise Latin America. Details of land mass, population and capital cities are summarized in Table 1.1. A brief analysis of the table suggests that there is considerable diversity in terms of both land mass and population, ranging from the largest country, Brazil, to El Salvador, the smallest. Brazil also has the largest population: at 161 million, it is more than fifty times larger than that of Uruguay with just over 3 million people.

Table 1.1. The nations of Latin America: Land mass, population and capital city

Country	Land mass (sq. miles)	Population	Year	Capital city
Argentina	1,070,000	35,700,000	1998	Buenos Aires
Bolivia	424,162	7,414,000	1995	Sucre
Brazil	3,286,487	161,700,000	1998	Brasilia
Chile	292,257	14,210,429	1995	Santiago de Chile
Colombia	439,734	37,422,791	1993	Santafé de Bogotá
Costa Rica	19,652	3,333,223	1995	San José
Cuba	44,218	10,904,932	1993	La Habana
Dominican Republic	18,703	7,915,000	1995	Santo Domingo
Ecuador	106,178	11,698,496	1996	Quito
El Salvador	8,256	5,118,599	1992	San Salvador
Guatemala	42,042	10,621,226	1995	Ciudad Guatemala
Honduras	43,277	5,602,500	1995	Tegucigalpa
Mexico	762,530	96,500,000	1998	México D.F.
Nicaragua	57,145	4,539,000	1995	Managua
Panama	29,208	2,674,490	1996	Ciudad Panamá
Paraguay	57,000	4,828,000	1995	Ascunción
Peru	496,224	23,088,000	1994	Lima
Uruguay	72,172	3,186,000	1995	Montevideo
Venezuela	352,143	21,644,000	1995	Caracas

Sources: Nebrada Díaz de Espada (1996, p. 350), Europa Publications (1997), BTI (1999, p. 9), *Financial Times* (1999a; 1999b)

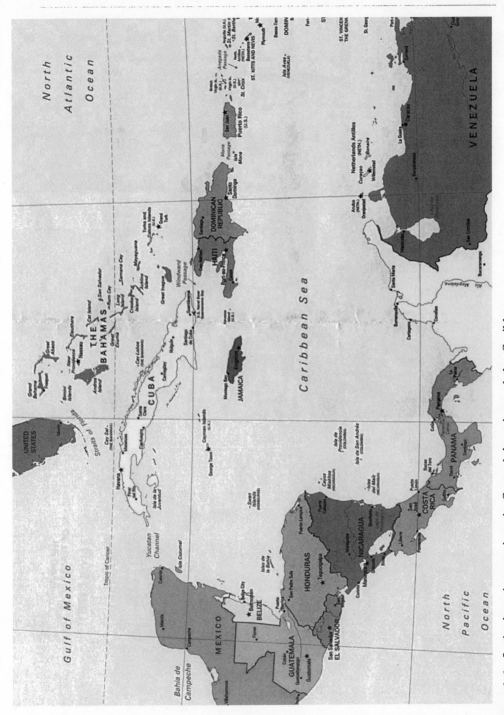

Figure 1.1. Latin American nations in Central America and the Caribbean

Figure 1.2. Latin American nations in South America

Terrain and Climate

The natural resources or physical attractions endowed in destination countries often form the main motivation to visit the region. Both landscape and climate are recognized as being fundamental assets in the development of the tourism offering (Seaton and Bennett, 1996, p. 360). The landscapes are immensely important world eco-systems of complex biological diversity, including the hydrological systems of the Amazonas, Orinocco, Paraná and Río de la Plata. Of great significance is the way in which relatively large tracts of land still remain virtually untouched by human development, particularly the tropical forests of the Amazonas. At the dawn of the twenty-first century, however, these areas are increasingly subject to degradation through all forms of development including tourism, particularly the Amazon region and the southern parts of Argentina and Chile – an issue that is raised later in the book.

In general terms the nations of Latin America encompass all climatic zones, from the arid deserts of Northern Mexico, through the Central American rainforest, to the Antarctic wastes of Tierra del Fuego in the south. Going east from Lima, a traveller would cross the magnificent Andean mountain range, passing through the clear air of the Peruvian-Bolivian *altiplano* region. Crossing into Brazil, the highlands of the Mato Grosso are reached, before descending into the tropical vegetation near Vitoria. Further to the north lies the vast Amazon jungle and to the south the *pampas* grasslands of Argentina, Uruguay and the Río Grande do Sul in Brazil. There are areas of desert near the sea, such as the Atacama in Northern Chile, and sub-tropical valleys surrounded by steep mountain ranges.

It is this diversity of terrain that accounts for the equally wide diversity of climatic conditions to be found throughout the region. Some areas (such as the Bogotá valley) enjoy the equivalent of a temperate spring for much of the year round, as in northern Europe or New England; others, by contrast, have a seasonal climate that varies considerably. Paraguay, for example, can be roughly divided into two zones: the Northwest and the Southeast, each with its own distinctive climate. (Box 1.A.) The climate in Paraguay contrasts with the

---

Box 1.A. Climate in Paraguay

The northwest of this landlocked country, the Chaco region, lies within the tropics and has very hot, wet and humid summers (October to March) and warm but drier winters ... In the southeast, summers are not quite as hot but are more rainy than in the north and winters are cooler because the terrain is higher. Rain increases the further east you go.

(Harding, 1996, p. 65)

Atacama Desert in northern Chile, parts of which receive no rainfall for years at a time. This region is described by the Chilean Tourism Promotion Corporation (TPC) as 'the world's driest desert' (TPC, 1996, p. 9). However, Cole points out that much further north, in Colombia, the same Pacific coastline receives between 6000 and 7000 mm. of rain a year (1970, p. 37). The climatic variation is considerable, and is a consequence of altitude, proximity to the sea and distance from the equator.

As a consequence of geographical location and terrain, some countries can offer the visitor extensive geographic and climatic variations entirely within their national boundaries. Chile represents the point well: to the north of the country lies the Atacama Desert, which is visited by neighbouring Bolivians and Peruvians, in addition to European visitors. Progressing south from the Atacama, there is a Mediterranean zone, where the major agricultural sectors are located and the capital, Santiago de Chile, is to be found.

Progressing further south the temperate zones are reached, where the climate and vegetation are more akin to that of northern Europe. Vast pine forests and numerous lakes give this region its name: 'The Lake District'. The whole region is bordered by the vast Andean mountain range to the east and the Pacific Ocean to the west. This area has been described by Hatchwell and Calder as: 'one of the most stunning parts of Chile, its landscape of mountains, lakes, volcanoes, waterfalls, primeval rainforest and white water rivers having a wild splendour' (1992, pp. 427–8).

At the southern extreme is the sparsely inhabited Tierra del Fuego and Patagonia, which, to this day, is considered one of the world's 'remotest regions' (Heywood, 1991). Patagonia is described by the Chilean authorities as 'The Silent South', and despite the overtly promotional emphasis, in essence its natural attractions form the major focus of the region's promotion. (See Box 1.B.) Taking an east–west cross-section of the country (centred on Santiago de Chile) gives another example of the climatic and physical diversity of Chile.

Box 1.B. Patagonia

South of the South, where silence reigns, the majestic landscapes and nature in all of its power are simply awe-inspiring. Pampa, mountains, lakes, rivers, forests running down to the water's edge, archipelagos, fjords, and glaciers flowing from the huge Campos de Hielos (ice-fields), succeed one another in an endless series. Here, where the ice of the glaciers plunges into the sea, the wind howls through every nook and cranny sculpturing fantastic shapes in the mountainside. Today, when nearly every corner of the world has been discovered and explored, Patagonia still silently waits.

(TPC, 1998, p. 2)

Viña del Mar, one of the premier Chilean Pacific ports, has a Mediterranean ambience, with palm-lined promenades and, as the name implies, a climate suitable for the cultivation of grapes.

Moving inland, the hilly, wooded terrain gives way to the fertile agricultural valley in which the capital, Santiago de Chile, is built. Rising up almost immediately to the east of the city are the foothills of the Andes. These lead to the massive mountain peaks, many of which remain snow covered throughout the year, and then to the border with Argentina, no more than 100 miles from the Pacific coast.

There are other countries with equally varied and interesting eco-systems, not only in South America, but also in the Central American isthmus: perhaps one of the most important of these is Costa Rica. As it encompasses a relatively small land mass and has both a Pacific and a Caribbean coastline, Costa Rica has a highly varied terrain and climate, which means that it is readily accessible to visitors at all times of the year. The country can be crossed by vehicle in a matter of hours, rather than days, and the variations in topography and climate have provided the potential for eco-tourism. The variations in climate and terrain are described in the *Costa Rican Tourist Orientation Guide* (see Box 1.C).

Box 1.C. Costa Rica: Contrasts in terrain and climate

From the forested slopes of its volcanoes to the coral reefs off its coastline, the country offers visitors a phenomenal variety of environments to explore. Rain forests, white water rivers, pastoral mountain valleys, sun-swathed beaches ... the list goes on and on ... This incredible biological diversity is the result of Costa Rica's location, topography and climate. The country is located in the middle of a land bridge between North and South America, so it is part of a biological corridor through which life forms have moved between the two continents over the millennia, leaving Costa Rica with plant and animal forms native to both North and South America, as well as many species that can only be found in Central America, or only in Costa Rica. And because of its precipitous topography and variation in rainfall from region to region, there are many different ecosystems within the country, which creates niches ... for a variety of plants and animals.

(MEPRO, 1994, p. 12)

Summary

The diversity of terrain and climate, and the consequent plethora of flora and fauna, give Latin American destinations a spectacular tourism offering. In its broadest sense, any climatic condition or type of terrain can be enjoyed by the visitor at virtually any time of the year, in one or other of the Latin American republics. Furthermore, in many instances differing terrains and climates can be enjoyed within the same country. Thus, in terms of landscape and climatic variety, almost every Latin America country has a significant natural environment, in addition to the existence of several major urban conurbations throughout the region, such as Mexico City, Buenos Aires and São Paulo.

Most Latin American nations now recognize the importance of tourism as a means of stimulating economic development: the benefits associated with economic growth, such as employment, increased wealth and improved living conditions, are often cited. However, other longer term impacts have been experienced, such as environmental degradation and potentially negative socio-cultural impacts (Wilkinson, 1989). Certainly the natural geo-climatic attractions of the region have resulted in increasing visitation during the latter half of the twentieth century, as has its cultural heritage. The pre-Hispanic cultures of the *Mayan*, *Aztec*, *Inca* and *Chibcha* civilizations have given Peru, Bolivia and Colombia architectural sites as breathtaking as any in the world and more spectacular than most. Many tour operators offer packages with a blend of both nature and culture: a typical example of this is illustrated in Box 1.D, in which the cultural heritage is viewed against the backdrop of the spectacular Andean vistas.

Box 1.D. Cradle of the Incas

This trip explores the lands of the Inca and the Nazca civilisations, with nights spent in local hotels. At Cusco, you can explore the Inca ruins and have the choice of either trekking the Inca Trail or taking the train to Machu Picchu. At Nazca there is the option of flying over the Nazca Lines … You will cross the great Lake Titicaca, and have the chance to meet the indigenous Indian peoples in their remote villages.

(Dragoman, 1999, p. 69)

HISTORICAL-POLITICAL DEVELOPMENT

Introduction

A third major element of the destination mix is culture 'interwoven with history' (Mill and Morrison, 1992, p. 269), with a richness that is often understated in the context of Latin America. Whilst it is beyond the scope of this book to trace in any detail the complexity of historical and political development of the various Latin American republics, it is, nevertheless, appropriate to provide a short overview of the region's historical development. This is a key factor in that the various republics have shared a common pattern of development; this contributes to their status as 'Latin American' nations.

The Hispanic occupation of the region began in 1492 when Columbus sailed on behalf of the Spanish Crown to explore the lands to the west. The two major indigenous civilizations, the Aztecs (mainly inhabiting what is now Mexico) and the Incas (mainly occupying modern-day Peru and Bolivia), were defeated and the area occupied and settled by the Spanish. Portuguese adventurers achieved similar occupation in what is modern-day Brazil. Years of colonial organization and development, agricultural reorganizaton and the exploitation of mineral wealth left their mark, with large-scale population movements and the near-destruction of some native civilizations.

One social consequence of the development of local primary industries was the growing need for labour, a need which could not be satisfied by using the existing population (Schmink and Wood, 1992). The Spanish, and more particularly the Portuguese, solved this problem by importing large numbers of slaves from West Africa. In Portuguese colonies they were used principally to work on the sugar estates. Estimates vary, but between 1601 (the beginnings of the slave trade) and 1810 (the beginnings of the Independence period), some 0.9 million slaves were shipped to Spanish America and some 2.5 million to Brazil (Thomas, 1994, p. 28). The consequences of this enforced migration can be seen today, in the large negroid populations of Brazil and the Spanish Caribbean – such as in Cuba.

It is difficult to identify the precise moment at which the Hispanic American provinces rose in revolt against control from Europe, as rebellions began in different areas at different times. Mexico, for example, is generally accepted as being the first country to attempt to break free from Spain. The revolt in Mexico was led by Father Miguel Hidalgo y Costilla, in 1810; it failed and he was executed by the Spanish, providing Mexico with its first national hero. In his honour, Hidalgo's name adorns at least one street in most Mexican towns and cities.

Unlike Brazil, which achieved its independence from Portugal relatively peacefully, Spanish colonial independence was only won through force of arms and in many instances it was a decidedly bloody affair; the Spanish-American independence wars lasted many years and resulted in considerable loss of life. It has been speculated that it was precisely this process of violent rebellion that gave the Latin American military leaders such a relatively important role in their respective republics: it was the Military that won independence through force of arms and not, generally, civilian leaders. Furthermore, on gaining independence, it is argued that the Military provided the only element capable of maintaining a structured society and enforcing law and order in the newly independent nations (Villanueva, 1962; del Solar, 1976).

The independence wars cannot be mentioned without including two important figures: Simón Bolívar and José de San Martín. These two generals have since become heroes in their respective countries (Colombia and Argentina) and throughout much of South America. As with Hidalgo, their legacy is evident today in street names, famous buildings, national holidays, and even countries – Bolivia is named after Bolívar. Bolívar liberated most of modern-day Colombia, Panama, Venezuela, Ecuador and Bolivia; San Martín gained independence for Argentina, Chile and southern Bolivia and Peru. To appreciate the importance of this period of history is to understand something of the historical outlook of many modern Latin American nations.

It is a sad irony that, once independence had been achieved, at such a high cost to human life, those republics that shared common socio-cultural, historical, political and economic bonds should spend their formative post-independence years in conflict with one another. It is almost as if the Military, having achieved independence, could only survive or function by engendering some form of conflict.

In terms of post-independence developments, the cases of Brazil, Chile and Mexico illustrate the different forces at work and show how events of the mid-late nineteenth century have affected the existing politico-geographic structures in some countries today.

Brazilian independence was achieved relatively peacefully in 1824, yet a year later the country was involved in a war with Argentina. This lasted three years and ended in the formation of Uruguay as a 'buffer' between the two South American giants. Twenty years later, Brazilian forces intervened in Argentina to assist in the overthrow of the dictator Rosas. Between 1865 and 1870, Brazil (in alliance with Argentina and Uruguay) fought the War of the Triple Alliance against Paraguay. Brazilian losses were heavy, but they did not begin to match those suffered by Paraguay – estimated by some scholars to have reached 20 per cent of the entire population (Keen, 1992, p. 200). The legacy of mistrust felt by many Paraguayans towards Brazil is evident even today, as is the resentment over the loss of land. This latter point is particularly pertinent, as some of the territory ceded to Brazil includes the Igazú Falls, a major tourist attraction of spectacular natural beauty and one that Paraguayans feel they should benefit from far more than is currently the case.

Chilean post-independence history took a slightly different course; independence was won in 1817, and eleven years later the country was torn apart by a series of civil wars which lasted until 1830. A short period of peace was brought to an end in 1836 with the outbreak of the war against the Peruvian-Bolivian Confederation (1836–9). The 1840s saw alternating periods of peace and civilian unrest, until the country was plunged into civil war once again in 1851.

No sooner had the unrest caused by this civil war subsided than the country was at war with Peru and Bolivia again, in 1879. The War of the Pacific was one of the most significant events of the late nineteenth century and has had a direct effect on the modern-day boundaries of the nations concerned: it established Chile as the major Pacific coastal power, reducing the dominance of Peru, and deprived Bolivia of its coastline (Burr, 1965; Basadre, 1978). The effects of this last point are only too apparent today in the tourist sectors of both Chile and Bolivia. The Chileans, as has been previously noted, market the Atacama region as a major attraction: it is precisely this region that was taken from Bolivia in 1879. The Bolivians visit the region in their thousands every year, but now only as tourists in a foreign country – doubtless the irony is not lost on the tourist authorities of both countries.

The Mexican experience was different again, yet just as bloody and probably more tragic, as the country suffered a series of civil wars and rebellions, attempts at reoccupation by Spain, and occupation by France. This was in addition to persistent intervention by the USA. Following the Mexican declaration of independence in 1821, Spanish forces attempted to retake the country in 1829, precipitating a civil war between those loyal to the Spanish Crown and those who wished for an independent state. The Mexican general Santa Anna declared himself President in 1832 and four years later his forces put down a successionist rebellion in the Mexican state of Texas. The battle of the Alamo is a well-known chapter in the history of the USA and it provided the catalyst that led to Texan independence from Mexico a year later.

Taking advantage of a weak and demoralized Mexico, the French invaded, plunging the country into yet another civil war, which culminated with the overthrow of President Santa Anna. In 1845 a recently independent Texas joined the USA, thus effectively transferring a large part of Mexican territory to the USA – a fact that is the subject of some resentment on the part of Mexicans to this day. It also led to a serious breach of US–Mexican diplomatic relations, which in turn led to the Mexican-American War of 1846–8. This was to prove disastrous for Mexico, as at the Treaty of Guadaloupe (1848), Texas, California and New Mexico were officially ceded to the USA. The end of the war brought about increased Mexican hostility to the USA, and many politicians focused on the return of this territory as an issue of national unification.

Unfortunately for Mexico, the country was embroiled in yet another civil war, which lasted for five years, until 1862, when the country underwent a period of temporary unification in the face of yet another attempted invasion by the French. Taking advantage of Mexican political instability, the French installed Archduke Maximillian of Austria as Emperor of Mexico, but their influence ended with their defeat by nationalist forces and Maximillian was shot in 1867. Peace was still to elude Mexico, however, as in 1872 a full-scale rebellion broke out in the north of the country, led by Porfirio Díaz – he was to become dictator and lead Mexico through the process of modernization.

Thus the post-colonial history of Mexico could be summed up as a series of civil wars and rebellions, interspersed between a disastrous war against the USA and repeated attempts at intervention by the USA and France. When viewed in this context modern Mexican xenophobia becomes more understandable, and in particular their distrust of the USA, which they still regard as having 'stolen' nearly one-third of Mexican territory. As Porfirio Díaz is frequently quoted as saying: 'Poor Mexico, so close to the United States and so far from God.'

Immigration

The early twentieth century saw a rise in European immigration to Latin America; whilst all countries experienced some immigration, it was particularly heavy and concentrated in Argentina, Chile, Uruguay and Brazil. In addition to the many thousands of immigrants from Spain, who settled in every country, there were certain destinations that received particularly large numbers from other countries, which had a direct influence on the cultural development of those nations. Perhaps the best case in point is Argentina: government statistics gave the population for 1914 as 70 per cent of Argentinian origin (i.e. born in Argentina), and 30 per cent of foreign origin. Of these, the largest group (12.1 per cent) was Italian, followed by Spanish (10.7 per cent). Even by 1980, the Italian population still amounted to just over 25 per cent of the 1,903,159 foreign-born Argentinians (Carlevari, 1993, p. 151).

The USA and Latin America in the Twentieth Century

Disputes between the various republics and the USA increased in frequency, culminating in the Spanish-American-Cuban War of 1898–1902. Having evicted the Spanish occupiers, the USA installed itself as the neo-colonial power in Cuba, using economic and political leverage, rather than direct occupation.

This policy was to typify US involvement in Latin America for the following 78 years. The relationship is summed up by Foner:

> The instrument through which American domination was established in this part of the world and steadily reinforced was neo-colonialism, and Cuba was the model. Cuba illustrated how American monopolies could gain a protected sphere of influence with a form of independence masked by US intervention and control.
>
> (1972, p. 672)

American influence increased throughout the whole of Latin America: US forces occupied Veracruz in Mexico in 1914, and two years later a military expedition led by General Pershing invaded Mexican territory in pursuit of the bandit Pancho Villa.

Another effective and less costly method of maintaining US control over the region was to encourage (or at least not to prevent) the rise of dictators, who would control their country in line with US interests. If this failed, direct military intervention could always be resorted to; between 1898 and 1933 the USA intervened on nine occasions in Cuba, the Dominican Republic, Mexico, Nicaragua and Panama.

Perhaps the most infamous symbol of US involvement in Central America was the United Fruit Company, which epitomized the extent to which US commercial interests controlled large segments of some Latin American economies, and the political control they exercised in the maintenance of these commercial interests (Pearce, 1982, pp. 12–17; Acker, 1988). By 1950, according to Niedergang, the company:

> owned a fleet of 50 ships, symbolizing power and luxury ... It controlled port development, railway lines and roads in all states with which it had signed contracts ... It owned telephone lines ... cable companies ... and most of the shares in twenty or so firms or companies whose operations were directly or indirectly connected with the tropical fruit trade.
>
> (1971, pp. 298–9)

Revolution in Latin America

It was perhaps inevitable that the consequence of US domination and the excesses of domestic tyrants would be revolution throughout Latin America. The fall of the Arbenz government in Guatemala in 1954 is generally credited with having inspired Fidel Castro and Ernesto Guevara to take up arms in Cuba (Gott, 1973, p. 64). With the success of the Cuban Revolution in 1959, it appeared as if the whole continent was ripe for revolt: the 'domino-effect' (a momentum of geographical proximity) was the scenario most feared by the USA, as this could not only have weakened US influence in the area, but also have opened the door to Soviet involvement.

Guerrilla groups (some supported by the Cubans, others by the Russians or the Chinese), mushroomed throughout the region in the 1960s. In Colombia, for instance, the old FARC (Colombian Armed Revolutionary Forces) founded in the late 1940s by Moscow-inspired communists, was joined in the early 1960s by the ELN (National Liberation Army), which received its backing from Cuba.

Whilst the guerrilla struggles in Colombia are perhaps the most complex and prolonged, similar groups were emerging throughout the entire continent – inspired either by overseas communist states or by the injustices and inequalities evident in their own societies. Guerrilla actions were particularly widespread in Guatemala, Peru and Venezuela. Only in Chile did an anti-establishment coalition achieve success through the ballot box, with the election to the Presidency of the Marxist Salvador Allende in 1970.

The rise of guerrilla movements led to a right-wing backlash; military governments, blaming civilian ineptitude and inability to control the rising violence and disorder, took control in many countries from the mid-1960s. This first took place in Brazil, where the Military, backed by opposition groups, seized power in 1964. The Chilean military ousted Allende in 1973, and in Argentina, a military *junta* seized control in 1975. Unfortunately, the seizure of power was not apparently considered sufficient to neutralize the threat posed by the various subversive groups. The Military began a reign of terror and slaughter of the civilian population, on the pretext of combating terrorist groups: the so-called 'dirty war', which was fought with particular ferocity in Argentina and Chile. Davis, for instance, suggests that the true number of casualties that occurred during and immediately after the Chilean military *coup* may never be known, but range from 2500 to 80,000 (1985, p. 368). The kidnappings and killings continued for many months after the *coup* had so obviously succeeded.

Today, the Military have been replaced in all countries by elected civilian governments of varying degrees of competence and honesty. Throughout the continent, dictatorship and other forms of oppressive government are giving way to elected democracies, although the process is slow in some cases and there is still a strong military presence in some countries (Hunter, 1997). Ironically, it is now only Cuba which still has a dictatorship (Centero and Font, 1997).

Guerrilla groups have (for the most part) been silenced, a spectacular example being the capture by the Peruvian Army of Anibal Guzmán, the leader of *Sendero Luminoso*. Some groups still cause problems, however, such as in Colombia, where the guerrillas now appear to be operating in a loose alliance with the drug barons against the government forces, and together these pose a serious threat to the stability of the country (Robinson and Wilson, 2000).

Summary

Since the 1980s there has been a transition to elected democracies and this has led to more peaceful regimes in Latin America, but this has not been without tensions and dilemmas (Dominguez and Lindenberg, 1997). It is hoped that the presence of civilian governments will bring sustained, peaceful development in the region. One way in which the new democrats have strengthened their position is through the process of *apertura* or 'opening up' of their economies. By seeking greater integration into the world trade and by playing a more active part in international organizations, the new leaders have calculated that the potential for disruption by guerrilla groups or the military will be reduced. This is based on the assumption that there is a correlation between economic growth and political stability. It is within this context that the book discusses the development of tourism.

REFERENCES

Acker, A. (1988) *Honduras: The Making of a Banana Republic*, South End Press, Boston, Mass.

Basadre, J. (1978) *Perú: Problema y Posibilidad*, Banco Internacional de Perú, Lima.

BTI (1999) *British Trade International: Mexico*, Mexico Desk, British Trade International, London.

Burr, R. N. (1965) *By Reason or Force: Chile and the Balancing of Power in South America, 1830–1905*, University of California Press, Berkeley and Los Angeles, Calif.

Carlevari, I. (1993) *La Argentina 1993: Estructura Humana y Económica (9th edition)*, Ediciones Macchi, Buenos Aires.

Centero, M. A. and Font, M. (eds) (1997) *Towards a New Cuba? Legacies of a Revolution*, Lynne Reiner Publishers, Boulder, Colo.

Cole, J. P. (1970) *Latin America: An Economic and Social Geography*, Butterworth, London.

Davis, N. (1985) *The Last Two Years of Salvador Allende*, I. B. Tauris, London.

del Solar, F. J. (1976) *El militarismo en el Perú*, Solarte Libros C. A., Caracas.

Dominguez, J. I. and Lindenberg, M. (eds) (1997) *Democratic Transitions in Central America*, University Press of Florida, Miami.

Dragoman (1999) *Discover the Dream: Adventure Holidays & Overland Journeys (1999/2000)*, Dragoman Overseas Travel, Stowmarket.

Europa Publications (1997) *Europa World Year Book (1997) (Vols 1 and 2)*, Europa Publications, London.

Financial Times (1999a) 'FT file: Brazil', *Financial Times Survey: Brazil*, 2 November.

Financial Times (1999b) 'FT file: Argentina', *Financial Times Survey: Argentina*, 15 December.

Foner, P. S. (1972) *The Spanish-Cuban-American War and the Birth of American Imperialism (Vol. II: 1898–1902)*, Monthly Review Press, New York.

Gott, R. (1973) *Rural Guerrillas in Latin America*, Penguin Books, Harmondsworth.

Harding, M. (1996) *Weather To Travel: The Traveller's Guide To The World's Weather*, Tomorrow's Guides, London.

Hatchwell, E. and Calder, S. (1992) *Travellers Survival Kit : South America*, Vacation Work Publications, Oxford.

Heywood, D (1991) 'World's End', *The Sunday Times* (8 December).

Hunter, W. (1997) *Eroding Military Influence in Brazil: Politicians Against Soldiers*, University of North Carolina Press, NC.

Keen, B. (1992) *A History of Latin America: Vol. II, Independence to the Present* (4th edition), Houghton Mifflin, Boston, Mass.

MEPRO (1994) *Costa Rica: Tourist Orientation Guide (1994)*, Mercadeo Profesional Mepro, San José.

Mill, R. C. and Morrison, A. M. (1992) *The Tourist System*, Prentice Hall, Englewood Cliffs, NJ.

Nebrada Díaz de Espada, A. (1996) 'Apendice Estadístico' in J. M. Arriaga Fano and F. Fernández Rodríguez (eds), *Situación 1996: América Latina* (pp. 349–58), Banco Bilbao Vizcaya, Bilbao.

Niedergang, M. (1971) *The Twenty Latin Americas (Vols 1 and 2)*, Penguin Books, Harmondsworth.

Pearce, J. (1982) *Under The Eagle: US Intervention in Central America and The Caribbean*, Latin America Bureau, London.

Robinson, G. and Wilson, J. (2000) ' "New Vietnam" Seen in Colombia Drugs War', *Financial Times* (30 March).

Schmink, M. and Wood, C. M. (1992) *Contested Frontiers in Amazonia*, Columbia University Press, New York.

Seaton, A. V. and Bennett, M. M. (1996) *Marketing Tourism Products: Concepts, Issues and Cases*, International Thompson Business Press, London.

Thomas, A. (1994) *Third World Atlas* (2nd edition), The Open University Press, Milton Keynes.

TPC (1996) *Tourism Manual 1996*, Tourism Promotion Corporation, Santiago de Chile.

TPC (1998) *Patagonia: The Silent South*, Tourism Promotion Corporation, Santiago de Chile.

Villanueva, V. (1962) *El militarismo en el Perú*, Empresa Gráfica T. Scheuch S.A., Lima.

Wilkinson, P. (1989) 'Strategies for Tourism in Island Microstates', *Annals of Tourism Research*, Vol. 16, pp. 153–77.

CHAPTER 2

Tourism and the Economy

INTRODUCTION

This book focuses on tourism in Latin America, mainly from a business perspective, and within this context there are a number of definitional issues to resolve. Tourism is essentially about human activity, which involves travel from an originating area to a destination for the purpose of business or pleasure or just business. Researchers often refer to tourism within the context of an origin-destination matrix. Pearce, for example, comments:

> Tourism is thus a multi-faceted activity and a geographically complex one as different services are sought and supplied at different stages from the origin to destination. Moreover, in any country or region there is likely to be a number of origins and destinations, with most places having both generating (origin) and receiving (destination) functions.
>
> (Pearce, 1989, p. 2)

It embraces cultural, economic and social exchange processes and this is why the consumption of tourism (a composition of services, which make up tourism supply) is different from the market for consumables or tangible products. The elements of tourism are bound together in a mesh of activity, which we refer to as travel and tourism.

Tourism Definitions

The definitions adopted in this book are those which have been agreed by a number of institutions. It has nevertheless taken several decades to achieve agreement between governments as to which categories of travellers or visitors should be included in the definition of tourism. There is also still a question of the validity of statistical comparisons, because governments do not collect statistics for the same reasons, nor in a similar manner. The World

Tourism Organization (WTO) has, however, presented a definition which is both workable and has gained acceptance on a global basis. It is outlined in Figure 2.1.

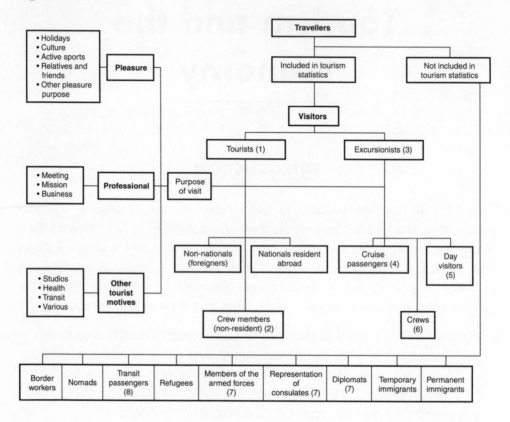

Key
1 Visitors who spend at least one night in the country visited.
2 Foreign air or ship crews docked or in lay over and who use the accommodation establishments of the country visited.
3 Visitors who do not spend the night in the country visited although they may visit the country during one day or more and return to their ship or train to sleep.
4 Normally included in excursionists. Separate classification of these visitors is nevertheless recommended.
5 Visitors who come and leave the same day.
6 Crews who are not residents of the country visited and who stay in the country for the day.
7 When they travel from their country of origin to the duty station and vice-versa (including household servants and dependants accompanying or joining them).
8 Who do not leave the transit area of the airport or the port. In certain countries, transit may involve a stay of one day or more. In this case, they should be included in the visitors statistics.

Figure 2.1. Classification of travellers

Source: WTO (1993)

It has only been in recent years that the day excursionist or day visitor has been included in the statistics, yet day visits clearly make up an important sector of the tourism business in many economies. In relation to Latin America, the main excursionist flows are on the Mexican-USA border and across the Rio de Plata between Argentina and Uruguay.

Of the many definitions listed, for example by Burkhart and Medlik (1989, p. 42), or Middleton (1994, pp. 8–9), the one which has increasingly gained acceptance is that by Mill and Morrison (1992, p. 9) as it is more comprehensive. It recognizes the importance of pre- and post-trip activity as well as activities at the destination. The implications for the tourism researcher in understanding the entire process, rather than simply concentrating on the travel journey and destination, are fundamental:

> Tourism is the term given to the activity that occurs when tourists travel. This encompasses everything from the planning of the trip, the travel to the place, the stay itself, the return, and the reminiscences about it afterwards. It includes the activities the traveller undertakes as part of the trip, the purchases made and the interactions that occur between host and guest. In sum, it is all of the activities and impacts that occur when a visitor travels.
>
> (Mill and Morrison, 1992, p. 9)

This definition encompasses four overlapping phases of consumer activity:

- pre-purchase activity, such as finding information, discussing the prospect with friends and family, booking the holiday or travel arrangements for a day visit, and preparation before travel;
- the journey to and from the destination, possibly including an overnight stop en route;
- the activities undertaken at the destination, which might be uniform or characterized by a very wide range of activities;
- post-consumptive behaviour such as processing photographs and talking about experiences.

These overlapping phases provide a useful framework for the analysis of the tourism business. They provide an insight into why and how travel is purchased, the elements of a holiday which people really value and how a destination can secure repeat business. However, it is also important to augment this framework with the political, social and environmental processes and impacts which make tourism more than simply a closed business sector or sectors.

Principles of Tourism

Whilst definitions vary according to discipline, perspective, or purpose, there tends to be some common ground in the literature. Therefore, many analyses of tourism refer to a number of defining principles which have been summarized by Burkhart and Medlik (1989, pp. 39–40):

- Tourism is an amalgam of phenomena and relationships.
- Two elements, the journey to the destination (dynamic element) and the stay (static element), are fundamental.
- This type of activity takes place away from the normal place of residence and work and is therefore different from those enjoyed by residents in the areas through which the visitor travels or stays.
- Movement is short term and is intended to be of a temporary nature.
- Visits to destinations take place for a number of reasons, but exclude taking up permanent residence or employment, which is remunerated.

Add to these three further characteristics:

- Tourism includes the activities of day visitors or excursionists, some of which might be local residents enjoying their own area (Middleton, 1994, pp. 8–9).
- It concerns primarily the consumption of a wide range of products and services, provided by public and private organizations (Jefferson and Lickorish, 1988, p. 1; Middleton, 1994, p. 11; Morgan, 1996, pp. 8–9).
- It is not an entirely neutral process but can involve considerable benefits and disbenefits to society (Burns and Holden, 1995, pp. 14–21).

The combined eight general principles underlie the core definition, but there are also a number of technical descriptions which enhance understanding of both the scope of tourism and the components which make up the overall structure of the system.

Technical Terms

These are particularly salient, for example, when attempting to analyse quantified data on a comparative scale, possibly between supply sectors or across countries.

Therefore, terms such as day excursion, short break, and distinctions between domestic and international travel, inbound and outbound make up a necessary vocabulary used in the analysis of the tourism system. There is little dispute about the terms themselves or what they mean. The discussion tends to focus on the lack of consistency in the collection of tourism data between countries, the validity of the statistics collected and the difficulties of comparative analysis (Smith, 1995, pp. 9–10; Cooper *et al.*, 1998, pp. 46–7). This presents a particular problem in developing countries. Different countries afford different levels and methods of data collection in relation to tourism. On the one hand, Mexico has a sophisticated and continuous form of data collection which is easily verified but, in contrast, poorer countries such as Bolivia and Guatemala are unable to conduct continuous surveys, nor do they include domestic or internal tourism in their data.

The core terms are:

- Visitor or Tourist
  The terms used to describe a person travelling (sometimes also referred to as a traveller) to and staying in a particular place away from their usual environment, for more than one night but less than one year, for leisure or business purposes.
- International Tourism
  Travel between countries for the purpose of tourism. Long haul refers to very long distances, for example, over 1000 miles. Journeys from the northern states of the USA, Canada and Europe to Latin America are long haul. Short haul refers to shorter distances, for example, 250–1000 miles. A trip from Nicaragua to Costa Rica would be short haul.
- Inbound and Outbound
  Inbound or inward tourism refers to visits of a country by non residents, hence importing overseas currency. Outbound or outward refers to trips by residents of one country to another, hence an outward flow and an export of currency.
- Internal or Domestic Tourism
  Travel by residents in their own country, or trips made by foreign visitors wholly within one country.
- Excursionist/Same Day Visitors
  Visitors who begin and end their visit at home or from a holiday base within the same 24-hour period.

Business perspective

This book is written from a tourism business perspective. It focuses mainly on the consumption and supply of travel and tourism. However, the tourism manager needs to be able to manage the interaction between supply and demand within appropriate social and environmental constraints and in line with the principles of sustainability. This requires an understanding of tourism from a variety of disciplinary approaches. McIntosh, Goeldner and Ritchie (1995, pp. 17–21) provide a useful outline, of which some are mentioned below to illustrate the diversity:

- Institutional Approach: This focuses on the functional aspects of travel intermediaries, technically classified as a subset of the management approach.
- Managerial Approach: Exploration of the management of tourism enterprises to meet changing patterns of demand in society.
- Economic Approach: An economic perspective relating to aspects of supply and demand, employment and balance of payments but also development and economic gain.
- Geographical Approach: Specializing in the spatial and development aspects of tourism but very wide-ranging in approach.
- Interdisciplinary Approaches: Reference to other disciplines such as anthropology, psychology and political science in the understanding of culture and other societal dimensions of tourism.

Tourism Models

The presentation of models which explain the growth of tourism are essential to the understanding of developing countries. Models which are often quoted, such as that by Mathieson and Wall (1982, pp. 15–16) and Lea (1988, p. 17), suggest that an elementary stage of tourism development inevitably leads to the next. In reality, this might be the case, but not necessarily so; nor might it occur at a scale, or timeframe envisaged in the model. Cuba and the Dominican Republic, for example, have developed within very short time scales. Tourism development is discussed further in Chapter 3.

ECONOMIC OVERVIEW

The importance of tourism to the development of the various republics has been one of considerable discussion but what is its relative importance across Latin American countries? Table 2.1 outlines the per capita GDP (Gross Domestic Product), a basic comparative measure of the economic wealth of the individuals of each nation. This illustrates the considerable disparity of wealth

Table 2.1. GDP and GDP per capita

Country	Year	GDP (US $ millions)	GDP per capita (US $)
Argentina	1997	322,700	9,520
Brazil	1997	786,400	4,799
Mexico	1997	334,700	4,747
Chile	1997	74,200	4,700
Uruguay	1997	18,100	4,600
Venezuela	1997	67,300	4,102
Panama	1997	8,200	3,160
Costa Rica	1998	10,500	2,995
Peru	1997	62,400	2,502
Colombia	1997	85,200	2,305
El Salvador	1997	10,400	1,970
Paraguay	1997	10,100	1,904
Guatemala	1997	17,700	1,600
Ecuador	1997	18,800	1,590
Cuba	1994	12,900	1,172
Bolivia	1997	8,100	1,005
Dominican Republic	1991	7,100	986
Honduras	1997	4,400	784
Nicaragua	1997	1,900	431

Sources: Crawford (1990), ABECOR (1992a; 1992b), Fidler (1992; 1994; 1997), *Financial Times* (1995 and 1999), Bauer (1996), Flanders (1996), Europa Publications (1997), Pilling and Bowen (1997), Jolly (1998), Lapper (1998), Tricks (1998), BTI (1999a, 1999b), Latin America Press (1999, p. 6)

and is a stark reminder of the erratic development patterns and levels of poverty that typify many Latin American nations. The prosperity of Argentina (with a per capita figure of US $9520 for 1997) is only relative; it is, however, approximately twice that of the next highest, Brazil, which has US $4799. At US $4747 per capita, Mexicans enjoy roughly similar levels of wealth as do Brazilians. Three more countries all average above $4000 per capita: Chile (US $4700), Uruguay (US $4600) and Venezuela (US $4102). At the other end of the spectrum, two of the poorest countries are to be found in Central America: Honduras (US $784) and Nicaragua (US $431).

There is also a major issue regarding debt: the majority of Latin American nations are highly indebted to both internal and external creditors. Many of these external debts have their origins in the nineteenth century, when the newly independent countries turned to countries such as Great Britain and the USA for finances to develop their infrastructres, domestic industries and Armed Forces (Rippy, 1971, p. 10; Greenhill and Miller, 1973; Marichal,

1988). These and additional debts incurred subsequently have proven difficult to repay and are now ever-growing burdens on the economies, despite continued and regular servicing. For example, the Brazilian foreign debt rose from US $83,205 million in 1982 to US $119,742 million in 1987 (ABECOR, 1988). Debt servicing became an important economic and political issue for many nations, resulting in Brazil imposing a moratorium on repayments in 1988. Interestingly, one of the solutions adopted was the 'debt for nature' swap, in which large tranches of external debt would be written off in return for government cooperation in protecting the rainforest:

> Holland's deputy prime minister, Rudolf de Korte, told Brazilians that if the Amazon is lost, the resulting greenhouse effect would, amongst other things, flood Holland. He proposed that part of Brazil's huge foreign debt could be 'swapped' for a project to save the Amazon.

> (Schwarz, 1989)

Levels of debt, however, have continued to grow, putting greater pressure on governments to develop tourism as an income generator in order to counterbalance the increasing drain on their earnings. For example, Table 2.2 illustrates levels of external debt, and what these represent as percentages of GDP for selected Latin American nations.

Table 2.2. External debt 1997 (selected nations)

Country	External debt (US $ millions)	External debt as % of GDP
Argentina	193,600	38.1
Bolivia	5,248	64.7
Brazil	193,663	24.6
Chile	31,440	42.3
Colombia	31,777	37.3
Ecuador	14,918	79.0
El Salvador	3,282	31.5
Guatemala	4,086	22.9
Honduras	4,698	104.6
Mexico	149,690	44.7
Nicaragua	5,677	288.1
Panama	7,715	93.8
Paraguay	2,053	24.6
Peru	30,496	48.8
Uruguay	6,652	36.5
Venezuela	35,542	52.7

Source: Latin America Press (1999, p. 6)

In economic terms, the region has begun to witness the benefits from the development of various free trade and common market zones, especially in terms of the direction of trade, although this does generally tend to reflect the increasing economic influence of the USA (Bulmer-Thomas and Dunkerley, 1999). The most important of these trading zones are summarized in Table 2.3.

There are obvious benefits for tourism in terms of the increased flows of goods and services between the countries shown in Table 2.3, both in terms of the increased ease of access for tourists, and the growing 'business tourism/urban tourism' market. An analysis by the 'Argentina Desk' of the British Department of Trade and Industry (DTI) suggested that, in the period January–September 1997 Brazilian imports to Argentina amounted to some US $4942 million (22.5 per cent of total import value). In the same period exports to Brazil were valued at US $5618 million (some 29 per cent of total export value). Argentinian exports to Uruguay and Paraguay during the same period amounted to US $522 (3 per cent of total export value) and US $427 million (2.2 per cent) respectively, giving a total Argentinian export value to Mercosur members of US $6567 million, or

Table 2.3. Key trading zones in Latin America

Organization	Membership
Andean Community (Comunidad Andina)	The CA was formed in 1969 initially as a Common Market, and known as the 'Andean Pact' (Pacto Andino). Today, its membership comprises Bolivia, Chile, Colombia, Ecuador, Peru, Venezuela.
Central American Common Market (Mercado Común de América Central)	Costa Rica, El Salvador, Guatemala, Honduras, Nicaragua. The aim of this Common Market is to enhance the influence of the various Central American republics through collective decision-making and the sharing of common politico-economic goals.
North American Free Trade Agreement (NAFTA)	Formed initially in 1989 as a Free Trade Area Agreement between the USA and Canada, the NAFTA was officially formed in 1994, after the accession of Mexico. It is unique in the Americas, as it represents a free trade zone between two developed economies and one developing economy, Mexico.
MERCOSUR (Southern Market)	Mercosur was also initially formed as a Free Trade Agreement, in this instance between Argentina and Brazil in 1988. It expanded to its present size in 1990 with the accession of Paraguay and Uruguay. Bolivia and Chile both hold associate membership.

34 per cent of total exports by value (DTI, 1998, pp. 49–50). It has also been suggested that Mercosur has improved the level of peace and security between constituent countries, which, in previous decades, had been involved in territorial disputes (Dávila-Davies, 1992, p. 275; Chudnovsky and Porta, 1995).

Sector Contributions to GDP

Whilst GDP indicates an overall level of wealth in each particular country, it does not explain how this wealth is generated, nor which sectors make the most important contribution. The three sectors that comprise economic activity are: primary (agriculture, forestry, fishing, mining); secondary (manufacturing, construction, power generation); tertiary (services, including retail, transportation, tourism, education, administration, health, and finance). An analysis of the contribution of each sector to GDP shows, once again, a relative imbalance in terms of development of certain economies (see Table 2.4).

Table 2.4. Sector contributions to GDP

Country	Year	Percentage contribution to GDP by sector		
		Primary	Secondary	Tertiary
Argentina	1994	4.9	30.1	65.0
Bolivia	1994	18.1	32.6	49.3
Brazil	1995	12.8	38.4	48.8
Chile	1995	8.1	32.9	59.0
Colombia	1995	13.1	33.9	53.0
Costa Rica	1995	17.3	24.5	58.2
Cuba	1995	6.9	31.3	61.8
Dominican Republic	1995	12.7	31.7	55.6
Ecuador	1994	12.0	38.0	50.0
El Salvador	1995	13.8	28.0	58.2
Guatemala	1994	24.5	19.6	55.9
Honduras	1995	24.5	29.0	46.5
Mexico	1995	8.2	27.8	64.0
Nicaragua	1995	33.2	21.3	45.5
Panama	1995	8.1	18.6	73.3
Paraguay	1995	26.4	25.5	48.1
Peru	1995	13.3	42.0	44.7
Uruguay	1995	8.6	25.2	66.2
Venezuela	1995	5.7	40.7	53.6

Source: Europa Publications (1997)

Countries such as Nicaragua, Paraguay, Guatemala and Honduras are still heavily reliant on agriculture, with the primary sector accounting for up to one-third of GDP in Nicaragua. In Nicaragua, Honduras and Guatemala, a large proportion of agricultural output is in the form of tropical fruits and coffee: the top four Guatemalan exports (by value) are coffee (US $267 million), sugar (US $143 million) bananas (US $98 million) and tobacco (US $40 million) (Dallas, 1994, p. 40).

By contrast, some countries (such as Panama) have important tertiary sectors: the very high contribution of over 73 per cent of GDP reflects the relative importance of the banking and retail sectors to the Panamanian economy – in particular the attraction of the Colón Free Zone (CFZ), which is one of the world's largest free trade zones. According to the manager of the CFZ, in 1996 it accounted for 14 per cent of GDP alone, employing some 13,000 people directly and another 5000 indirectly (Colitt, 1997).

Other strong primary contributions are generally in the form of mining and extractives. A recent survey valued the Chilean copper industry at around US $35,000 million, some 40 per cent by value of all exports (Mark, 1998). Copper is also important to the Peruvian economy, whilst in Venezuela it is oil which, according to another economic survey, accounts for 'more than 70 per cent of the country's export revenue and over 25 per cent of its gross domestic product' (Luce, 1997). Whilst the primary sector remains important, a gradual shift away from this sector towards the secondary and tertiary sectors has occurred since the early 1900s. Nowhere is this more in evidence than in Argentina (see Table 2.5).

Table 2.5. Argentina: Changes in GDP contribution, 1900–94

| Year | Sector contribution as a percentage of GDP | | |
	Primary	Secondary	Tertiary
1900	32.0	23.0	45.0
1935	28.7	24.0	47.3
1970	16.6	40.3	43.1
1975	15.0	34.0	51.0
1980	15.0	33.0	52.0
1985	19.0	27.0	54.0
1986	17.0	28.0	55.0
1987	16.0	27.0	57.0
1994	4.9	30.1	65.0
% change	− 27.1	+ 7.1	+ 20.0

Source: Based on Carlevari (1993, p. 191) and Europa Publications (1997)

Summary

Whilst the figures in Table 2.4 give an indication of the overall balance of a nation's economy, indicating the growing importance of the tertiary sector in all countries, tourism is but one relatively small element of the broader services sector in many countries, which is growing throughout Latin America. The next section focuses on the relative importance of tourism to the economy.

TOURISM AND THE ECONOMY

Introduction

Whilst domestic tourism has always existed over the last century, it has generally been of very little commercial value in Latin America, confined to a few wealthy travellers, who mostly stayed in the larger cities. Ironically, as the means of travel became easier and less expensive, there has been a corresponding tendency amongst the wealthy to travel to Europe and/or the USA. Thus, apart from business-related travel to major cities, domestic tourism is generally regarded in most countries as being of secondary importance. There is, in many cases, a positive correlation between a nation's prosperity and the level of domestic tourism; it is unsurprising, therefore, that there are only a few nations in which domestic tourism has begun to assume relatively significant proportions: principally Argentina, Brazil, Chile and Mexico.

Referring to domestic tourism in Chile, SERNATUR (the government-backed tourism authority) concludes that the increased demand is a consequence of a number of factors, including increased levels of income and improved employment prospects, the growing involvement of women in the labour market, easier access to consumer credit and an increased level of private vehicle ownership (SERNATUR, 1998, p. 28). However, for the large percentage of the population of most Latin American countries that live at subsistence levels, tourism is not an option in their lives.

Since the advent of international mass tourism in the late 1950s/early 1960s, Latin American governments have focused on incoming tourism as an increasingly important contributor to the nation's economy. This is particularly the case with some economies: for example, the Economist Intelligence Unit in London (EIU) reported that, in 1990, tourism represented 10 per cent of the Dominican Republic's GNP (EIU, 1990, p. 21), whilst by it was claimed that in Costa Rica: 'Tourism became the biggest earner of foreign exchange in the economy in 1993 ... a role which had traditionally been filled by coffee, the historic motor of the Costa Rican economy' (Monet, 1996, p. 8).

At the macro-economic level, tourism provides much needed income and foreign exchange and, in theory, it can reduce the balance of payments and unemployment, help towards an increase in standards of living of certain sectors of the population, and encourage inward investment. For example, the President of Chile, Eduardo Frei Ruiz-Tagle, is quoted as crediting tourism with 'generating income, creating employment, encouraging investment and encouraging the decentralisation of production throughout the country' (SERNATUR, 1998, p. 1). The Venezuelan Tourism Corporation (CTV) gives its prime mission as: 'To optimise the contribution tourism makes to the development of the country, and to heighten international awareness of the country' (CTV, 1995, p. 1).

What makes inbound tourism particularly attractive to many governments is their belief that, in relation to other sectors, the level of financial investment required to stimulate tourism is minimal in comparison to manufacturing. For instance, investment in luxury hotels is sought from international hotel groups, simply because capital is not readily available in the home market (WTO, 1994, p. 51). For example, the Venezuelan government recently coordinated an investment programme between the Hotel Humbolt and the Caracas Cable-car Company, for a joint development project located in the *El Avila* National Park. Foreign companies involved in funding this project were from Germany, Austria, Spain, the USA and Brazil.

In perspective, however, overall levels of investment are low; one commentator noted that of the 'world's 200 most important hotel chains, only four are South American' (Rizzotto, 1992, p. 33). Whilst this has implications for future revenue generation, it also implies that, at least initially, foreign multinationals provide some of the necessary investment required, which would otherwise not be available from the domestic Latin American markets. Another aspect of tourism development which is sometimes overlooked is that of 'public goods', such as beaches and other 'natural' areas, which constitute a basic appeal to the market. The exploitation of these 'public goods' by governments and the private sector is one of the benefits of tourism development in Latin America, but also remains one of the key issues of sustainability.

Economic Contribution

There are three major areas in which incoming tourism makes a positive addition to a country's economy: (1) contributing to GDP (2) encouraging inward investment; and (3) increasing opportunities for employment.

Contributing to GDP

Tourism's contribution to GDP levels varies considerably from country to country (see Table 2.6). There are three basic groupings that emerge from an analysis of Table 2.6. These are: countries in which tourism plays a relatively important role in contributing to GDP; countries in which tourism contributes a relatively modest percentage of GDP; and countries in which the contribution tourism makes to GDP is very small.

Those countries in the first category, in which the tourism sector contributed to between 7 and 10 per cent of the country's GDP, include the Dominican Republic (10 per cent), Costa Rica (8.2 per cent), Brazil (8.0 per

Table 2.6. Tourism earnings and GDP

Country	Year	Tourism receipts (US $ million)	Tourism receipts as % of GDP
Dominican Republic	1989	640.0	10.0
Costa Rica	1996	654.8	8.2
Brazil	1994	1924.0	8.0
Bolivia	1996	160.0	7.8
Peru	1994	402.0	6.7
Guatemala	1995	276.6	6.6
Cuba	1993	1000.0	5.6
Panama	1992	291.6	5.3
Colombia	1994	794.0	5.0
Nicaragua	1996	58.4	4.2
Argentina	1993	3614.0	4.0
Chile	1994	833.0	4.0
Uruguay	1994	632.2	3.8
Honduras	1996	115.0	3.6
Venezuela	1994	639.0	3.2
Paraguay	1993	204.0	2.4
Mexico	1992	5997.0	2.0
Ecuador	1996	253.0	1.6
El Salvador	1996	44.2	0.5
Mean		**1000.9**	**3.1**

Sources: EIU (1990, p. 21), IPAT (1993, p. 27), Euromonitor (1994, pp. 6–7), Yunis (1994, pp. 29–30; 53; 70–1; 100; 123; 166; 175–6; 199; 212), Kendall (1995), Lora and Vallejo (1995, p. 1), Secretaria de Turismo (1995, p. 7), Haynes (1996, p. 8), Pilling (1996), Monet (1996, p. 7; 1997, p. 87), Europa Publications (1997), Bowen (1997), Martin de Holan and Phillips (1997, p. 785), Secretaria Nacional de Turismo (1997, p. 73), Dex (1998, pp. 3–6)

cent) and Bolivia (7.8 per cent). Whilst tourism is obviously of great benefit to these countries, with the exception of Brazil their economic base is comparatively narrow. For example, Costa Rica is still heavily dependent on agriculture, as is the Dominican Republic, whilst the Bolivian economy is dominated by mining. Brazil, by comparison, has a highly diversified economic base, ranging from agriculture and fishing, through mining and forestry, to manufacturing – particularly motor vehicle and the aerospace industries.

By contrast, those countries in which tourism plays a relatively less important role, form the majority of destinations in Latin America. Several of these countries are generally in a much stronger position, as they have a greater diversification to their economic base, with tourism only accounting for between 3 and 7 per cent of GDP: they are Peru, Guatemala, Cuba, Panama, Colombia, Nicaragua, Argentina, Chile, Uruguay, Honduras and Venezuela. For example, in Cuba in 1994, tourism contributed around 5.0 per cent of GDP, as compared with manufacturing which accounted for 26.0 per cent and agriculture, forestry and fishing – 6.8 per cent (Fidler, 1995a). The position, however, is changing, with a greater emphasis being placed on coastal tourism development.

The final cluster includes those countries in which tourism contributes to less than 3 per cent of GDP: Ecuador, Paraguay, Mexico and El Salvador. The inclusion of Mexico in this group may appear surprising at first, in view of the great numbers of tourists that visit the country. However, despite the importance of tourism to the Mexican economy, it is still only relatively minor when compared to the country's oil revenues, manufacturing sector (especially motor vehicles) and agricultural exports.

Encouraging Inward Investment

One of the major problems facing most developing countries is the lack of available domestic capital for the development of the tourism infrastructure. Thus, in order to stimulate investment for new accommodation or resort areas, a country or a destination often has to seek overseas developmental capital – an issue which has already been discussed in terms of the levels of external debt.

Historically, Latin America has suffered from a funding gap in this sector and governments, with the notable exception of Mexico, have been equally reluctant to invest in substantial tourism projects, given the diversity of other development issues with which they are faced. Hence tourism in Latin America has been relatively starved of the investment necessary to stimulate growth in recent decades. The Inter American Development Bank has approved projects such as the restoration of the historic quarter of Quito, Ecuador, but other initiatives have been rare. The World Bank (IBRD) has played a limited role in supporting tourism-related projects in Bolivia, Brazil, Colombia and Peru. Mexico has been a major benefactor of IBRD money. There has also been support through the World Bank's Multilateral Guarantee Agency (MLGA), which, since 1993, has supported a number of tourism studies and investor forums, plus a rainforest aerial tram and the building of Marriot International and Radisson hotels in Costa Rica. It has also helped the McDonald's Corporation to establish a restaurant in Chile (Travel and Tourism Analyst, 1998, p. 83).

This type of investment is, nevertheless, highly significant in developing countries, not only in terms of encouraging other private investment, but also in that it signals a level of confidence in the country to the worldwide financial markets. The resident population should also benefit from improvements to infrastructure such as roads, rail links, water treatment programmes, slum clearances, etc. A report in 1991 on investment opportunities in Argentina illustrates the problems facing the government when trying to stimulate tourism investment (see Box 2.A).

Box 2.A. Tourism investment in Argentina

The prospect of an influx of high-spending foreign visitors calls for massive investment in top-range hotels and other facilities ... Projects tendered are expected to concentrate on hotel construction and the development of tourism-orientated infrastructure like roads. In addition, investors in tourism in the poorer northern provinces of La Rioja and Catamarca may deduct the entire cost of new equipment and housing from their corporate tax base under law number 22021/79.

(Doggart, 1991, p. 48)

By 1995, however, the situation had improved. Hotel expansion in Argentina was well advanced, driven by the expanding Argentinian economy; one study claimed a total of eight five-star hotels in Buenos Aires, giving a total capacity of 2000 rooms, with 'possibilities for further expansion' (Mazzia, 1995). By 1997, the issue of the privatization of airports had become an important subject of national political debate and has fuelled an increase in tourism sector development, mainly in the capital (Obarrio, 1997). A similar pattern of investment incentives have been encouraged by the Costa Rican government with a degree of success in stimulating improvements to existing accommodation, and in attracting new investment (Coffey, 1993, p. 88).

The Chilean government has also been proactive in stimulating investment in tourism and public services, concluding that support and investment will continue to be necessary for public goods and services if they are to compete in terms of the quality of existing tourism offerings (SERNATUR, 1998, p. 8). Other investment has been directed towards training, such as outlined by the Bolivian government in their 1997 training programme for employees in the tourism sector, which was backed by the World Bank (Secretaria Nacional de Turismo, 1997, p. 77). However, whilst the financial climate for tourism development is changing in favour of Latin America overall, there is still considerable inequality in terms of those sectors that receive the greatest benefit, as the principal benefactors are still largely cities and integrated resorts. Furthermore, inequalities of investment are also apparent at a national level, with the poorest countries failing to attract the same levels of investment as their more economically advanced neighbours. In the medium-to-long term this is likely to exacerbate the differences between the levels of prosperity in certain countries.

Increasing Opportunities for Employment

This is a significant area, as unemployment remains one of the most intractable problems for governments throughout Latin America, especially since the financial crises that have hit the region since 1995. In Argentina, for example, unemployment peaked in 1995 at 18.4 per cent of the economically active population (Lapper, 1998). The real problem is underemployment, with the public sector (in particular, government and administration) absorbing more people than budgets permit. In Ecuador, according to a survey: 'The public sector is also bloated and inefficient, and its employee unions resist change ... The government has retired voluntarily close to 45,000 of the 430,000 workers employed by the public sector' (Fidler, 1995b).

The far-ranging privatizations and de-regulations that have taken place throughout the region, coupled with an opening of domestic markets to exports, have meant that much of this *underemployment* has turned into *unemployment,* or a new informal economy, with consequent socio-economic problems. Whilst automation and computerization may well lead to greater levels of production efficiency, they will also contribute to *higher* levels of unemployment, at least until the appropriate level of skills can be acquired by the workforce. The issue has been discussed by a number of researchers, such as Cubitt, who comments that: 'There is some evidence to show that foreign investment encourages capital intensive industrialisation, which leads to high levels of unemployment/underemployment' (1995, p. 42). In this respect, the advantage that tourism has over traditional manufacturing industry is that it is labour-intensive. Whilst adopting the latest technology such as Computerized Reservation Systems, tourism remains very much a 'people'-based sector,

Table 2.7. Guatemala: Projected employment in the tourism sector, 1994–2005

Year	Number employed in tourism sector
1994	57,800
1995	63,800
1996	67,100
1997	70,400
1998	73,900
1999	77,600
2000	81,400
2001	85,500
2002	89,800
2003	94,300
2004	99,000
2005	104,000

Source: INGUAT (1995, p. 52)

where levels of direct contact between visitor and host are essential elements of the tourism marketing mix.

In many countries there has been a significant increase in the numbers employed in the tourism sector, either directly through government bodies such as Tourism Authorities, or more usually through private sector organizations. For example, figures compiled by the Guatemalan Tourism Institute show that employment within the tourism sector is expected to nearly double over the ten years from 1994 (see Table 2.7).

Local Tourism Economies

Whilst most studies have concentrated on international tourism and Latin American countries, there are relatively few studies that have given consideration to the economic impacts of visitor spending and employment creation within different local economies, either at a regional level or at a destination level of a country. O'Hare and Barrett, in their investigation of Peru, argue that, as a consequence of the improving economy in the late 1990s following the neo-classical model of privatization and free trade, tourism flows have noticeably improved. However, they claim that the regional distribution of tourism income remains uneven:

Very little is known about the local and regional impact of tourism in Peru. Many of the poorer Departments with low foreign tourist flows do not gain much external currency from international visitors and are effectively by-passed by this source of revenue. This study has shown, however, that the tourist (hotel and restaurant) sector in Peru is highly important in terms of regional wealth and employment creation, providing between 4.1 percent and 30.9 percent of each Department's total GDP ... It seems, however, that both the large-scale hotel and the small-scale *hostal* are poor generators of wealth for the local community.

(1998, p. 60)

Incoming Tourism Arrivals

In a global context, tourism in Latin America is not as yet significant, as the region only accounts for approximately 7 per cent of all international arrivals. These international visitor arrivals (excluding cruise ship tourism) amounted to 38,214,000 in 1995, which represented 34.8 per cent of the total number of arrivals in the Americas. International visitor arrivals had risen to 44,903,000 by 1998, a 14.8 per cent increase in three years. In terms of numbers of arrivals, there is considerable variation between the various nations (see Table 2.8).

However, these aggregate figures in Table 2.8 tend to understate the dynamism of the market in relation to international arrivals in Latin America.

Table 2.8. Incoming tourists by destination 1988–98 (000's)

Country	1988	1990	1992	1994	1996	1998
Argentina	2,119	2,728	3,031	3,866	4,286	4,860
Bolivia	167	217	245	320	592	387
Brazil	1,743	1,091	1,692	1,853	2,666	4,818
Chile	624	943	1,283	1,634	1,450	1,767
Colombia	829	813	1,076	1,027	1,343	1,600
Costa Rica	329	435	611	761	779	943
Cuba	309	327	455	617	999	1,390
Dominican Republic	936	1,305	1,415	1,717	1,926	2,309
Ecuador	347	362	403	472	494	508
El Salvador	134	194	314	181	283	542
Guatemala	405	508	541	537	520	636
Honduras	250	202	231	228	255	318
Mexico	14,142	17,176	17,146	17,182	21,405	19,810
Nicaragua	75	106	167	238	303	411
Panama	199	214	291	324	362	439
Paraguay	284	280	334	406	426	350
Peru	359	317	217	386	663	815
Uruguay	1,035	1,267	1,561	1,884	2,152	2,163
Venezuela	373	525	446	496	759	837

Source: WTO (1999)

An analysis of the aggregate global figures during the 1990s indicates a slowing of the annual growth rate of demand; by contrast, in Latin America the reverse is true, as the annual level of international arrivals is increasing rapidly, especially in contrast to the more mature North American destinations.

THE MARKET FOR TOURISM

Domestic Markets

Of the statistics which are publicly available, least is known about domestic tourism markets in Latin America. A significant proportion is business tourism generated by the major commercial centres and capital cities, for example, between São Paulo and Brasilia, Buenos Aires and Córdoba, Mexico City and Guadalajara. There are also well-established resorts which gain from the conference and short break markets such as Cartagena in Colombia, frequented by wealthy travellers from Bogotá, or Mar del Plata which the *Porteños* (natives of Buenos Aires) prefer for weekend breaks.

In the larger economies such as Argentina, Brazil, Chile and Mexico more information tends to be available for the researcher, especially in Mexico, which has enjoyed a longer history of holiday-taking than many other Latin American countries. In the late 1980s–early 1990s the government encouraged domestic tourism, and in 1992 over 38 million Mexicans took their main holiday in their own country, amounting to 36.4 million overnight stays in hotels or similar serviced accommodation (Euromonitor, 1994, p. 125). Many of the traditional resorts such as Acapulco serve primarily the domestic market.

Tourism practitioners and authorities recognize that elsewhere there is an insufficient resource base to enable an improved level of tourism data to be collected. The following example illustrates the paucity of data available and how tourism researchers often have to derive demand patterns from other sources. In a study of tourism undertaken in preparation of a Tourism Master Plan for Panama in the early 1990s, there was no known data available on domestic tourism. An estimate of demand was constructed on the basis of an analysis of household incomes drawn from the census data of 1990. A total of 10,000 households (amounting to some 40,000 residents), located mainly in Panama City, were surveyed in 1992 on behalf of the Instituto Panameño de Turismo. It was discovered that these residents had made on average 4.2 pleasure trips in the previous year involving at least one overnight stay, thereby generating 170,000 trips per year.

The study assumed that this segment would form the nucleus of the domestic market, i.e. that it constituted a core domestic market primarily making trips to the interior of the country. Almost a third (28.9 per cent), for example, took a trip to La Amistad, located within the confines of La Amistad International Park, and also to the nearby Barú Volcano National Park. The rich bio-diversity of the tropical rainforests, especially noted for bird-watching, as well as popular walking routes to the craters of the extinct volcano, make this a popular destination. The report, however, acknowledges that Panamanians prefer to visit the area for the events at Boquete rather than to visit the areas of the Park itself (IPAT, 1993). It is this type of incremental data which typically has been used by tourism authorities to evaluate the nature of domestic markets. For the most part, the domestic pleasure market sector is considered to be small and far less attractive, in terms of revenue potential, than international markets.

Whilst governments and local tourism authorities may well give greater consideration to the collection of data in the future, tourism analysts meanwhile have to rely on gathering disparate sources of information in each country. The major limitation is that this does not allow accurate comparative analysis between countries. There is, however, a limited amount of qualitative data available. Research undertaken by Lumsdon and Swift (1999) in South America found that tour operators do not envisage any significant change in domestic markets in the short term. The authors discussed the question in a series of interviews with over 40 tour operators in Argentina, Chile, Uruguay and Paraguay. The majority of respondents thought that there would be a far greater increase in intra-regional tourism than in domestic markets. First, it was argued that many domestic resorts were lacking in infrastructure and therefore would find it increasingly difficult to compete in either the domestic or international markets. Secondly, the respondents considered that competitor destinations, especially Cuba, Mexico and the Caribbean, could offer superior quality holidays, very often at a similar or lower price than a domestic break in some instances.

Nevertheless, there are indications that the independent domestic travel market might be developed, albeit on a small scale. The 'Strategic Plan' published in 1995 by the Instituto Hondureño de Turismo (IHT) highlighted the existence of a relatively high level of domestic demand: in 1994 an estimated 586,000 Hondurans sought overnight accommodation. It was also suggested that in fact the number of domestic tourists might be even higher, as the Honduran middle classes make frequent use of friends' houses (VFR market) rather than hotels (IHT, 1995, p. 14).

The advantage for each country is that, by encouraging a domestic market to take holidays at home, there will be a lessening of the balance of payments deficit in tourism. Not only has Mexico continued to promote to its domestic market, but in Brazil the National Tourist Organization, *Embratur*, had launched in the late 1990s a major television campaign to encourage Brazilians to discover their own country.

Intra-regional Tourism

Tourism in Latin America is primarily concerned with intra-regional flows, mainly between neighbouring countries (Schlüter, 1991). It accounts for between 70 and 75 per cent of all international arrivals. An analysis of the data points to the major flows between Argentina, Chile, Uruguay and Brazil, for example. This is not the case elsewhere; there are very limited flows between other countries such as Ecuador and Peru, or Venezuela. There are also weaker flows between countries in Central America and a large proportion of this is accounted for by business tourism. Thus, of the 332,850 inbound visitors recorded in Panama in 1993, 79 per cent were on business (IPAT, 1993). Table 2.9 illustrates that the major markets were mainly near neighbours, with the exception of the USA, and this is principally due to the Panama Canal.

Intra-regional tourism is growing. The reasons for this growth vary from country to country but are similar to the underlying factors stimulating long

Table 2.9. Major markets for Panama

Generating country	Percentage of incoming visitors to Panama
Near neighbours	
Costa Rica	14
Colombia	13
Dominican Republic	10
Ecuador	7
Venezuela	6
Nicaragua	6
Total percentage	56
Others	
USA	16
Europe	7
Others	21
Total percentage	44

Source: adapted from IPAT (1993)

haul tourism to Latin America. The growth is explained by increasing political stability, rising standards of living amongst urban dwellers, and improved business confidence across several Latin American countries. It is also attributable to a reduction of the price of air transport and better packaging of holidays including the charter air market, although the level of reliability of this sector has been subject to criticism. It is also likely that the recently formed trading zones established in the 1990s, such as Mercosur, have removed some of the barriers to travel. Table 2.10 outlines the major arrivals from neighbouring countries as a percentage of total arrivals in 1994.

Therefore, the outbound market in most countries reflects travel across near borders, with Argentina, Chile, Colombia and Uruguay enjoying very high levels of cross-border tourism. The exception is Venezuela, which attracts only a small proportion of its visitors from near neighbours and a far larger percentage from the USA and Europe.

There is, however, an increasing trend towards the wealthier urban market in the South taking package holidays in Brazil, Cuba and Mexico. Similarly, a growing demand for long haul outbound trips to the USA and Europe has been identified (Lumsdon and Swift, 1999). This is reflected in the number of Latin American countries featured in the world's top 60 tourism spending countries, as calculated by the World Tourism Organization. Brazil is Number 18 on the list, spending US $5825 million a year on international travel, followed by Mexico at Number 25, Argentina at 30, and Venezuela which, at 32, spent US

Table 2.10. South America: Arrivals from neighbouring countries as a percentage of total arrivals, 1994

Destination	Percentage of total arrivals and markets (neighbouring countries)
Argentina	71.7% (Bolivia, Brazil, Chile, Paraguay, Uruguay)
Bolivia	42.5% (Argentina, Brazil, Chile, Paraguay, Peru)
Brazil	60.2% (Argentina, Bolivia, Colombia, Paraguay, Peru, Uruguay, Venezuela)
Chile	71.1% (Argentina, Bolivia, Peru)
Colombia	73.1% (Brazil, Ecuador, Panama, Peru, Venezuela)
Ecuador	45.4% (Colombia, Peru)
Paraguay	54.8% (Argentina, Bolivia, Brazil)
Peru	27.2% (Bolivia, Brazil, Chile, Colombia, Ecuador)
Uruguay	92.3% (Argentina, Brazil)
Venezuela	7.2% (Brazil, Colombia)
Average	**54.55%**

Source: Yunis (1996, p. 14)

$2251 million in 1996. The spend is low, however, in comparison to that of the major tourism spenders, such as Germany (US $50,815 million). Colombia, Chile, Costa Rica and Peru are also included towards the bottom of the list (WTO, 1997).

The International Long Haul Market

The long haul market is already of importance to the tourism economies of Latin American, not in *volume*, but in terms of the *value* it represents. National tourism offices and other trade associations seek to develop these high spending markets, and this is evidenced in the marketing investment directed towards international travel fairs in Europe and North America. It is possible to define a long haul trip by distance, a trip over 1000 miles, or by journey time, for example over six hours air travel time or three days by ship. Using either form of measurement Latin America is a substantial distance from the major generating markets of the world. Distance has traditionally been cited as a major barrier to market development, even in the case of Mexico which is close the USA, but a significant distance from the affluent north-eastern states.

Prior to the 1980s, the long haul market to Latin America was dominated by exclusive, up-market independent travel, with a much smaller adventure-explorer segment seeking long stay discovery holidays. During the past two decades the market for long haul travel has been widened, principally because of three reasons. The tour operator supply sector, in both generating and receiving countries, has grown in terms of the numbers of companies and the range of holidays offered. It has also become more influential, having gained substantial experience of the market. In particular, speciality companies have opened up a wide range of opportunities for adventure, nature and culture tourism to niche market segments.

Secondly, several national tourism organizations, or their equivalent, have sought to develop long haul markets by encouraging airlines and tour operators to offer all-inclusive packages to major coastal resorts in their particular country. This has occurred mostly in Brazil, Costa Rica, Cuba, the Dominican Republic and Mexico.

Thirdly, the cruise market has grown substantially in Latin America, with fly-cruise packages offered throughout the world, via Miami and other ports for departures to the Caribbean and Latin America.

Thus, the annual average growth rate of arrivals to North America between 1980 and 1996, for example, was 3.7 per cent and a similar figure was recorded for Central America. By contrast, South America witnessed a growth rate of 5.9 per cent during the same period (WTO, 1999). US outbound travel

Table 2.11. South America: Arrivals from Europe and the USA, 1994

| Destination | Visitors from Europe | | Visitors from the USA | |
	Number	% of total arrivals	Number	% of total arrivals
Argentina	480,000	12.4	261,000	6.7
Bolivia	104,000	32.5	35,000	10.9
Brazil[a]	338,000	22.9	118,000	8.0
Chile	162,000	10.0	91,000	5.6
Colombia[b]	78,000	7.4	112,000	10.7
Ecuador	81,000	16.8	93,000	19.3
Paraguay	42,000	10.4	18,000	4.7
Peru	109,000	28.2	81,000	21.0
Uruguay[c]	39,000	1.8	17,000	0.8
Venezuela	194,000	45.1	108,000	25.2
Total	1,627,000		934,000	

Notes:
(a) data for 1992; (b) data for 1993; (c) includes Uruguayans resident in the USA or in Europe.

Source: Yunis (1996, p. 15)

is important for Latin America, particularly Mexico, which accounts for 30 per cent of US outbound trips. However, this includes border visitors, with large numbers of cross-border day excursions. The remainder of Latin America (and the Caribbean), receives 16.2 per cent of the US outbound market (Travel and Tourism Analyst, 1998, p. 29).

An analysis by Yunis (1996) indicates that Europe generates 13 per cent of the total number of visitors to South America, and North America generates between 7 and 8 per cent. These flows are illustrated in Table 2.11. It is probable that these overestimate demand as many of the arrivals will be participating in a multi-country holiday and may well therefore be recorded several times. The table also illustrates the importance of the long haul market to Bolivia, Peru and Venezuela where between 23 to 45 per cent of arrivals are from Europe. Generation of visitor arrivals by different countries in Europe is uneven. The three main generators are Germany, Italy and Spain. Italy is a major contibutor of visitors to Brazil and Venezuela, and Spain generates a major flow to Argentina and Uruguay (Yunis, 1996, p. 16).

The question of travel motivation and selection of visitor destination is one which has received increased attention in the literature during the past decade. Um and Crompton (1990), Laws (1995) and Moscardo *et al.* (1995) argue that it is possible to understand destination choice not only through travel motivation but also in relation to preferences in terms of activity and features of preferred destinations. The research involved a large-scale study of the Australian outbound market and there are a number of parallels which could be drawn in relation to the Latin America market.

Brown (1997) investigated the relationship between visitation and destination attributes, concentrating on what has been described as pull factors in motivational studies. He undertook a comparison between the destination feature of Central/Southern Africa in comparison to Latin America and the Caribbean. His empirical work featured two European countries where the populations have a high propensity to purchase long haul holidays, Germany and the UK. In the study, Brown identifies the demographic characteristics of visitors to Latin America as is shown in Table 2.12.

A factor analysis was undertaken, based on the six attraction factors of: (1) heritage/cultural; (2) city enclave; (3) comfort/relaxation; (4) beach/resort;

Table 2.12. UK and German visitors to Latin America

Demographic characteristic	UK (225) (%)	German (76) (%)
Marital status:		
Single	38.1	56.0
Married	57.1	10.7
Age:		
Under 35	34.6	44.7
36–50	30.8	32.9
50 and over	34.6	22.4
Educational level:		
Primary School	34.8	14.5
Jr High School	17.4	35.5
Technical School	9.6	7.9
High School	–	22.4
University	30.4	19.7
Occupation:		
Retired	7.7	10.5
Owner	23.1	17.1
Manager	–	13.2
Professional	26.9	40.8
Student	30.8	9.2
Other	11.5	9.2

Source: based on Brown (1997, p. 306)

(5) outdoor resources; (6) other factors. The analysis suggested some broad differences and similarities in national motivations to travel:

- German visitors ranked beach/resort and heritage/cultural as the most important factors.
- UK visitors ranked 'other factors' (exotic atmosphere, shopping, fast food, budget restaurants, nightlife) first, and heritage and culture second.
- Both German and British visitors ranked 'city enclaves' as least important.

Whilst it is inappropriate to draw far-reaching conclusions from this type of small-scale study, by applying the findings to a far more complex market, the study does provide a fascinating insight into the motivation of two European markets for long haul travellers to Latin America. There is clearly a need for more research in the area, such as a more detailed investigation of the attitudinal factors underlying destination choice within the Latin American context, perhaps relating overall perceptions and images to specific destination choice or activity choice.

SUMMARY

Tourism, whilst bringing the potential for development, also brings with it problems. The concern is that governments, eager to exploit the lucrative tourist markets of Europe and the USA, will be the catalyst for unchecked development throughout the region. This could have far-reaching and irreversible negative effects on sensitive eco-systems and the architectural heritage and be potentially damaging to cultural and social structures – an issue that is discussed in Chapter 9.

This process of unchecked development has already begun in certain countries. This has been most notable in Mexico, where despite government efforts to control development, such as through the General Law of Ecological Equilibrium and Environmental Protection (1988), resorts such as Acapulco had already deteriorated to such an extent in the 1990s that tourists began to turn to other destinations (Denton, 1993).

The challenge for both governmental and private organizations is to develop tourism as a key contributor to GDP, whilst at the same time maintaining unspoiled the very attractions which make the region so spectacular. However, it is necessary to recognize that, for many Latin American nations, the tourism sector forms only a small part of the overall process of economic development. Furthermore, the imperatives of many governments are to stimulate rapid economic development in the short term to improve levels of employment, regardless of potentially negative long-term impacts.

REFERENCES

ABECOR (1988) 'Brazil', *ABECOR Country Reports: December 1988,* Economics Department, Barclays Bank, London.

ABECOR (1992a) 'Colombia', *ABECOR Country Reports: July 1992,* Economics Department, Barclays Bank, London.

ABECOR (1992b) 'Bolivia, Paraguay & Uruguay', *ABECOR Country Reports: June 1992,* Economics Department, Barclays Bank, London.

Bauer, R. (1996) 'Deep Poverty in "Real Peru"', *Financial Times Survey: Peru* (7 March).

Bowen, S. (1997) 'Short on Promotion', *Financial Times Survey: Panama* (8 October).

Brown, D. O. (1997) 'German and British Tourists' Perceptions of African, Latin American and Caribbean Travel Destinations', *Journal of Vacation Marketing,* Vol. 4(3), pp. 298–310.

BTI (1999a) *Central America,* British Trade International, London.

BTI (1999b) *Bolivia,* British Trade International, London.

Bulmer-Thomas, V. and Dunkerley, J. (1999) *The United States and Latin America: The New Agenda,* Harvard University Press, Cambridge, Mass.

Burkhart, A. J. and Medlik, S. (1989) *Tourism: Past, Present and Future,* 2nd edition, Heinemann, Oxford, pp. 38–42.

Burns, P. M. and Holden, A. (1995) *Tourism: A New Perspective,* Prentice-Hall, Hemel Hempstead.

Carlevari, I. (1993) *La Argentina 1993: Estructura Humana y Económica* (9th edition), Ediciones Macchi, Buenos Aires.

Chudnovsky, D. and Porta, F. (1995) 'Antes y Después de la Unión Aduanera del Mercosur: Prioridades de Política', in P. Bustos (ed.), *Más Allá de la Estabilización: Argentina en la Epoca de la Globalización y la Regionalización* (pp. 35–42), Fundación Friedrich Ebert, Buenos Aires.

Coffey, B. (1993) 'Investment Incentives as a Means of Encouraging Tourism Development: The Case of Costa Rica', *Bulletin of Latin American Research,* Vol. 12(1), pp. 83–90.

Colitt, R. (1997) 'Tropicana Wholesale', *Financial Times Survey: Panama* (8 October).

Cooper, C., Fletcher, J., Gilbert, D., Shepherd, R. and Wanhill, S. (1998) *Tourism: Principles and Practice,* Longman, Harlow.

Crawford, L. (1990) 'A Cautious Sell-off Approach', *Financial Times Survey: Uruguay* (15 October).

CTV (1995) *Plan de Mercadeo Estrategico, 1995–2000,* Corporación de Turismo de Venezuela, Ministerio de Industria y Comercio, Caracas.

Cubitt, T. (1995) *Latin American Development,* 2nd edition, Longman Scientific & Technical, Harlow.

Dallas, R. (1994) *Pocket Latin America and the Caribbean,* Penguin, Harmondsworth.

Dávila-Davies, D. R. (1992) 'Competition and Cooperation in the River Plate: The Democratic Transition and Mercosur', *Bulletin of Latin American Research,* Vol. 11(3), pp. 261–77.

Denton, D. (1993) 'Acapulco Renaissance', *Business Mexico,* Vol. 3(3), pp. 15–16.

Dex, R. (1998) 'Ecuador', *International Tourism Reports, No. 3, 1998,* Economist Intelligence Unit, London.

Doggart, S. (1991) *Investment Opportunities in Argentina,* The Southern Development Trust, London.

DTI (1998) *Argentina: Hints to Exporters*, Foreign & Commonwealth Office and Department of Trade & Industry, London.

EIU (1990) 'The Dominican Republic', *International Tourism Reports*, No. 1, 1990, Economist Intelligence Unit, London.

Euromonitor (1994) *Travel and Tourism in Latin America*, Euromonitor, London.

Europa Publications (1997) *Europa World Year Book (1997) (Vols 1 and 2)*, Europa Publications, London.

Fidler, S. (1992) 'It Looks Better, But It May Not Last', *Financial Times Survey: Dominican Republic* (27 February).

Fidler, S. (1994) 'Debt Burden Has Been Eased', *Financial Times Survey: Bolivia* (9 November).

Fidler, S. (1995a) 'Budget Deficit Cut By More Than 70%', *Financial Times Survey: Cuba* (26 September).

Fidler, S. (1995b) 'A Little War, Then Back to Business', *Financial Times Survey: Ecuador* (27 July).

Fidler, S. (1997) 'Oil and a Policy Switch Put Economy Back on Track', *Financial Times Survey: Venezuela* (21 October).

Financial Times (1995) 'Cuba: Key Facts and Indicators', *Financial Times Survey: Cuba* (26 September).

Financial Times (1999) 'Brazil: Key Facts and Indicators', *Financial Times Survey: Brazil* (2 November).

Flanders, S. (1996) 'All Eyes on Second Chapter', *Financial Times Survey: Brazil and The State of Bahia* (6 June).

Greenhill, R. G. and Miller, R. M. (1973) 'The Peruvian Government and the Nitrate Trade, 1873–1879', *Journal of Latin American Studies*, Vol. 5(1), pp. 103–11.

Haynes, L. (1996) 'Cuba', *International Tourism Reports, No. 3, 1996*, Economist Intelligence Unit, London.

IHT (1995) *El Turismo: Una Alternativa Para El Desarrollo de Honduras*, Instituto Hondureño de Turismo, Tegucigalpa, M.D.C.

INGUAT (1995) *Guatemala: Desarrollo Turístico Sustenable Hacía el Año 2005*, Instituto Guatemalteco de Turismo, Guatemala, C.A.

IPAT (1993) *Plan Maestro de Desarrollo Turistico de Panama: 1993–2002*, Instituto Panameño de Turismo, Departamento de Desarrollo Regional I Medio Ambiente, Panama.

Jefferson, A. and Lickorish, L. (1988) *Marketing Tourism*, Longman, Harlow.

Jolly, A. (ed.) (1998) *Doing Business With Latin America*, 2nd edition, Kogan Page, London.

Kendall, S. (1995) 'Exotic Treasures Need Constant Protection', *Financial Times Survey: Ecuador* (27 July).

Lapper, R. (1998) 'Argentina: Fitting a Financial Shock Absorber', *Financial Times Survey: Argentina* (27 July).

Latin America Press (1999) 'The Debt Crisis in Statistics', *Latin America Press* (20 December).

Laws, E. C. (1995) *Tourism Destination Management – Issues, Analysis and Politics*, Routledge, London.

Lea, J. (1988) *Tourism and Development in The Third World*, Routledge, London.

Lora, E. and Vallejo, C. (1995) *Competitividad Internacional del Turismo*, FEDESARROLLO, Santafé de Bogotá.

Luce, E. (1997) 'Finding a Balanced Approach', *Financial Times Survey: Venezuela* (21 October).

Lumsdon, L. M. and Swift, J. S. (1999) 'The Role of the Tour Operator in South America: Argentina, Chile, Paraguay and Uruguay', *International Journal of Tourism Research*, Vol. 1(6), pp. 429–39.

McIntosh, R.W., Goeldner, C. R. and Ritchie, J. R. B. (1995) *Tourism, Principles, Practices, Philosophies,* John Wiley, Toronto.

Marichal, C. (1988) *Historia de la Deuda Externa de América Latina,* Alianza Editorial, Madrid.

Mark, I. (1998) 'Dependence on Copper in Sharp Focus', *Financial Times Survey: Chile* (12 March).

Martin de Holan, P. and Phillips, N. (1997) 'Sun, Sand, and Hard Currency', *Annals of Tourism Research,* Vol. 24(4), pp. 777–95.

Mathieson, A. and Wall, G. (1982) *Tourism: Economic, Physical and Social Impacts,* Longman, Harlow.

Mazzia, Y. (1995) 'Un Negocio de Cinco Estrellas', *Clarin* (Buenos Aires) (19 March).

Middleton, V. T. C. (1994) *Marketing in Travel and Tourism,* 2nd edition, Butterworth-Heinemann, Oxford.

Mill, R. C. and Morrison A. M. (1992) *The Tourism System,* 2nd edition, Prentice Hall, Englewood Cliffs, NJ.

Monet, R. L. (1996) 'Costa Rica', *International Tourism Reports, No. 4, 1996,* Economist Intelligence Unit, London.

Monet, R. L. (1997) 'Guatemala', *International Tourism Reports, No. 4, 1997,* Economist Intelligence Unit, London.

Morgan, M. (1996) *Marketing for Leisure and Tourism,* Prentice Hall, Hemel Hempstead.

Moscardo, G., Yang, C., Cai, L., Pearce, P. L. Te-Lang, C. and O'Leary, J. T. (1995) 'Understanding Destination Choice Through Travel Motivation and Activities', *Journal of Vacation Marketing,* Vol. 2(2), pp. 109–22.

Obarrio, M. (1997) 'Aeropuertos: Diputados del PJ ven con Desagrado el Decreto', *La Nación* (23 March).

O'Hare, G. and Barrett, H. (1998) 'Regional Inequalities in the Peruvian Tourist Industry', *The Geographical Journal,* Vol. 165(1), pp. 47–61.

Pearce, D. (1989) *Tourist Development,* 2nd edition, Longman, Harlow.

Pilling, D. (1996) 'Stay, Just a Bit Longer', *Financial Times Survey: Uruguay* (29 May).

Pilling, D. and Bowen, S. (1997) 'The Final Wave of a Long Goodbye', *Financial Times Survey: Panama* (8 October).

Rippy, J. F. (1971) *Latin America and the Industrial Age,* Greenwood Press, Westport, Conn.

Rizzotto, R. A. (1992) 'Hotels in South America', *EIU Travel & Tourism Analyst,* No. 1, 1992, Economist Intelligence Unit, London.

Schlüter, R. G. (1991) 'Latin American Tourism Supply: Facing the Extra Regional Market', *Tourism Management,* Vol. 12(3), pp. 221–8.

Schwarz, W. (1989) 'Stirrings of Hope in the Forest', *Guardian* (14 March).

Secretaria de Turismo (1995) *Argentina: El Turismo en Cifras (Años 1990 a 1994),* Secretaria de Turismo, Buenos Aires.

Secretaria Nacional de Turismo (1997) *Estrategia de Desarrollo Turistico: Bolivia,* Secretaria Nacional de Turismo, La Paz.

SERNATUR (1998) *Política Nacional de Turismo,* Servicio Nacional de Turismo/Chile, Ministerio de Economia, Santiago de Chile.

Smith, S. J. (1995) *Tourism Analysis,* 2nd edition, Longman, Harlow.

Travel & Tourism Analyst (1998) 'Outbound Markets: USA Outbound', *Travel & Tourism Intelligence,* No. 4, London.

Tricks, H. (1998) 'Hurt by the Global Pinch', *Financial Times Survey: Mexico* (7 October).

Um, S. and Crompton, J. L. (1990) 'Attitude Determinants in Tourism Destination Choice', *Annals of Tourism Research,* Vol. 17(2), pp. 432–48.

WTO (1993) Briefing information. World Tourism Organization, Madrid.

WTO (1994) *Global Tourism Forecasts to the Year 2000 and Beyond: Volume 3, The Americas*, World Tourism Organization, Madrid.

WTO (1997) Statistics supplied by World Tourism Organization, Madrid.

WTO (1999) Statistics supplied by World Tourism Organization, Madrid.

Yunis, E. (1994) *Prospects for Tourism in South America*, Travel & Tourism Intelligence, Economist Intelligence Unit, London.

Yunis, E. (1996) *Main Tourism Trends in Latin America*, Travel & Tourism Intelligence, Economist Intelligence Unit, London.

PART II

The Tourism Offering

CHAPTER 3

The Supply of Tourism

INTRODUCTION

As discussed in Chapter 2, the growth of international visitor arrivals during the 1990s has been important to Latin American tourism. Pizam (1999, p. 576) estimates that an increase of 31 per cent, or 7.1 per cent per annum, was recorded between 1991 and 1995. The growth trend has continued during the late 1990s, although Latin America's share of the world market still remains at approximately 2 per cent of the total number of international visitors.

Spending on tourism in Latin America accounts for 7 per cent of all consumption in the region, and this level is approximately half that experienced in Europe or North America. Pizam estimates that its market share of international receipts is falling at an average rate of 1.7 per cent per annum. Projected growth of consumption up to the year 2005 remains low in comparison to other developing markets such as South East Asia and China, or Eastern Europe. The explanation relates primarily to the low level of income per capita in Latin American countries. There is little prospect of this changing in the short term. In reality, the growth in volume and household consumption in Latin America is commencing from a relatively low base.

Thus, in the perspective of world tourism, Latin America has yet to emerge as a major sector; Mexico is exceptional in this respect, as the country is recognized as one of the top world destinations, accounting for 3.6 per cent of world arrivals (in World Tourism Organization statistical tables, Mexico is featured in the North Americas). This is a slight improvement from 1980, when it was Number 8, but accounted for 4.19 per cent of world arrivals. Argentina ranks 29th, and Brazil, Chile, the Dominican Republic and Uruguay also feature in the lower cohorts of the top 60 world destinations. As a region, Latin America is only just beginning to emerge as a major tourism destination.

Tourism Policy and Planning

It is impossible to discuss the inter-relationship of the public and private sector in tourism provision without first discussing the framework of policy and planning. The adoption of formal tourism policies in Latin American countries stems mainly from governmental interest in stimulating economic development. This has especially been the case in Mexico (Zizumbo, 1991; Rodriguez, 1993). It also signals an attempt to maintain control over a process which can produce a number of dis-benefits such as the degradation of natural habitats, cultural attrition, pollution and distortion of local economies (Edgell, 1987, p. 22). Tourism policy can be described as follows:

> A policy may be defined as a course of action calculated to achieve specific objectives. Objectives are general directions for the planning and management of tourism, and are based on identified needs within market and resource constraints ... In simple terms, policies attempt to maximize the adverse effects of tourism, and as such are part of the planned development in a region which is necessary to create develop, conserve and protect tourism resources.
>
> (Brown and Essex, 1989, p. 533)

In Latin America, as elsewhere in the developing world, the traditional approach to tourism development in the past decade has been driven by national governments. Public sector tourism has, for the most part, been the responsibility of a ministry of tourism or a quasi-governmental national tourism organization (NTO). They have been charged with the duty to devise a tourism policy and in some cases to implement it. In many respects this remains very appropriate for a number of reasons. First, there has been a lack of interest or capability on the part of the private sector to invest in tourism. Furthermore, in the earlier decades, when Latin American countries were essentially closed economies following import substitution policies, tourism development, in reality, could only be guaranteed by governments. Thus, for the most part, both tourism policy and consequent development lay firmly in the hands of government; it was facilitator and in many cases also the owner/operator of tourism facilities. This was an approach adopted by Mexico during the 1970s and 1980s when successive governments endorsed the establishment of a number of organizations responsible for planning, funding and executing tourism policy. There remains a strong centralized approach to tourism policy in Mexico in comparison to other Latin American countries (Secretaría de Turismo, 1991; Molina, 1999).

In the 1990s, with the re-emergence of open economies throughout Latin America and the increased interest by inward bound hotel and tour companies, a neo-liberal framework of economic development has been re-established.

This is reflected in increased privatization of sectors such as transport and communications and in some countries the state-owned hotel groups, all of which are fundamental to tourism development. The shift in ideology also prompted greater involvement in tourism development by the private sector with joint government–private sector funding and policy formation being taken forward in partnership.

The key point is that tourism policy sets a framework in which planning at a country and provincial level can take place, and that it can be systematic in approach (Liu, 1994). This also involves implementation of policy guidelines at a regional and destination or resort level (Gunn, 1994, p. 427). In the case of many Latin America countries, the NTOs very often used the services of international consultants based in the North to develop Tourism Master Plans for their particular country. These documents invariably offered a diagnosis of the problems and prevailing issues, set out major opportunities and presented broad-brush strategic directions. In most cases, they featured very little detailed work on how the strategies would be resourced, by whom and in which particular timeframe. Thus, there tends to be a gap between broad policy frameworks, many of which were researched and written in the mid-1990s, and what actually happens in terms of tourism development at the resort or destination level.

Tourism Development at the Destination

The development of tourism at a destination level, either in terms of new building, as in the case of integrated resorts, or in terms of the restoration of old resorts and quarters of cities, is a fundamental part of tourism development. At a destination level this might involve estimating future demand, as in a feasibility study, but increasingly emphasis is being placed on a multi-disciplinary approach to evaluating the likely impacts of any development, both in a strategic dimension and in more detail at the resort level.

Management Techniques

Strategic Environmental Assessment is an analysis of impacts relating to the changes of travel patterns, investment, employment and environmental factors resulting from a major project such as an airport extension or an integrated resort. This would usually include an environmental impact study which refers to areas in close proximity to a proposed development. This is the type of analysis expected when local developments are planned in sensitive areas, such as a lodging complex at the periphery of a national park. In reality, the process of lodging development near national parks or coastal strips is often far more incremental as planning regulations are missing or flaunted by private entrepreneurs.

The four analytical concepts are environmental audit, environmental impact analysis, carrying capacity and community assessment techniques.

Environmental Audit

As part of the sustainable development process of destinations it has been suggested that they review their policies and practices in the form of a checklist of all proposals, likely impacts and possible forms of mitigation. Goodall and Stabler (1992) provide a framework for environmental evaluation, set out in five stages:

1 Consideration Stage: scoping/review
2 Formulation Stage: sustainable tourism policy
3 Implementation Stage: environmental impact assessment/environmental audit
4 Decision Stage: development approval
5 Operational Stage: monitoring progress/impacts.

Environmental Impact Analysis

Increasingly, there is concern that major developments such as integrated resorts will lead to heavy impacts on the environment. For example, at Cancun in Mexico there are currently concerns that the large number of visitors will lead to an irreversible destruction of a coral reef. An Environmental Impact Assessment attempts to set out the nature, magnitude and degree of importance of particular impacts which would occur as a result of a major piece of infrastructure being built. An environmental assessment would be expected to include:

- a comprehensive description of the development proposed including the site, designs envisaged, size or scale of development;
- sufficient data to allow the assessment of the main effects which the development is likely to have on the environment;
- a discussion of the likely significant effects relating to humans, flora and fauna, soil, water and air, climate and the landscape, material assets and cultural heritage;
- a note of caution about serious adverse effects and suggested alternative measures.

Increasingly, throughout the world tourism developers are becoming involved in this type of work alongside designers and tourism authorities.

However, there is considerable variation in terms of practice which is affected by the degree of planning regulation adopted in a given state, region or country, the effectiveness of monitoring regulation, the extent to which corrupt practices are tolerated, and the level of interest expressed by international non governmental organizations.

Carrying Capacity

Another important concept is the Carrying Capacity. This concept relates to the relationship between level of demand and magnitude of impacts, reflective of all aspects of community life from the ecological, economic and socio-cultural norms (Canestrelli and Costa, 1991). Cooper *et al.* (1998, pp. 94–107) define it as 'that level of tourist presence which creates impacts on the host community, environment and economy that is acceptable to both tourists and hosts, and sustainable over future time periods'. Cooper rightly refers to the 'tourist presence', because it is not simply a measure of tourist numbers but reflects length of stay, degree of concentration, seasonality and what visitors actually do when at a destination. This has become a major issue in terms of cruise ship arrivals at many Caribbean islands, where large numbers of passengers disembark for short periods of time, thus bringing intensive levels of intrusion within very short timeframes.

There are a number of indicators measuring thresholds of capacity (Elliot, 1990):

- the level above which the character of the place is damaged and the quality of the experience is threatened;
- the level above which physical damage occurs;
- the level above which irreversible damage takes place;
- the level above which the local community suffers unacceptable side effects.

Harrison (1992, p. 12) refers to a number of these in relation to developing countries. For example, the trip index is a measurement of the proportion of a trip undertaken at a particular destination. The calculation involves dividing the length of stay at a destination by the length of the total trip, multiplied by 100. This allows a measurement of the intensity of the visitation over time.

Whilst carrying capacity techniques offer opportunities for diagnosis, invariably the evaluation of a saturation point at a given stage in the destination's life cycle (O'Hare and Barrett, 1997) is subject to a degree of subjectivity. Thus, there is a tendency to allow continual development at Latin American resorts, as the concept is rarely applied in any scientific manner while there is a prospect of gaining more visitor spending and employment.

Another major issue in Latin America is that there is a distinct lack of resources available to control excessive levels of demand which bring major dis-benefits.

Community Assessment Techniques

The case for community participation in the development of destinations and the particular form that it might take is reasonably well documented in the literature (Getz, 1983, pp. 239–63; Haywood, 1988, pp. 154–67; Keogh, 1990, pp. 449–65). This is particularly the case when the ratio of tourists to visitors is high, as might be expected at many Latin American resorts.

The result has been the development of a number of models, based on surveys or observations at Northern destinations; these stress that the host community participation should be an integral part of the tourism development process. The case for community involvement in tourism planning is well researched but some authors, such as de Kadt (1992), are concerned that this should be genuine participation by a wide range of groups in society and not simply by those with a potential to gain commercially. This is particularly the case in Latin America where the emergence of populist local groups in recent decades has increased as a reaction to a lack of involvement in participatory processes in the past. Despite this re-emergence of populism, there is nevertheless still a lack of resident input into tourism development. In most cases the issues of privatization and prices, lack of social care, education and violence are seen as overwhelmingly more important, and tourism issues are afforded a lower level of commitment.

Murphy (1985, pp. 36–8) argues that there is a need to balance a pure business and development approach with a more community-oriented approach which 'views tourism as a local resource. The management of this resource for the common good and future generations should become the goal and criterion by which the industry is judged.' The four main areas of consideration are:

- management issues, such as bringing all parties together;
- social and cultural considerations, such as local heritage;
- business and economic considerations;
- environmental and accessibility matters.

Perhaps the most sophisticated approaches have been in relation to non-governmental organizations working with indigenous communities, in order to secure local control of tourism development. It is this type of tourism development framework which offers a promise of positive long-term tourism benefit. It would be unrealistic to present it as a panacea for all development processes, but quite clearly this approach fits into a framework of sustainable development.

Tourism development in Latin America is becoming a more important issue than hitherto. Tourism policies are increasingly being adopted formally and measures taken to progress them are the concern of the public and private sectors. There are a number of reasons. There is greater international awareness and development and imagery are vital to attract overseas markets (Echtner and Ritchie, 1993, p. 3; Gartner, 1993; Meethan, 1996). There is also an increasing number of resorts which have reached maturity in their overall life cycle and hence there is a need for strategic commitment (Butler, 1980, p. 5; Choy, 1992; Douglas, 1996). Major concerns remain, however, about a lack of resources to follow through plans, about unintended consequences of planned developments and about incremental unplanned development of pristine coastal and nature destinations, which can negatively affect both quality and image. In the context of Mexico, Casado (1997) argues that planning is less effective than might be the case, given the imperfections of the political and social system where corruption, for example, is still prevalent.

Furthermore, without government regulation it will be difficult to deter degradation. Further regulation is unlikely in the short term for, as Jenkins (1994) argues, while governments are still important in the development of tourism in developing countries, the balance has shifted to encourage more private sector tourism planning and management:

> It does not mean that government has no role to play in tourism. It is very much the 'hidden hand' which guides policy while ensuring that services which, to a large extent make up the satisfaction for foreign tourists, are actually offered by those best able to provide them. If there is a concept which guides our understanding of future tourism development in the third world, it must be 'government should not do what the private sector is able and willing to do'.
>
> (Jenkins, 1994, p. 8)

THE TOURISM OFFERING

Introduction

In the discussion of the provision of tourism, several authors refer to the term 'tourism product' (Lewis and Chambers, 1989; Middleton, 1994), on the basis that the range of products and services which make up tourism can be assumed under the greater generic term 'product'. In contrast, other authors refer to the tourism experience or tourism service within a context of service marketing, reflecting a balance between the tangible and intangible benefits accruing from travel (Vellas and Bécherel, 1999). There are, furthermore, a number of additional factors, such as symbolic, or psychological associations (i.e. perceptions regarding ambience, cultural attributes of destination populations, etc.). The balance of opinion would appear to be very much in favour of intangibility and of looking at relationships in terms of host–guest interaction. Therefore, the authors favour the term 'tourism offering', which is defined by Lumsdon (1997, p. 143) as: 'a combination of services which delivers primarily intangible, psychological benefits but which also includes tangible elements'.

This section identifies the key components which make up the tourism offering in Latin America. It has been argued that the major barrier to the development of international tourism in many Latin American countries is the lack of infrastructure. Poor road and rail transport, a narrow range of accommodation and lack of communications are considered limitations on the supply side which are holding back the growth in visitor numbers. Several commentators suggest that the gradual improvement in investment experienced in recent years is beginning to bring benefits for visitors and that these successes can be measured by a sustained increase in international travel to and within Latin America (Poole and Bowen, 1998).

The following analysis of the supply sectors presents an overall picture of uneven provision, a wide variation of standards and rapidly changing conditions in several sectors. The process of privatization and de-regulation in the transport sector, for example, has brought a succession of changes such as the withdrawal of rail services and the collapse of competing airlines in some countries. This will continue to thwart those who seek to establish a stable marketing environment in which to develop tourism.

Accommodation Sector

The accommodation sector aims principally to provide overnight accommodation for either business or pleasure travellers or a mixed market as in many city destinations. According to the WTO (1997) there were an estimated 945,000 rooms available in Latin America in 1996: 370,000 rooms in Mexico, 48,000 in Central America and 527,000 rooms in South America. This is likely to be a substantial underestimate, given that there will be rooms sold for tourism purposes which are not registered formally and hence are not recorded. Furthermore, with the growth of hotel and inclusive resorts during the past five years it is likely that, between 2000 and 2005, the availability of rooms will exceed 1 million within the tourism sector.

The range of accommodation varies from the very basic *hostal* accommodation to 5-star hotels and inclusive resorts. The latter present a classic form of enclave tourism, where all needs of the visitor are catered for at one centre of accommodation which, according to some authors, is generally separated from the local community. This is the most recent form of accommodation to be developed throughout Latin America, and public–private sector cooperation in Mexico and the Dominican Republic have advanced the concept more in these two tourism economies than in other countries. It has been suggested that the continued innovation and profitability of inclusive resorts will position them to 'become a very powerful force' in Latin American tourism (Poon, 1998, p. 76). In Mexico, a number of recently created integrated resorts, newly built destinations designed to incorporate all of the needs of the overseas visitor, constitute the hallmark of tourism development, and this is discussed in detail in Chapter 4. These 'mega-resorts' are located in coastal regions but there are smaller scale examples of similarly fashioned mountain resorts designed for ski-ing, such as at Bariloche in Argentina.

Whilst the literature discusses the acquisitions, mergers and branding of major hotel groups in Latin America, it is often forgotten that the accommodation sector is dominated by small-scale companies and the average size of hotel at many destinations reflects this. The exception is Cuba, where there is a strong degree of state control. Elsewhere, many hotels are family owned and managed and have suffered a lack of investment, especially during the lean years of the mid-1980s and early 1990s. This is, of course, not peculiar to Latin America, but reflects a pattern repeated in many countries where much of the older, traditional accommodation stock has failed to invest in line with market expectations. The result is that in many Latin American city destinations there remains a large stock of medium- to low-range hotels which lack the degree of modernity desired by North American and European markets and which cater primarily for low-yielding packaged tourism from near markets.

The growth in the international tourism market has stimulated international hotel operators to enter the Latin American market, and at the same time this new provision reinforces the process of tourism development. The increased level of investment in Latin America during the late 1990s is partly explained by market growth, but also by increased business confidence in addition to loss of markets elsewhere. In general terms, the development matches six key global trends identified by Go and Pine (1995) in their discussion of the formulation of hotel strategies:

- The maturity and hence slow growth in industrialized countries, thus encouraging territorial expansion into newly developing countries.
- Increasing price-consciousness of price-value by guests.
- The rise of short breaks in domestic markets and a rapid rise in long haul travel.
- The continued interest in corporate mergers and acquisitions.
- Internationalization and accessibility of global distribution systems.
- Shortage of skilled labour in the hotel sector.

The main reasons for increasing interest in Latin America relates to a number of factors which are summarized below:

- Overall market trends in Latin America during the 1990s point to a sustained and stronger growth than in other regions of the world.
- The democratization of Latin American countries and increased stability has improved investor confidence, although not entirely.
- The willingness of several governments to assist in development has made investment opportunities more worthwhile. Nicaragua, for example, offered a ten-year tax incentive in the mid-1990s to international hotel groups.
- Improvement of economies in several Latin American countries has stimulated business tourism, particularly in Argentina, Chile, Colombia and Mexico.

For example, the Florida-based Choice Atlantica Hotels is in the process of building or operating over 100 hotels in Latin America. It holds the franchise for developing branded hotels such as Comfort and Quality Inns and Clarion Hotels in South America. In 1998 it set out a plan to develop up to 12 mid-range Quality hotels during the next decade in Buenos Aires, Argentina and in the capital of Uruguay, Montevideo. These hotels usually feature fitness centres and business suites to attract the business tourism sector. It is an investment which amounts to approximately US $100 million. Grupo Posadas, the Mexican-based chain, has acquired the franchise for the Caesar Park hotel brand in Latin America, which is also well known in the North American market. Development to date includes hotels in Rio de Janeiro, São Paulo and Buenos Aires.

The continued interest by North American companies, such as the Marriott chain, indicates a degree of commitment to the Latin American market which had not been evidenced in previous decades. There has also been a continued commitment to privatization of state-owned hotel groups. For example, in Peru, the state-owned Enturperu group has been sold or leased to international groups. Thus, in the early years of the twenty-first century, Latin America is witnessing a growth of high standard accommodation provision in capital cities and key resorts, in many respects following a pattern evidenced in Mexico in the 1960s.

The issue as to whether this type of investment is beneficial to local economies is a subject of much discussion. Protagonists of growth argue that international investment is essential to stimulate the building of hotels at resorts and large-scale up-market hotels in city destinations. Large-scale investments are often too capital intensive for local companies or public authorities. Thus, external investment, in many instances backed by supportive local public sector involvement, is the only way to increase accommodation capacity to any significant extent. Once the capacity is available there is a *raison d'être* for airlines and tour operators to increase their commitment to a destination. This is the model justified by several Tourism Master Plans and numerous tourism development projects throughout Latin America.

McQueen (1989) is critical of this argument on a number of grounds. Transnational hotels seldom invest large amounts of their own capital in developing countries. Instead they seek support funds from local private and public sources to allay risk. Frequently, they rely on national or local governments to provide all other associated infrastructure. Furthermore, Lea (1988) comments that they are more interested in maximizing profits through charging management fees, licensing or franchising and other service agreements rather than investing in direct ownership at a given destination.

TRANSPORT

Transport is recognized as one of the most significant factors in the development of tourism in that it is a necessary requirement for tourism to take place (Leiper, 1990; Page, 1999). In terms of the transport component of any given holiday there are a number of fundamental distinctions to be made:

- The provision of transport between originating zones and destinations.
- Transport systems at the destination.
- Transport designed for utilitarian purposes which might also be used by visitors.

- Transport designed for tourism purposes in order to enhance the visitor experience, or offered as a form of visitor attraction.

Another essential ingredient is where 'the quality of the transportation experience becomes an important aspect of the tourist experience and therefore, a key criterion that enters into destination choice' (Lamb and Davidson, 1996, p. 262). Thus, whatever the type of transport used, the most important aspect is the degree of confidence of the visitor when booking, the degree of reliability and safety when travelling and the expected levels of comfort. As elsewhere, these are crucial issues in the development of transport systems for tourism in Latin America (see Box 3.A).

Box 3.A. Key forms of transport in Latin America

Form of transport	Importance in Latin American tourism	Examples
Air travel: Short haul/long haul flights.	Major importance to international travel. Charter flights limited, mainly scheduled flights.	Most tour operators offer triangular flights between major destinations, for example, Miami, Rio, Caracas-Lima-Miami.
Highways: Car, hire car and coaches.	Poor infrastructure in most countries, and low levels of private car ownership means limited development. Coach travel involves long hours, and lacks personal safety.	There is a coach sector in each country which deals with international visitors, for example 'Turbus' in Santiago de Chile. Most car-based tourism is of a domestic nature. Mexico is developing an independent traveller coach tourism market. Guided minibus or bus tours are popular at many destinations such as the famous charabanc tours around Cartagena in Colombia which include a live band on board, drinks and scheduled stops for dancing.
Road transfers: Taxi, minibuses.	Of major importance at all destinations but personal security and standardization have been a major concern of tourism authorities.	In Buenos Aires a system of recognized hotel-based taxis, known as a 'Remise', has been established to offer secure transfers at a fixed price between hotels and airport.
Rail: Urban metro and intercity.	Rail networks in decay throughout Latin America with the exception of Mexico. City metro systems overcrowded.	Mexico is developing its rail-based network for the USA market. In most other countries the railway systems have been truncated but there are a number tourism trains such as the Train to Machu Picchu in Peru, and the Train to the Clouds in Salta, Argentina.

Form of transport	Importance in Latin American tourism	Examples
Marine: Cruise and ferries.	Cruise liner tourism in growth. Local ferries and river boat tourism buoyant.	An increasing number of cruises call at Puerto Limón, Costa Rica. Many also call at Rio de Janeiro and Buenos Aires.
Non-motorized: Horse-back, cycling, walking, kayak.	Very small international market.	Walking as a way of getting around tourism destinations is popular but not always pleasant because of chaotic traffic systems, pollution and lack of personal security. Long distance walking, cycling and trekking are well established and offered to niche markets as a tourism experience. Despite inherent problems of personal security it is growing; for example eco-tourism groups in Costa Rica are invariably chaperoned by local guides.

Within the Latin American context the situation is complex, not least because many countries are in the process of privatizing many transportation systems. The first candidate, in most countries, has been the airlines. Whilst each country has approached the issue in a different way, the standard approach appears to have been to sell off all or part of the national carrier, whilst at the same time de-regulating the industry and encouraging the establishment of new, privately owned carriers.

Air Travel

There is an extensive network of scheduled airline services across Latin America which provides the key to international tourism from North America and Europe. The airline hubs are Miami in Florida and to a lesser extent Houston in Texas. In Latin America, most countries have a direct link to either the USA or Europe via the capital city, but not always. Tourism authorities in Paraguay consider that attempts to generate long haul tourism are being held back by the lack of long haul arrivals by any carriers. A trip requires a change at either Rio de Janeiro or Buenos Aires.

Air travel in Latin America has been the subject of a process of de-regulation during the 1990s, as has been experienced throughout the entire airline industry (Wheatcroft, 1994). The consequences have been noticeable in Latin America, for the privatized flag carriers have in some instances been challenged by emergent airlines, sometimes referred to as the 'New Breed', such as *Lapa* in

Argentina, *Aces* in Colombia and *Aerocontinente* in Peru. The number of new entrants has been significant. However, it is argued that the 'flag carriers' still enjoy government protection, and that new airlines experience considerable barriers when competing against incumbents. The Argentinian government allowed Aerolineas a period of five years before competitors were allowed to compete for regional routes and ten years in relation to long haul routes:

> The coexistence of one airline in monopolistic and competitive segments of the same market has probably led to the appearance in Argentine air transport of a phenomenon that tends to arise under these circumstances – the emergence of cross-subsidization from domestic services (monopolistic) to international services (competitive).
>
> (Gerchunoff and Colonia, 1993, p. 276)

The de-regulation process has affected the market for air travel in Latin America in several other respects. First, it has stimulated price reductions, but not extensively. The Department of Commercial Aviation in Brazil has allowed fare discounting in recent years and this has encouraged competitive pricing during the low season, September to November. However, competition has been short-lived. Declining revenue has brought about a reduction in the overall number of companies operating in some countries, for example in Peru where there are now only two airlines offering domestic flights.

Secondly, it has provided a market environment receptive to integration. The general global trend towards airline alliances has been replicated in Latin America. The nature of these alliances takes many forms: joint marketing initiatives or a sharing of resources in the operation of a network of services, and code sharing of long haul routes. The marketing power gained by airlines from such alliance building has been subject to criticism on the grounds that it distorts competition in favour of those who design and hence control the information supply of the distribution systems (Bennett, 1993).

The development and implementation of computerized reservation systems and electronic global distribution systems, such as Amadeus, Galileo, Sabre and Worldspan, have been extensive and this has accelerated the process of gaining market power and consolidation of supply. These systems enable major airlines to monitor, with a degree of immediacy, patterns of demand and the level of revenue for any particular route. It also provided in the earlier years of development a commercial advantage to those who own the systems, in that the airline could prioritize its own flights or those of the alliance in favour of competitors at the point of sale, such as at the travel agent. This advantage is now negligible as the level of information is available to all partners. However, the practice of sharing codes, where two airlines can use the same code to highlight a transatlantic flight and a feeder link, allows alliances to gain market share on long haul routes. The shared code allows both flights to be recorded as a single routing and hence is afforded a higher priority on the booking system than a connecting flight denoted by another code.

The issue of air transport is also significant, as depending on how successful it is, other sectors of the infrastructure may be privatized, such as airports, docks, railways, buses, telephones and postal systems. In Argentina, for instance, the programme of privatization began in early 1990 and has embraced all sectors of the economy, especially the public utilities, transportation and communications sectors, with state-owned airlines, gas and electricity companies all being affected (Barham, 1993). Other measures include the de-regulation of the construction industry, which, it is hoped, will benefit tourism by reducing costs in this sector by up to 25 per cent (De Simone, 1994). Iberia, the Spanish airline, increased its holdings in Aerolinas Argentinas to 85 per cent in 1995, whilst in April of that year the International Finance Corporation (an arm of the World Bank) announced a US $81 million package for the construction of a new 31 km highway from the Buenos Aires International Airport of Ezeiza to the city of Cañuelos and improvements to the existing road connecting the airport with Buenos Aires (Lapper and Pilling, 1995). There is even a government department charged with overseeing the process of privatization (Subsecretaria de Privatizaciones) which, in 1994, began the mammoth task of privatizing the shipyards (Barcelona, 1994). It has progressed both air and rail transport privatization, but without recourse to the social context of regional transport policy (Keeling, 1994, p. 499).

Road Travel

With the exception of Mexico, where substantial investment in the 1990s has greatly improved the road system between major cities and tourism destinations, road-based tourism have been retarded by the lack of infrastructure. Congestion and pollution have a major negative impact on tourism in capital cities: Mexico City and Bogotá are extreme examples. The exception is La Habana, where imposed rationing of petroleum means that bicycles and public transport dominate in favour of private vehicles.

The investment has been made primarily in the inter-urban highway sector for the purposes of industrial development and on occasion this may have a secondary consequence of opening up tourism destinations. The expansion of a tourism infrastructure alongside major highways would also change the nature of the tourism offering, which currently signifies rurality rather than urbanization. Nevertheless, there has been a continued improvement of highways in recent years. In Brazil, for example, Embratur with others are investing in both road and air transport improvements in the north-east of the country, and improving access to the Amazon and the Pantanal which is expected to be beneficial to tourism.

Outside the major cities, car hire, or car touring, is rare. Most international tourism relies on packaged coach travel, for example, from ports where cruise liners dock or from capital cities to the surrounding tourism hinterland. There are well-established coach operators in most countries such as *Turbus* in Chile. They have attempted to develop a new demand for coach tourism, but many find it difficult to compete on long-distance routes with airlines.

Inadequate, or poorly maintained, public transport affects not only the visitor, but also the resident populations of many large cities (Dimitriou, 1992). Overcrowding, poverty, a lack of investment, and an inability to maintain minimum standards on vehicles (in particular buses), have led to uncomfortable, unreliable, dirty, and potentially dangerous, public transport facilities. A 1996 report on the Colombian transportation infrastructure noted that:

> there are few real highways and only 314 km of paved road per million inhabitants. Fifty per cent of the main roads wind through steep *cordilleras*, with bridges and tunnels in constant need of repair. The rail system, which carries about a million tons of cargo a year, has less than 1,700 km of line in service.

(Kendall, 1996)

Rail Travel

Rail is not a significant form of transport in most Latin American countries. It varies enormously from country to country, as is indicated in Table 3.1. Use of the fragmented network for tourism purposes is very limited, and is estimated to be at best static in most countries and in decline in others. In

Table 3.1. Rail passenger traffic: Selected countries, 1996

Country	Railway company/organization	Number of passengers carried
Cuba	Unión de Ferrocarriles de Cuba	11,724,600
Mexico	Ferrocarriles Nacionales de México	6,727,383
El Salvador	Fenadesal	313,143
Bolivia	Empresa Ferroviaria Oriental S.A.	303,906
Venezuela	Ferrocar	1,173

Source: adapted from material supplied by the Asociación Latinoamericana de Ferrocarriles (1997)

Peru, the privatization of many of the lines currently operated by state-owned Enafer is expected to stimulate innovative practices on a number of lines where there is tourism potential. The service from Cuzco to Machu Picchu is the best known, but the prospects are still limited. In Argentina the privatization of the railways, and attempts to seek regional government support for passenger service provision, has led to the withdrawal of most rail services, including the line between Buenos Aires and Córdoba, which had considerable tourism potential (Calvert, 1996, p. 151).

There are, unsurprisingly, few celebrated tourism routes remaining in Latin America, such as the Train to the Clouds from Salta in Argentina and the Lemon Express in Costa Rica. To date, the most promising revival in the use of the rail network for tourism purposes has been in Mexico, such as the Train to Copper Canyon.

THE CRUISE MARKET

A cruise has been defined as a 'floating hotel with a different destination every day' (Gibbons, 2000, p. 13). Marine tourism has grown dramatically in Latin America during the past three decades, partly as a response to passenger interest as cruises become more fashionable again and partly as companies increase capacity through investment in new ships and seek a wider market through aggressive pricing. The market is dominated by the USA, which accounts for approximately 80 per cent of world cruises (Morrison *et al.*, 1996). Most of these depart from Miami, Port Everglades and Port Canaveral. There is a much smaller but increasing fly-cruise market from Europe.

An analysis of Table 3.2 suggests that Mexico is still by far the most popular cruise destination, followed by Costa Rica. This is still small in comparison with the Caribbean, which received 9,718,000 cruise passengers in the same year (Travel & Tourism Analyst, 1998, p. 12).

Table 3.2. Cruise visitors: Selected countries, 1996

Destination	Estimated arrivals
Mexico	2,142,000
Costa Rica	159,000
Dominican Republic	111,000
Colombia	100,000
Panama	14,000
Cuba	2,000

Source: WTO (various years)

Typical of the cruise market offering is the 'South American Discovery' package sold by Titan Tours. This is a 14-day cruise, starting at Viña del Mar on the Chilean coast and proceeding south around the Cape to Buenos Aires, with stops *en route* at Puerto Montt, Puerto Chacabuco, Punta Arenas, Ushuaia, Port Stanley in the Falkland Islands, Puerto Madryn and Montevideo.

Box 3.B. 'South American Discovery'

A unique opportunity to visit one of the last remaining virtually unspoiled regions of the world on this spectacular cruise down the Chilean Coast and around Cape Horn. With more mountains than the Alps, more glaciers than Alaska and more fijords than all Scandinavia, Chile is a natural wonderland rivalling any in the world. This holiday commences with a stay in the vibrant capital of Chile, Santiago, before setting sail on an unparalleled journey through breathtakingly spectacular scenery – snow-capped mountains, towering volcanoes, emerald-green lakes, glaciers and islands ...

(Titan Tours, 1999, p. 26)

TRAVEL TRADE: DISTRIBUTION

Introduction

The travel trade, sometimes referred to as the intermediary within the distribution system, is of vital importance in international travel, especially as facilitators and opinion leaders regarding destinations and different types of holiday destinations (Dimanche and Moody, 1998, p. 173). The structure of the travel trade comprises three key elements:

1 Wholesalers, tour operators and local ground handlers.
2 Travel agents.
3 Travel trade associations.

In all Latin American countries there is a distinction between wholesalers, tour operators and local ground handlers. The wholesaler designs and costs packages for inward and outbound tourism, then sells this on to a tour operator to brand and operate on a day-to-day level. However, the tour operator will also design and cost packages, as well as perhaps buy packages from wholesalers. In some instances they sell the packages through an associated chain of retail travel agencies. The ground handler is usually sub-contracted by the tour operator to provide local transfers, carriage of luggage and bookings to local attractions or on local public transport.

Most of the wholesalers and tour operators are situated in the capital city, although there will be specialist tour operators based at other destinations which are mainly responsible for ground handling and management of packages in that particular area. One of the interesting aspects of tour operation is the extent to which the internationalization of tour operators in Latin America has led to the development of international tourism business:

> The tour operator acts as a catalyst of demand – he interprets the market needs of his clients and packages these needs into destinations. His influence on the direction of demand is particularly significant to long haul, relatively expensive, destinations, i.e. most developing countries.
>
> (Jenkins, 1991, p. 274)

Lumsdon and Swift (1999) undertook a study of over 40 tour operators in Argentina, Chile, Uruguay and Paraguay. They concluded that in terms of the internationalization of the supply chain, tour operators in Europe and North America tend to dominate the relationship:

> tour operators have concentrated initially on intraregional supply, and in terms of developing long-haul markets have done so in association with major operators who provide a degree of security. This is especially the position with those operators who handle small volumes, and are almost totally reliant on the European or North American tour company to negotiate, design and administer an outbound tour on their behalf.
>
> (1999, pp. 437–8)

The World Wide Web

One of the fundamental changes in the travel trade sector is the rapidly increasing awareness and use of the internet (or the 'World Wide Web') by potential customers. This is a global trend but core international markets, especially the USA, have the highest penetration of internet usage in the world. According to a recent report in the *Financial Times,* the potential is considerable:

> those countries that have the greatest penetration of internet usage are also the countries that spend most heavily on tourism. The US, Germany, Japan and the UK dominate both internet usage and tourism expenditure. In 1997, these four countries alone accounted for 41 percent of worldwide tourism expenditure. They also accounted for 79 percent of the world's present internet population.
>
> (Richer, 1999)

The radical changes to lifestyles brought about by the internet, electronic mail, satellite TV and mobile phones (with internet capability) is also bringing changes to the provision of information and booking systems and hence to the entire distribution system in tourism. This is likely to have a number of impacts on the Latin American tourism market. First, the USA, Germany and the UK are three important markets and increasingly potential visitors will seek to book direct with airlines and specialist tour operators in any given country. A recent report suggested that of internet users in the USA, 31 per cent shop online; equivalent figures for Germany and the UK are 25 per cent and 24 per cent respectively (Rigby, 2000). Most tour operators and ground handlers have embraced the internet in order to compete more effectively in the international market and this is likely to become increasingly important in the future. Estimates vary, but one commentator has forecast that not only will travel be the 'biggest selling item over the internet within five to ten years' but 'airline tickets could account for 60 percent of these travel purchases' (Done, 2000).

The level of diffusion of ownership and the use of IT technology has been slower in developing markets, such as Latin America. However, the pattern is changing: according to a report for the Inter-Sectorial Unit for Tourism/OAS (ISUT, 1997), the trends in Latin America will be similar to those in North America, especially in Brazil, Chile and Mexico, which already account for 85 per cent of the internet users in Latin America.

Secondly, the travel agency sector in Latin American countries, which dominates the retailing of outbound markets, is likely to decline. Many travel agencies remain independent and small scale and rely on personal contact with consumers for much of their business. However, as the internet becomes more prevalent and visitors become more experienced, the pattern of buying holidays is predicted to change as elsewhere. It is likely that the transactional chain will become shorter as consumers gain more experience in purchasing holidays and other travel facilities directly from suppliers (Witt *et al.*, 1991, p. 31). Travel agencies will find it difficult to survive unless they embrace the new technologies, or seek a new role.

TRADE ASSOCIATIONS

There are numerous trade associations throughout Latin America which represent one or more of the tourism business sectors, lobby governments and international bodies for more investment and concessions. They are also involved in intra-regional trade fairs. Examples include ABAV (the Brazilian Association of Travel Agents), COTELCO (the Hotel Trade Association of Colombia), *Asociación Panameña de Hoteles* and LATA (the Latin American

Travel Association). The prime aim of these organizations is to secure favour with governments in terms of investment and development of tourism or the protection of the sector in times of austerity. Thus, there are extensive links between the wide range of associations and governmental tourism organizations, although the exact nature of the linkages and the degree of influence has not as yet been extensively researched. As well as seeking to influence policy, they also provide professional services to members, including the provision of databases, business-to-business marketing and training.

VISITOR ATTRACTIONS

The core visitor attractions of Latin America can be categorized into cultural/ heritage and natural. These are discussed in Chapters 4, 5 and 6. Almost every country has now devised thematic trails from the Gaucho Trail of Uruguay and Argentina to the Sundance Trail in Bolivia. They have also encouraged visitation to the important heritage sites, and there are a number of national museums such as Guatemala's National Archaeology Museum holding international appeal, for example, the renowned collection of Mayan artefacts. Throughout Latin American, there are also many small-scale museums and heritage centres interpreting local history and culture but these are not generators of large numbers of visitors.

As yet there has been little development of major entertainment attractions such as theme parks. The only park of any significance is Terra Encantada, located near Rio de Janeiro, which opened in 1998 following a US $300 million investment.

THE PUBLIC SECTOR

The national tourism organization (NTO) is a generic term used to describe an organization, structured and funded mainly by government, which is charged with a number of responsibilities in relation to tourism development, policy formulation, implementation and promotion. According to Jefferson and Lickorish (1991), NTOs also often have a number of other roles such as guardian of the country's image, coordinating between supply sectors, trailblazing new markets and monitoring results. The extent to which NTOs enjoy such influence varies according to governmental status (Mill and Morrison, 1992).

The purpose of NTOs is to represent the commercial interests of their members but they do have a number of other objectives:

- to encourage greater awareness of Latin America as a holiday destination;
- to develop closer working relationships between different supply sectors in the provision of tourism in Latin America;
- to improve the quality and quantity of media coverage;
- to organize promotional campaigns and particularly events to stimulate interest in tourism.

There are formal and informal linkages between the members of private trade associations and those government departments responsible for tourism promotion and development. In all countries the NTO has a primary responsibility for promotion to overseas visitors and, to a lesser extent, the domestic population. Thus, it often concentrates on evaluating the tourism offering in order to determine priority international markets to target. This is a complementary role to tourism suppliers and individual destinations. The mission statements, objectives, structures, and the degree of leverage each NTO possesses in the tourism process depends on a number of factors. These might include the extent of government commitment, the relative importance of tourism in the economy and the stage of development of tourism (Choy, 1993; Taylor, 1994). It might also be affected by the influence of the private tourism sectors and the extent to which they exert pressure as stakeholders within the political arena.

Many countries rely on their embassies or consular activities to promote tourism as they cannot resource an extensive network of sales offices in all markets. Thus, the trade sections within these governmental organizations are often the first line of contact for the independent traveller. A study undertaken at Staffordshire University in 1999 looked at the extent to which Latin American embassies in the UK influence potential visitor perceptions through their response to enquiries. Comparisons were made on the basis of the speed of response with which the embassies replied to enquiries, and the quantity and quality of information they provided:

- *Speed of response:* two months was allowed for a response before a follow-up telephone request was made.
- *Quantity/type of information:* this was classified as either a pamphlet, leaflet, magazine, brochure, booklet, or any other photocopied/printed information source (such as excerpts from the World Travel Guide).
- *Quality (of information):* this was expressed in terms of a 1–5 score, with 5 being the highest. Quality assessments were made on each piece of information received, and the combined total gave the overall 'quality of information' rating for each country.

As can be seen from Table 3.3, there was considerable variation between countries, both in the speed with which embassies sent out their promotional material and in the quality and quantity of information sent.

In Latin America the NTOs take a variety of forms (see Box 3.C). In a few countries tourism is represented at governmental level by a ministry of tourism and a formal governmental civil service structure exists to service the ministry. In many countries, however, the NTO is usually an agency reporting to a government department (generally Trade, Industry or Economics), and hence the level of status and resources it enjoys is usually lower in comparison.

For example, the NTO in Panama (IPAT, or the Instituto Panameño de Turismo) underwent restructuring in the mid-1990s, and Figure 3.1 shows a simplified version of the proposed structure.

Table 3.3. Initial perceptions based on embassy responses

Country	Speed	Information received Type	Quality
Argentina	7 days	1 pamphlet, 2 leaflets, 1 brochure, 20 × A4 photocopies	37
Bolivia	7 days	1 brochure	19
Brazil	5 days	2 pamphlets, 1 magazine	30
Chile	5 days	2 pamphlets, 5 magazines	30
Colombia	22 days	26 × double-sided A4 photocopies	26
Costa Rica	7 days	2 pamphlets, 4 magazines, 2 brochures, 2 photocopies	37
Cuba	2 days	8 pamphlets, 1 photocopy	28
Ecuador	11 days (after second contact)	7 pamphlets, 1 leaflet, 3 × A4 colour sheets	27
El Salvador	5 days	7 pamphlets, 1 leaflet, 1 × A4 colour sheets	27
Guatemala	9 days	8 pamphlets, 1 magazine	38
Honduras	6 days	3 pamphlets	34
Mexico	10 days	8 pamphlets, 1 leaflet	35
Nicaragua	9 days	7 pamphlets	30
Panama	8 weeks	12 pamphlets, 1 leaflet, 4 magazines, 1 booklet, 1 brochure	38
Paraguay	8 days	4 pamphlets, 1 leaflet	28
Peru	3 days	11 pamphlets, 5 × A4 photocopies	39
Uruguay	2 days (after second contact)	20 × A4 colour sheets	30
Venezuela	14 days	7 pamphlets, 1 × A4 photocopy	14

Note: No response was received from the Embassy of the Dominican Republic.
Source: Mistry (1999, pp. 74–8)

Box 3.C. National tourism organizations

Country	Organization
Argentina	Secretaria de Turismo de la Nación
Brazil	EMBRATUR
Bolivia	Viceministerio de Turismo
Chile	SERNATUR (Servicio Nacional de Turismo)
Colombia	Ministerio de Turismo
Costa Rica	Instituto Costarricense de Turismo
Cuba	Oficina de Turismo
Dominican Republic	Secretaria de Estado de Turismo
Ecuador	Ministerio de Turismo
El Salvador	CST (Corporación Salvadoreña de Turismo)
Guatemala	IGT (Instituto Guatemalteco de Turismo)
Honduras	IHT (Instituto Hondureño de Turismo)
Mexico	Secretaria de Turismo
Nicaragua	Ministerio de Turismo
Panama	IPAT (Instituto Panameño de Turismo)
Paraguay	Dirección de Turismo/Secretaria de Turismo
Peru	PROMPERU (Comisión para la Promoción del Peru)
Uruguay	Ministerio de Turismo
Venezuela	Corporación de Turismo

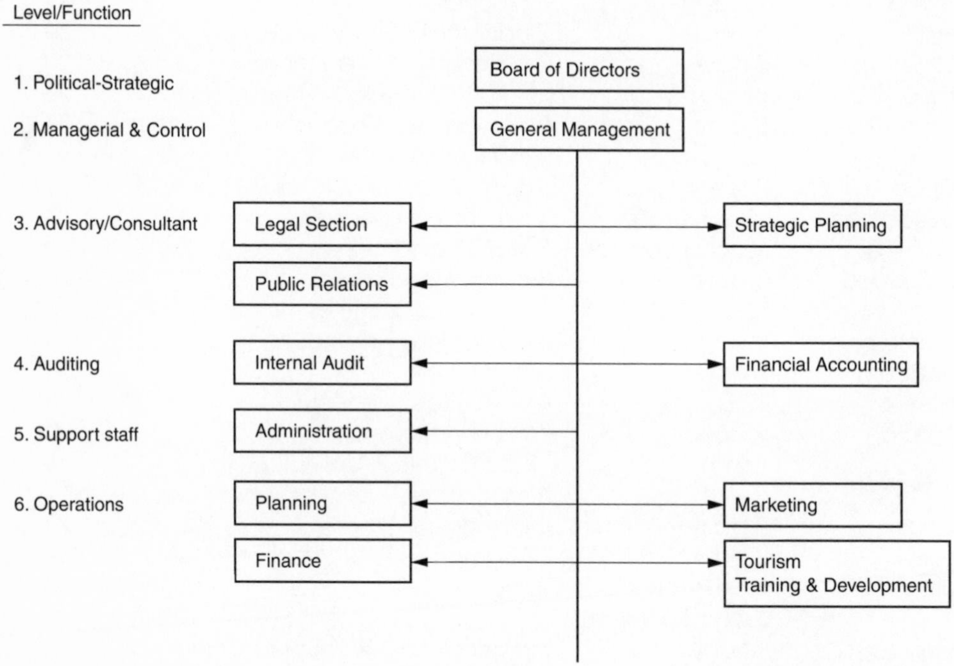

Level/Function

1. Political-Strategic — Board of Directors

2. Managerial & Control — General Management

3. Advisory/Consultant — Legal Section ← → Strategic Planning

Public Relations

4. Auditing — Internal Audit ← → Financial Accounting

5. Support staff — Administration ←

6. Operations — Planning ← → Marketing

Finance ← → Tourism Training & Development

Figure 3.1. Proposed structure for IPAT
Source: IPAT, 1993

The tasks and functions undertaken by NTOs in Latin America are usually set out by a directing body which involves members of government, and senior representatives from core trade organizations. Invariably, the most important function is that of promotion to markets, which involves a range of tasks from the establishment of a tourism office in originating markets to the hosting of familiarization trips by the media (Wahab *et al.*, 1976).

Other specific functions often included are listed in Box 3.D.

Box 3.D. The key functions of NTOs

Function	Example
Organization and attendance at workshops and trade fairs	The Secretaria de Turismo (Argentina) arranges to be present at between 15-20 shows per year in the USA, including the International Adventure Travel Show, Rosemont, Illinois.
Research	PROMPERÚ undertakes an annual survey of visitors who attend its stand at trade fairs; they are particularly interested in the effectiveness of the stand as a promotional tool, and in visitor perceptions of the image of Peru as a tourist destination.
Training and quality standards	As part of its development plan (1995-2000), SECTUR, the Mexican Tourism Ministry, introduced the 'National Crusade for Quality and Excellence in Tourism'. This was aimed at raising standards of customer service in government, the local community, business, labour and educational establishments.
Consumer classification standards	Several NTOs work with accommodation providers to establish a grading system for hotels.
Tourism policy	Advice relating to the development of tourism policy and planning.
Visitor education	The Costa Rican Tourism Authority (ICT) issues publicity material to advise visitors about the conservation of the environment and personal security.

One major function which all NTOs undertake is promotional activity, and this often absorbs a large portion of available budgets. In some countries it is the prime or sole function and is underpinned within the mission and aims of the NTO. The Honduran IHT, for example, recently outlined the major promotional objectives for the country's tourism industry:

- Improve the national image.
- Reinforce the country's reputation as a tourist destination.
- Strengthen relationships with tourism companies in the USA and Europe.
- Increase the level of state promotion of tourism.
- Increase the average tourist daily spend.
- Maintain a policy of sustainable development.

(IHT, 1999)

One area which is becoming increasing important is human resources. Whilst the education and training of employees in tourism remains a task undertaken primarily by the private sector, there is increasing pressure to encourage NTOs to raise the profile of the tourism sector as a source of employment. The private sector would like to see NTOs initiate policy guidelines and in some cases national training schemes to improve the human resource input in tourism. Pizam (1999) undertook a study of 209 travel and tourism enterprises and 17 NTOs in Latin America. The findings echoed that of a smaller study undertaken by Baum in the early 1990s (Baum, 1994) which highlighted the lack of qualified staff and poor skill levels in computer technology, marketing and foreign languages. The respondents were concerned that governments and political institutions afforded low priority to tourism and that educational institutions were not equipped to or failed to teach the skills appropriate to the business of tourism.

In summary, there has been considerable interest regarding the effectiveness of NTOs, such as studies comparing resources and the outcomes achieved by various organizations. For example, a study by Soteriou and Roberts concluded that:

Many NTOs represent government involvement in tourism and bear the features of governmental bureaucracies that include considerable organisational inertia. As such, an externally orientated, entrepreneurial approach (which is the essence of strategic planning) cannot be easily promoted in organisations of this type. In addition, the highly political nature of NTOs, especially those with considerable regulatory power, might inhibit establishing a process that aims to facilitate organisational decision-making.

(1998, p. 28)

CITY AND REGIONAL TOURISM AUTHORITIES

As well as governmental organizations there are also in some countries tourism authorities or departments responsible for coordinating tourism development and liaising with the private sectors to publicize tourism. These organizations vary in power and resource base. Smaller authorities often engage primarily in promotional activity. On the contrary, capital cities often collect data and are involved in training, the organization of trade fairs and the upgrading of the tourism offering.

A fundamental starting point is an understanding of visitor behaviour and feedback; some destinations have in place visitor tracking mechanisms to measure these factors (Haywood and Muller, 1988; Ryan, 1995). The example of Buenos Aires, the Argentinian capital and the major gateway to the rest of the country, offers an insight into the difficult task faced by the city. Attitudes of visitors are monitored on an annual basis by the *Dirección General de Turismo de la Municipalidad* (the Buenos Aires tourist authority). Interviews are conducted at the two airports of Buenos Aires (Ezeiza and Jorge Newberry), the seaport and the main bus station. The surveys undertaken in the early 1990s suggested that, whilst the majority of visitors had formed generally favourable impressions, those dislikes that were mentioned tended to reinforce some of the issues referred to previously. The major complaints by European tourists are indicated in Box 3.E.

Box 3.E. Survey of European visitors to Buenos Aires (1993)

Major dislikes of European visitors to Buenos Aires:

- delays caused by customs
- lack of hygiene in toilets and a lack of public toilets
- expensive taxi charges, especially from the airport
- time taken to get from the international airport (Ezeiza)to the city centre
- lack of long distance public telephones, and overall poor quality of telephonic communications
- suspected cheating by public officials
- begging in public places (especially restaurants)
- traffic congestion and noise
- uncomfortable public transport
- undesirable characters (referred to as 'sharks') offering services under false pretences at the airport
- lack of city information

(Taken from survey data held at the offices of the Dirección General de Turismo de la Municipalidad de Buenos Aires, Sarmiento 1551, Buenos Aires)

As a result of this, the tourism sector, in conjunction with the Buenos Aires city authority, combined with the tourism supply sector to implement a succession of development programmes to improve the city's position as an international centre. For example, the problem of communications is one with which the Argentinian government has long been familiar and, in an attempt to address the inadequacies of the network, it began a programme of privatization of the telephone system. Whilst this brought in new investment and expertise, it also brought a high level of disruption during the 1990s.

SUMMARY

During the 1990s tourism in Latin America grew both in terms of demand and supply. This has been a response partly to the increase in business tourism in the recently created economic markets, partly to meet the needs of international long haul tour operators and, to a lesser extent, to satisfy a new intra-regional demand for tourism.

The determination of tourism policy in many Latin American countries has been incremental. There also remains an underlying tension between the public and private sector as to what their roles should be in the process of development. The exceptions are Mexico and Cuba where the respective governments have set out a clear framework for the pattern of development. Tourism supply is likely to increase in the early years of the twenty-first century but the process will be uneven across the continent.

REFERENCES

Asociación Latinoamericana de Ferrocarriles (1997) personal communication.

Barcelona, E. (1994) 'Submarinos: Darían en Concesión la Fábrica', *La Nación* (Buenos Aires) (26 March).

Barham, J. (1993) 'Buying into Argentina Was the Easy Bit', *Financial Times* (7 December).

Baum, T. (1994) 'National Tourism Policies: Implementing the Human Resource Dimension', *Tourism Management*, Vol. 15(4), pp. 259–66.

Bennett, M. (1993) 'Information Technology and Travel Agency: A Customer Service Perspective', *Tourism Management*, Vol. 14(4), pp. 259–66.

Brown, G. P. and Essex, S. J. (1989) 'Tourism Policy in the Public Sector' in S. Witt and L. Moutinho (eds), *Tourism Marketing and Management Handbook*, Prentice Hall, London.

Butler, R. W. (1980) 'The Concept of a Tourist Area Cycle of Evolution: Implications for Management of Resources', *Canadian Geographer*, Vol. XXIV(1), p. 5.

Calvert, P. (1996) 'Privatisation in Argentina', *Bulletin of Latin American Research*, Vol. 15(2), pp. 145–56.

Canastrelli, E. and Costa, P. (1991) 'Tourist Carrying Capacity, A Fuzzy Approach', *Annals of Tourism Research,* Vol. 18, pp. 295–311.

Casado, M. (1997) 'Mexico's 1989–94 Tourism Plan: Implications of Internal Political and Economic Stability', Vol. 12 (Summer), pp. 44–51.

Choy, D. J. L. (1992) 'Life Cycle Models of Pacific Island Destinations', *Journal of Travel Research,* Vol. 30(3), pp. 26–31.

Choy, D. J. L. (1993) 'Alternative Roles of National Tourism Organisations', *Tourism Management,* Vol. 14 (October), pp. 357–65.

Cooper, C., Fletcher, J., Gilbert, D., Shepherd, R. and Wanhill, S. (1998) *Tourism: Principles and Practice,* Longman, Harlow.

de Kadt, E. (1992) 'Making the Alternative Sustainable: Lessons from Development for Tourism' in V. L. Smith and W. R. Eadington (eds), *Tourism Alternatives: Potentials and Problems in the Development of Tourism* (pp. 47–75), University of Pennsylvania Press and the International Academy of Tourism Study, Philadelphia.

De Simone, E. (1994) 'Plan Para Bajar en un 25% El Costo de la Construcción', *La Nación* (Buenos Aires) (20 March).

Dimanche, F. and Moody, M. (1998) 'Perceptions of Destination Image: A Study of Latin American Intermediary Travel Buyers', *Tourism Analysis,* No. 3, pp. 173–80.

Dimitriou, H. T. (1992) 'Transport and Third World City Development' in H. T. Dimitriou and G. A. Banjo (eds), *Transport Planning For Third Worlds Cities* (pp. 1–30), Routledge, London.

Done, K. (2000) 'Airlines Take Online Route to Soft Landing', *Financial Times* (24 February).

Douglas, N. (1996) 'Applying The Life Cycle Model to Melanesia', *Annals of Tourism Research,* Vol. 24, No. 1, pp. 1–22.

Echtner, C. M. and Ritchie, J. R. B (1993) 'The Measurement of Destination Image: An Empirical Assessment', *Journal of Tourism Studies,* Vol. 34(4), pp. 3–13.

Edgell, D. L. (1987) 'The Formulation of Tourism Policy: A Managerial Framework' in J. R. B. Ritchie and C. R. Goeldner (eds), *Travel, Tourism and Hospitality Research* (pp. 22–3), John Wiley & Sons, New York.

Elliot, H. (1990) 'Task Force Ordered to Assess Tourism Impact', *The Times,* 2 August.

Gartner, W. C. (1993) 'Image Formation Process', *Journal of Travel and Tourism,* Vol. 2, pp. 191–216.

Gerchunoff, P. and Colonia, G. (1993) 'Privatisation in Argentina' in M. Sánchez and L. Corona (eds), *Privatisation in Latin America* (pp. 276–301), Inter-American Development Bank, Washington.

Getz, D. (1983) 'Capacity to Absorb Tourism: Concepts and Implications for Strategic Planning' *Annals of Tourism Research,* Vol. 10, pp. 239–63.

Gibbons, W. (2000) 'The Cruise Market', *Tourism,* Spring.

Go, F. M. and Pine, R. (1995) *Globalisation Strategies in the Hotel Industry,* Routledge, London.

Goodall, B. and Stabler, M. (1992) 'Environmental Auditing in the Quest for Sustainable Tourism: The Destination Perspective.' Paper presented to Tourism in Europe, the 1992 Conference, Durham, 8–10 July.

Gunn, C. A. (1994) *Tourism Planning,* Taylor & Francis, Washington DC.

Harrison, D. (1992) 'International Tourism and the Less Developed Countries: The Background' in D. Harrison (ed.), *Tourism and the Less Developed Countries* (pp. 1–19), John Wiley, Chichester.

Haywood, K. M. (1988) 'Responsible and Responsive Tourism Planning in the Community', *Tourism Management,* Vol. 9(2), pp. 105–18.

Haywood, K. M. and Muller, T. E. (1988) 'The Urban Tourist Experience: Evaluating Satisfaction', *Hospitality Education and Research Journal,* Vol. 12, pp. 453–9.

IHT (1999) *Plan de Mercadeo, 1999,* Instituto Hondureño de Turismo, Tegucigalpa, M.D.C.

IPAT (1993) *Plan Maestro de Desarrollo Turísticode Panamá: 1993–2000*, Instituto Panameño de Turismo, Departmento de Desarrollo Regional y Medio Ambiente, Panama.

ISUT (1997) *Sustaining Tourism by Managing New Technology for Destination Markets,* Inter Sectoral Unit for Tourism, Washington DC.

Jefferson, A. and Lickorish, L. (1991) *Marketing Tourism: A Practical Guide,* Longman, London.

Jenkins, C. L. (1991) 'Tourism Policies in Developing Countries' in S. Medlik (ed.), *Managing Tourism* (pp. 269–78), Butterworth-Heinemann, Oxford.

Jenkins, C. L. (1994) 'Tourism in Developing Countries: The Privatisation Issue' in A. V. Seaton *et al.* (eds), *Tourism: The State of the Art* (pp. 3–9), John Wiley, Chichester.

Keeling, D. (1994) 'Regional Development and Transport Policy in Argentina: An Appraisal', *The Journal of Developing Areas*, Vol. 28, July, pp. 487–502.

Kendall, S. (1996) 'Long Route to Good Roads', *Financial Times Survey: Infrastructure in Latin America* (13 September).

Keogh, B. (1990) 'Public Participation in Community Tourism Planning', *Annals of Tourism Research*, Vol. 17, pp. 449–65.

Lamb, B. and Davidson, S. (1996) 'Tourism Transportation in Ontario, Canada' in L. Harrison and W. Husbands (eds), *Practising Responsible Tourism: International Case Studies in Tourism Planning, Policy and Development* (pp. 261–76), John Wiley, Chichester.

Lapper, R. and Pilling, D. (1995) 'IFC Announces $81m Argentine Toll-road Funding', *Financial Times*, 19 April.

Lea, J. (1988) *Tourism and Development in the Third World*, Routledge, London.

Leiper, N. (1990) *Tourism Systems: An Interdisciplinary Perspective*, Massey University, North Palmerston.

Lewis, C. C. and Chambers, R. E. (1989) *Marketing Leadership in Hospitality,* Van Nostrand Reinhold, New York.

Liu, Z. H. (1994) 'Tourism Development – A Systems Analysis', in A. V. Seaton *et al.* (eds), *Tourism: The State of the Art* (pp. 20–30), John Wiley, Chichester.

Lumsdon, L. M. (1997) *Tourism Marketing,* International Thompson Business Press, London.

Lumsdon, L. M. and Swift, J. S. (1999) 'The Role of the Tour Operator in South America: Argentina, Chile, Paraguay and Uruguay', *International Journal of Tourism Research*, Vol. 1(6), pp. 429–39.

McQueen, M. (1989) 'Multinationals in Tourism' in S. F. Witt and L. Moutinho (eds), *Tourism Marketing and Management Handbook* (pp. 285–91), Prentice Hall, Englewood Cliffs, NJ.

Meethan, K. (1996) 'Place, Image, and Power: Brighton as a Resort' in T. Selwyn (ed.), *The Tourist Image, Myths and Myth Making in Tourism*, John Wiley, Chichester.

Middleton, V. T. C. (1994) *Marketing in Travel and Tourism*, 2nd edition, Butterworth-Heinemann, Oxford.

Mill, R. C. and Morrison, A. M. (1992) *The Tourism System*, Prentice Hall, Englewood Cliffs, NJ.

Mistry, L. (1999) 'The Image of Latin America', unpublished Msc dissertation, Staffordshire University Business School, Stoke-on-Trent.

Molina, S. (1999) *Turismo sin Límites*, Cientur, Mexico City.

Morrison, A. M., Yang, C., Cai, L., Nadkarni, N. and O'Leary, J. T. (1996) 'Comparative Profiles of Travellers on Cruises and Land-Based Resort Vacations', *Journal of Tourism Studies*, Vol. 7(2), pp. 54–64.

Murphy, P. E. (1985) *Tourism: A Community Approach*, Methuen, New York.

O'Hare, G. and Barrett, H. (1997) 'The Destination Life Cycle: International Tourism in Peru', *Scottish Geographical Magazine*, Vol. 13(2), pp. 66–73.

Page, S. (1999) *Transport and Tourism*, Longman, New York.

Pizam, A. (1999) 'The State of Travel and Tourism Human Resources in Latin America', *Tourism Management*, Vol. 20, pp. 575–86.

Poole, C. and Bowen, S. (1998) 'Tourist Trade ... Latin America', *Latin Trade*, Vol. 6(8), pp. 11–17.

Poon, A. (1998) 'All Inclusive Resorts', *Travel & Tourism Analyst* 6, Economist Intelligence Unit, London.

Richer, P. (1999) 'Agents Must Adapt or Pack Their Bags', *Financial Times* (18 November).

Rigby, E. (2000) 'Does E-commerce Give the Consumer More Power?', *Financial Times Survey: Information Technology* (1 March).

Rodriguez, M. (1993) 'La Planeación del Turismo en Mexico. Reflexiónes y Perspectivas', *Estudios y Perspectivas en Turismo*, Vol. 2(1), pp. 31–8.

Ryan, C. (1995) *Researching Tourist Satisfaction: Issues, Concepts, Problems*, Routledge, London.

Secretaria de Turismo (1991) *Programa Nacional de Modernización del Turismo*, Secretaria de Turismo, Mexico City.

Soteriou, E. C. and Roberts, C. (1998) 'The Strategic Planning Process in National Tourism Organisations', *Journal of Travel Research*, Vol. 37 (August), pp. 21–9.

Taylor, G. D. (1994) 'Research in National Tourist Organisations' in J. R. B. Ritchie and C. R. Goeldner (eds), *Travel, Tourism and Hospitality Research: A Handbook For Managers and Researchers* (pp. 147–54), John Wiley, New York.

Titan Tours (1999) *Quality Escorted Cruise and Tour Holidays Worldwide (January 2000 to May 2001)*, Titan Travel Ltd, Redhill.

Travel & Tourism Analyst (1998) 'The North American Cruise Market', *Travel & Tourism Intelligence, No. 4*, London.

Vellas, F. and Bécherel, L. (1999) *The International Marketing of Travel and Tourism*, Macmillan, Basingstoke.

Wahab, S., Crampon, L. J. and Rothfield, L. M. (1976) *Tourism Marketing: A Destination Orientated Programme for the Marketing of International Tourism*, Tourism International Press, London.

Wheatcroft, S. (1994) *Aviation and Tourism Policies: Balancing the Benefits*, Routledge, London.

Witt, S. F., Brooke, Z. and Buckley, P. J. (1991) *The Management of International Tourism*, Unwin Hymes, London.

WTO (1997) Data supplied by Division of Economics & Market Research, World Tourism Organization, Madrid.

Zizumbo, L. (1991) 'El Turismo: Antecedents y Desarrollo', *Ollin*, Facultad de Turismo de la UEAM, Mexico City, pp. 4–30.

CHAPTER 4

Beach Tourism and Integrated Resorts

INTRODUCTION

The term 'visitor destination' refers to any place which has touristic appeal at an international, national or more local level. Hu and Brent Ritchie (1993, p. 25) define it as: 'a package of tourism facilities and services, which like any other consumer product, is composed of a number of multi-dimensional attributes'. The destination experience is still considered to be the 'fundamental product' in tourism (Brent Ritchie and Crouch, 2000, p. 1). Four integral elements have been identified by Lumsdon (1997) as prime attractors, the built environment, supporting supply services, and atmosphere or ambience. The concept 'ambience' is often expressed in terms of sense of place, or the cultural patterns of the residential community, which are represented in the local ways and expressed in everyday living. In the context of Latin America, with its rich tapestry of heritage, landscape form and climatic diversity, the appeal of adventure, culture and wildlife have tended to dominate destination imagery. The importance of beach tourism to several Latin American countries has, in contrast, been understated in the literature. Not only are the integral ingredients of sunshine and warmth abundant throughout the year, but also the quality of the beaches, in terms of the softness of the sand, slope and features, are important. These factors are in addition to an often exceptional background landscape, which make resorts such as Rio de Janeiro internationally renowned in the tourism sector. Riotur, the City of Rio de Janeiro tourism authority, naturally emphasizes the beach as one of the city's principal tourism attractions in its promotional campaign (see Box 4.A).

Box 4.A. Copacabana Beach, Rio de Janeiro

It's almost impossible for visitors to Rio to resist the charm of the city's eighty kilometers of beaches. Framed by the wavy black and white mosaics of Avenue Atlântica, Copacabana is one of the main reasons for this fascination. In fact, there are two separate beaches here: Leme (one kilometer) and Copacabana (just over three kilometers). A centre of activity both night and day, the beach is lined with kiosks, a bicycle path and racks, lifeguard posts, public showers and bathrooms, hotels, bars and open-air restaurants.

(Riotur, 1999, p. 9)

BEACH TOURISM

Five countries, namely Brazil, Cuba, the Dominican Republic, Mexico and Venezuela, are noted for beach tourism (Getino, 1990); they are discussed below. Several other Latin American countries, however, possess extensive and numerous beach resorts. These have been primarily the preserve of a domestic market, or that of a neighbouring country. Such beach offerings may well not be significant in appealing to a long haul European or North American market, but are important within an intra-regional setting (Schlüter, 1991).

For example, for decades the beach resorts of Uruguay have served the middle classes of Buenos Aires, along with their other favourite destination, the coastal resort of Mar del Plata, which received 2500 visitors in the period December 1996 to March 1997. Most people visited at the weekends and put intense pressure on the scarce mid-range hotel supply, causing La Asociación Empresaria Hotelera y Gastronómica de Mar de Plata to note in March 1997 that 'nobody else comes' to Mar del Plata because of the scarcity of hotel supply (Farchi, 1997).

In contrast, the Paraguayans favour the coastal resorts of southern Brazil and tour operators in the capital of Asunción compete to offer coach holidays throughout the season to Torres and Tramandai. In Chile there are a number of coastal resorts, of which Viña del Mar is the most popular. There are other resorts, for example, in the Arica area to the north, but these are not as well known internationally. It is difficult to estimate the level of demand of this type of domestic or neighbouring country market as the flows are not always measured. Demand nevertheless has been sustained and sufficient to encourage the development of sizeable coastal resorts in several countries.

Cities that offer seascape and beaches in South America include Cartagena and Santa Marta (Colombia); Montevideo and Punta del Este (Uruguay); Mar del Plata (Argentina); Lima (Peru); Rio de Janeiro, Pôrto Alegre, Salvador,

Recife and Fortaleza (Brazil); and Valparaiso and Viña del Mar (Chile). In Central America and the Caribbean, Mexico has the largest concentration of seaside towns, including Puerto Vallarta, Cancún, Acapulco, Veracruz, Campeche, Cozumel and Mazatlán. Other destinations include Colón (Panama); Limón and Puntarenas (Costa Rica); Puerto Barrios (Guatemala); Havana (Cuba); and Santo Domingo in the Dominican Republic. (See Box 4.B.)

Box 4.B. Classic beach resorts in Latin America

Argentina:	Mar del Plata
Brazil:	Recife, Rio de Janeiro, Salvador
Chile:	Viña del Mar
Colombia:	Cartagena, Santa Marta, Isla San Andrés
Costa Rica:	Guanacaste
Cuba:	Varadero
Mexico:	Acapulco, Cozumel, Puerto Vallarta
Uruguay:	Punta del Este

Brazil

With over 5000 miles of coastline, Brazil has some of Latin America's finest beaches, primarily situated in the states to the northeast, Santa Catarina and Rio Grande do Sul. An early project, known as TURUS, aimed to develop seaside resorts for the international market. In reality the resorts have subsequently attracted mainly Argentinians (Schlüter, 1994, p. 250). Demand for beach tourism is still generated mainly by visitors from Argentina and Paraguay. In global terms, the Copacabana beach at Rio de Janeiro is the most famous, but in the late 1980s–early 1990s it has suffered from a negative press because of theft and muggings.

Cuba

Despite the US ban on their citizens visiting Cuba, and the equally staunch anti-American position held for well over 40 years by Cuba, the country has managed to re-build its coastal tourism offering despite the lack of a major near market. In the 1950s, prior to the revolution, Cuba enjoyed a strong US market which amounted to some 350,000 visitors per annum (Salinas Chavez, 1998). It now attracts a Canadian, European and Latin American market amounting to 600,000 visitors per annum and worth approximately 1.5 billion US dollars (Reuters, 1998). Its premier beach resort, Varadero, which was developed in the 1880s by the American textile manufacturer Dupont, has grown dramatically. During the 1990s other resorts have been built around many of Cuba's extensive beaches and small islands, destinations such as Cayo Largo. The sustained growth in supply signifies a decade of rapid tourism development (Avella and Mills, 1996, p. 57).

This was not always the case, however. During the 1960s and 1970s Cuba resisted tourism and concentrated on the production of sugar cane and tobacco. From the mid-1980s government policy changed dramatically. Tourism development was sanctioned by the socialist administration under the direction of President Fidel Castro as an economic necessity following the break up of the Soviet Bloc, and the consequent loss of trading support. The collapse of this trading accord, known as the Council for Mutual Economic Assistance, led to a severe decline of the Cuban economy in the late 1980s bringing devastating hardship for the Cuban people. It eventually led to the re-appraisal of tourism as a way of earning foreign exchange, in order to alleviate some of the crippling problems of a severely weakened economy (Perez-Lopez, 1994; de Holan and Phillips, 1997).

The encouragement of international tourism has brought with it a number of changes. First, it has led to a widening of foreign policy. It has also led to an acceptance of the need to meet the expectations of visitors from other countries, In addition, Cuba has had to make alliances with capitalist tourism enterprises, although this has been somewhat hampered by US foreign policy (Krohn and O'Donnell, 1999, p. 85). For example, Cubanacan (the government tourism organization) has signed up to joint venture capital and management projects with international hotel groups such as Grupo Sol (Spain), Golden Tulip International (the Netherlands) and Superclubs from Jamaica (Berman, 1994). In this respect, Cuba has engaged in normal trading deals in order to facilitate rapid tourism growth.

While sun and sand holidays predominate in Cuba, water sports such as sea fishing and scuba diving are growing as the visitor market widens; there is also growing interest in health tourism (Goodrich, 1993, p. 36). However, resorts still concentrate on beach tourism, characterized by a growing number of all-inclusive hotels and holiday clubs, such as SuperClubs from Jamaica, which are predominately enclavic by nature (Bleasdale and Tapsell, 1994, p. 103). There remains, however, a question over the quality of the overall beach tourism offering:

Cuban resorts tend to be basic brick-and-mortar structures built on decent beaches. There are few amenities; the food and beverage operations are simple; recreational activities are limited, in most cases, to the pool and beach area; night time entertainment is strictly on-site; and shopping is non-existent. The bottom line? For a tourist, there is little to do in Cuba other than enjoy the beaches and the tropical climate.

(Berman, 1994, pp. 12–13)

The Dominican Republic

More than any other Latin American country, the Dominican Republic has invested in tourism in order to improve its economic position, following the introduction of a major economic stabilization programme agreed with the IMF in 1992 (Betances and Spalding, 1996). As a consequence of this, the country is a far more important visitor destination than its neighbour, Haiti, which shares the island of Hispaniola. It has an indigenous population of 7.3 million people and receives 2.2 million visitors per annum. Resort development in the Dominican Republic has been rapid during the 1980s and 1990s, including the expansion of all-inclusive beach resorts at Bávaro, Boca Chica, Juan Dolio, La Romana, Playa Dorada, Puerto Plata, Punto Cana and Samaná.

Throughout the Caribbean and increasingly in Latin America, the inclusive beach complex is gaining in popularity and nowhere more than in the Dominican Republic. There are a number of companies, one of the fastest growing of which is Allegro Resorts, based on the island. This has nearly 30 such resorts, including several in Mexico and Venezuela (Poon, 1998). Most are located in the Caribbean, which is the key zone for such resorts, but it is predicted that Latin America will become far more important than it is at present.

The all-inclusive holiday, as a generic concept, involves the visitor paying for a package, which includes most or all ingredients of the holiday such as transfers, food and beverages, use of facilities on the complex, tips and taxes. In practice, there are variations. Some complexes might include use of all sporting facilities; others charge for instruction in the more costly pursuits. The trend is towards bringing all elements into the package. This is appealing to tourism suppliers because travel agents can get larger commissions, the entire vacation price is paid in advance, costs can be measured more accurately and resources can be utilized more effectively. It is argued that the overall benefit to the visitor is that such complexes offer value for money, personal security, and a wide range of sporting or health facilities often segmented for different market groupings. The all-inclusive concept has been subject to criticism primarily on two grounds: (1) visitors do not explore the host region or country, and (2) they do not spend as much in the local economy as they would if they toured around.

The hotel inventory of the Dominican Republic is estimated to exceed 40,000 bedrooms, which is small in comparison to Mexico. There has also been a considerable shift in terms of ownership from mainly local independent hotel operators to at least 50 per cent belonging to chains and in particular the larger hotels, such as Barcelo, Club Med, Inter Continental, Grupo Sol, Ramada International and Sheraton Hotels.

The number of inclusive resorts clubs, such as El Portillo Beach Club, Capella Beach Resort, Caribbean Village Luperon, Casa de Campo and the largest Hamaca Beach, have been developed in the 1980s and 1990s. There are now over 40 such complexes. The rapid rise of tourism on the island and the heavy impact of visitors has been the subject of criticism, especially the strain placed by tourism development on the supply of water, on sanitation and refuse disposal. In the wake of Hurricane George in 1998, the government allocated funds for re-building many of the damaged inclusive resorts, but at the same time set aside funds to improve water quality and to remove rubbish tips at several resorts (Travel & Tourism Intelligence, 1999). It is likely that tourism has reached a level of saturation on the island in terms of use of core resources.

Mexico

In terms of international appeal, Mexico has undoubtedly been the leader in the provision of beach tourism, although both Cuba and the Dominican Republic have increased their sea-and-sand offering dramatically during the 1990s. Mexico possesses a lengthy Pacific coastline in addition to the Gulf of Mexico and the Caribbean Sea. There are many exceptional beaches, which have for decades appealed to the domestic market, and more recently to a more adventurous North American market.

Mexico's traditional resorts such as Acapulco, Matzatlán and Puerto Vallarta have grown rapidly in the past 30 years to meet this increasing international demand, witnessing a rash of hotels, apartments, marinas and golf courses. The Mexican government, however, has chosen a different route to tourism development by investing mainly in new integrated resorts. These modern, self-contained resorts have become very attractive to European and North American markets, and have been promoted aggressively as safe havens in the warmth of the South. Nevertheless, development of traditional resorts has remained important to Mexico in terms of generating employment in regional economies. With regard to Puerto Vallarta, Chant (1992) refers to the pace of tourism development, for example, as population increases were registered at a level of 11–12 per cent per annum in the 1980s as a consequence of tourism.

However, in later research, she notes the decline in visitor spending in the early 1990s, which she attributes to the construction of an extensive self-contained marina development, built along the coast, only a short distance from Puerto Vallarta (Chant, 1994, p. 217). Chant's research has also revealed other social impacts arising from rapid tourism growth, which are discussed in Chapter 9.

Venezuela

Venezuela has approximately 2800 miles of Caribbean and Atlantic coastline, and this forms its major tourism offering. There are well over 100 beach resorts, many to the west of the capital Caracas. Along the coast near Puerto La Cruz, Maiquetia and near La Guiara are numerous resorts which serve a mainly domestic market. This tourism offering suffered during the heavy rains and mudslides of December 1999, which resulted in extensive damage to resorts and much loss of life.

Allegro Resorts, from the Dominican Republic, has opened two major all-inclusive resorts on Isla Margarita, which is often presented as a Caribbean destination for overseas visitors in the promotional material of tour operators. This type of beach tourism complex is being planned elsewhere.

Central America

With the exception of Costa Rica, the international appeal of beach tourism in Central American countries remains relatively unexploited, and consequently there remain many pristine beaches with relatively low levels of use. The main markets are primarily residents from nearby townships. As suggested, Costa Rica is the exception as beach tourism has been developed at Guanacaste and Quepos on the Pacific Coast. In Guanacaste, the Papaguayo project is expected to urbanize an entire coastal strip around the Bahia Culebra and is expected to be the largest project of its kind in Central America, accommodating approximately 30,000 visitors, although this is small in contrast to Mexican-style integrated resort development. This has been highly controversial in Costa Rica, as it signals the government's willingness to attract mass tourism. On the Caribbean coast there are also extensive beaches south of Puerto Limón, where many of them are within reserve areas and are relatively undeveloped.

There has been limited development of resorts in other Central American countries such as Montelimar and Pochomil on Nicaragua's Pacific Coast. However, beach tourism to date has not been a major feature of tourism promotion for many Central American countries, which have generally concentrated instead on cultural and nature-based tourism.

INTEGRATED RESORTS

Introduction

The term integrated resort refers to a newly built visitor destination which has been planned, implemented and promoted in a coordinated manner, usually by one agency following a master plan and following specific guidelines. This agency usually drives the concept forward by bringing a multiplicity of public and private sector organizations together in order to resource and implement the construction and operation of the resort. The end result is an essentially self-contained resort, which can be sold to an international market.

The criteria adopted for site selection of integrated resorts is outlined in Table 4.1. This table includes a summary of some of the major issues which have been the subject of academic debate in recent years.

Table 4.1. Integrated resorts

Core criteria	Explanation	Critical issues
Nature of the site: physical features and cultural heritage	A site should have major appeal(s), such as an extensive beach, marina, an impressive background landscape or an exceptionally strong cultural appeal.	Coastal development will impinge on natural features and/or cultural authenticity. Therefore, balance between new buildings and the setting is of crucial importance at design stage.
Climate	Primarily sun-drenched locations where potential threats such as hurricanes can be minimized.	Evaluation of micro-climate is important: Hurricane Gilbert damaged the development of Cancún, Mexico.
Land availability	Evaluation of land in relation to other possible uses.	Land ownership, and displacement of traditional elements of use (e.g fishing, farming), are all contentious issues.
Access	The degree of current or potential access by all forms of transport.	Air and car access are prioritized over more sustainable forms of transport. Travel within resorts can often lead to congestion or a poor quality environment. This fits uneasily with sustainable development.
Positioning in relation to existing resorts	Assessment of how a new resort might impact on existing nearby resorts.	Major disadvantage for existing resorts is the loss of markets and employees.

Core criteria	Explanation	Critical issues
Infrastructure	Resource commitment required to modify existing/build new infrastructure: water supply, power, communications, waste disposal.	Heavy use of resources such as water can create problems for agriculture. Evaluation of potential effects prior to construction is required.
Minimizing pollution	Necessary to determine a scale of development appropriate to locality, in order to minimize impacts and avoid excessive pollution.	Balance between optimum level of commercial development and minimization of negative impacts is a major issue for developers.
Host community	Need to evaluate local opinion, and incorporate economic and socio-cultural values within the development process, is an essential element in shaping new resort.	Techniques/approaches to evaluation of varied wants/opinions of host community can be superficial, or offer minimal commitment to participation.
Availability of labour and capital	Appraisal of private and public sector financing and availability of labour supply.	Wide ranging: from sourcing capital to recruitment and training of local workforce. Local ownership/employment *vis-à-vis* foreign involvement can be an issue.

Source: adapted from Inskeep (1994)

Investment in this type of resort has been justified on the grounds of meeting market expectations of the 'North' within the context of the 'South'. It is argued by practitioners that the integrated resort is essentially what the mass market wants, and that the level of demand vindicates the extent of development. Integrated resorts also bring a heightened level of personal security, and meet the needs of visitors who prefer heavily packaged holidays. They are what Lumsdon and Swift refer to as 'wealthy tourism enclaves separated from poor host communities' (1994, p. 362).

The core plans for an integrated resort are likely to include:

- Land use plans for hotels, attractions, shopping zones, residential areas, conservation areas, beach areas.
- Transport plans setting out access to and within the resort.
- Power and telecommunications.
- Water supply, sewerage and drainage plans.
- Communications and promotional plans.

Thus, the plans for the development of such coastal resorts are considered to be integrated into two respects: first, in line with other regional or national economic development plans and second, in terms of bringing all key tourism elements together in accordance with a planning blueprint for a new town.

Integrated Resorts in Mexico

Mexico has been the prime mover of integrated resort development in Latin America. The commitment to integrated resorts has always featured strongly in the succession of Mexican tourism master plans, and from the late 1960s has been supported by the highest levels of government as the cornerstone of tourism policy. The prime reason has been and remains the attraction of a mass market, especially visitors from the USA, in order to improve the balance of payments and to disperse tourism through different parts of Mexico rather than solely Mexico City and the border zone with the USA. In hindsight, it is clear that integrated resort development was sanctioned in order to improve the failing Mexican economy, more than any other factor. For example, after the *Tequila Crisis*, President Zedillo announced extended plans in 1996 to continue to expand tourism including integrated resort development in order to stimulate a new economy.

The government followed the recommendations of a Bank of Mexico study of tourism in 1969 and decided to plan five major integrated resorts: Cancún, Ixtapa, Los Cabos, Loreto and Las bahías de Huatulco. The planned resorts were designed and developed, initially by INFRATUR in the early 1970s; this then became part of FONATUR, which in turn is an agency of SECTUR, the Ministry of Tourism. These organizations planned the construction of, or the acquisition and subsequent lease of, property to the private sector. The government also provided financial assistance to encourage the private sector to respond to the opportunities afforded by the development of integrated resorts (Clancy, 1998). This included the operation of hotels in the resorts such as the state-owned Nacional Hotelera group (now privatized) during the earlier stages of the resort development, and financial incentives to the private sector to build and run other hotels within the resort.

The government decided to invest heavily in the early years of development on two integrated resorts, Cancún and Ixtapa. They have been referred to as mega projects although the others, Los Cabos, Loreto and Las bahías Huatulco, are well established, and promoted in the international market. Jesitus (1993), for example, refers to a golf-orientated mega resort at Los Cabos, known as Cabo del Sol, with an intention of applying international golfing standards to attract the North American market. According to Ayala

(1993) Huatulco is expected to become the largest of the mega project resorts, although it is unlikely that it will grow larger than Cancún.

Of the resorts, Cancún is currently the most important in terms of value and volume. It attracts approximately 4 million visitors per annum, generating an estimated 2 billion US dollars per year, approximately one-third of total income generated. The resident population is estimated to be over 400,000 and is projected to rise to 500,000.

There has been an element of criticism regarding the way in which the resort has developed, particularly in terms of the loss of cultural identity. The resort has attracted criticism, not only from Mexican nationalist groups but also from Western travel writers:

> Say Hello to Cancún and bid adios to Mexico. You can play golf or tennis, enjoy watersports, pay 2 dollars for a cup of coffee, try on a pair of Gucci shoes, and let the doorman at the Hard Rock pour tequila down your throat to help pass the time in the queue.
>
> (Wickers, 1989)

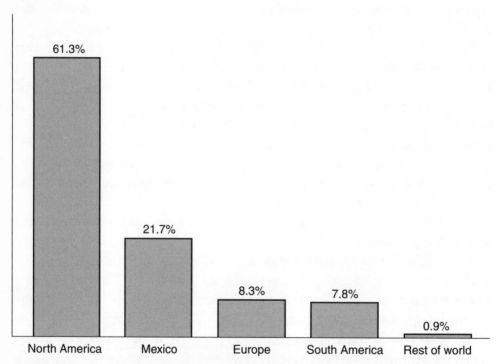

Figure 4.1. Distribution of visitors to Cancún (percentage contribution of markets to total visitors to Cancún, January to July 1998)
Source: Asociación de Hoteles de Quintana Roo (January–July, 1998) (Press Pack)

According to Inskeep (1994), integrated resorts such as Cancún have probably attracted visitors who would otherwise not have taken a holiday in Latin America. He has argued that such resorts have also been successful, both in terms of the environment and economically, in generating spending in a regional tourism economy. The project has also drawn in substantial private investment. For example, the Malecón Cancún project (a promenade, hotel, residences and a park) involved two large private investment groups, Grupo Coin and Grupo DSC, in a package amounting to over US $600 million (Farquharson, 1992). However, critics have pointed to the continued expansion of Cancún along the coast towards the Mayan site of Tulum. It is argued that this urbanization and hence continued demand for beach and water sports has led to the partial destruction of the coral reef along much of the shoreline.

Integrated Resorts in Colombia

Other Latin American countries are beginning to invest in integrated resorts. Colombia, which has a 1800-mile coastline, has few resorts of international appeal. It has invested heavily in one integrated resort, Barú, built on the island of Baús near Cartagena. The resort, named Playa Blanca Barú, was begun towards the end of 1993, with the aim of turning a virtually uninhabited peninsular into a tourist complex of some 150 hectares. Estimated costs were in the region of US $185 million, and the complex has been designed to include a heliport, commercial and conference centres, a 100-berth marina, an 18-hole golf course, 240 tourist flats, 180 villas, 102 mansions and hotel accommodation totalling 900 rooms (Garcia, 1994).

Critique of Enclave Tourism

Despite a preference for the development of enclave tourism by governments, as well as development companies and foreign visitors, several writers have questioned the appropriateness of this form of tourism development (Freitag, 1994). A critique of integrated resorts, and similarly all-inclusive resort complexes, indicates three major issues of concern:

Loss of Sense of Place

It has been argued that integrated resorts lose the essential element of tourism, which Seaton and Bennett (1996) describe as the 'destination factor'. Given that the integrated resort process conceptually attempts to homogenize the destination offering in terms of layout, design and facilities, the meaning of the place is lost. This could be a long-term weakness as more integrated resorts are built:

In today's competitive travel market, excessive replication of the same theme of tourism development dampens rather than fosters economic success. Travelers seek destinations because of special qualities of place. Otherwise, why travel? Every destination has a different set of geographic factors, traditions, relationship to markets, and host characteristics. Analysis of factors can lay the foundation for building upon the uniqueness of place.

(Gunn, 1994)

Enclave Tourism

The enclave nature of such resorts means that there is limited contact between the visitor and local community (Freitag, 1994). Matley argues that this 'can produce an "ocean liner" atmosphere, insulated from the outside world' (1992, p. 239). The concept has been justified in terms of minimizing visitor intrusion, but it is a reasoning which runs counter to the idea that visitors are often motivated to travel in order to learn about other cultures (McIntosh *et al.*, 1995).

Concentration of Spending

The third major criticism of both inclusive resort complexes and integrated resorts is that visitors do not spend in the local economy. Much of the spending is retained by the tour operator and travel agency in the host country or is leaked to the owner's host country. Spending by the visitor beyond the resort complex is minimal, and hence there is only a limited dispersal of revenue into the regional economy.

SUMMARY

The core concerns which tourism developers have to address relate to the potential economic, environmental and social impacts of coastal resort development. The concept of a resort's carrying capacity, which attempts to measure the relationship between the level of demand at a resort and the magnitude of impacts, will become of increasing significance in tourism (Canastrelli and Costa, 1991; Cooper *et al.*, 1998). It is currently not assessed with any degree of accuracy in relation to the economic benefits that might accrue from the development of existing resorts and future large-scale integrated developments. Resorts such as Rio de Janeiro in Brazil and Cartagena in Colombia reflect the inequalities of Latin American societies:

Cartagena exhibits the irony and stark contrasts inherent in Colombian society. Each November, thousands swarm the city to catch a glimpse of the Miss Colombia contestants, while its famed beaches and tepid waters attract foreign tourists despite the war. The bounty from the tourist harvest, however, fails to reach the city's marginalised population. In addition, people living in poverty are frequently forced to wallow in the waste discarded by the rest of Cartagena. Ciénaga La Virgen ... is literally built on an enormous pile of garbage – including toxic and organic waste – jutting out into the Caribbean Sea.

(Ludwick, 2000, p. 4)

Given that many coastal resorts in Latin America are in the growth stage, and that continued government and private sector development is likely to fuel growth towards maturity, the potential risk of degrading marine environments and damaging the cultural character of many destinations is high. Evidence from Mexico points to growing awareness of the issues, but as respective Latin American countries press ahead with resort urbanization of coastal strips, lessons which could be learnt from previous experience are being subordinated to economic imperatives to stimulate international tourism demand.

REFERENCES

Avella, A. and Mills, A. (1996) 'Tourism in Cuba in the 1990s: Back to the Future?', *Tourism Management*, Vol. 17, pp. 55–9.

Ayala, H. (1993) 'Mexican Resorts: A Blueprint With an Expiration Date', *The Cornell Hotel and Restaurant Administration Quarterly*, Vol. 34(3), pp. 34–42.

Berman, S. (1994) 'The Challenge of Cuban Tourism', *The Cornell Hotel and Restaurant Administration Quarterly*, Vol. 35(3), pp. 10–15.

Betances, E. and Spalding, H. A. (eds) (1996) *The Dominican Republic Today: Realities and Perspectives. Essays in English and Spanish*, Hemisphere Studies, New York.

Bleasdale, S. and Tapsell, S. (1994) 'Contemporary Efforts to Expand the Tourist Industry in Cuba: the Perspective From Britain' in A. V. Seaton (ed.), *Tourism: The State of the Art* (pp. 100–9), John Wiley, Chichester.

Brent Ritchie, J. R. and Crouch, G. I. (2000) 'The Competitive Destination: A Sustainability Perspective', *Tourism Management*, Vol. 21, pp. 1–7.

Canastrelli, E. and Costa, P. (1991) 'Tourist Carrying Capacity: A Fuzzy Approach', *Annals of Tourism Research*, Vol. 18 (2), pp. 295–311.

Chant, S. (1992) 'Tourism in Latin America: Perspectives From Mexico and Costa Rica' in D. Harrison (ed.), *Tourism and the Less Developed Countries* (pp. 85–101), Belhaven Press, London.

Chant, S. (1994) 'Women, Work and Household Survival Strategies in Mexico, 1982–1992: Past Trends, Current Tendencies and Future Research', *Bulletin of Latin American Research*, Vol. 13(2), pp. 203–33.

Clancy, M. (1998) 'Tourism and Development: Evidence From Mexico', *Annals of Tourism Research*, Vol. 26(1), pp. 1–20.

Cooper, C., Fletcher, J., Gilbert, D., Shepherd, R. and Wanhill, S. (1998) *Tourism Principles and Practice,* Longman, Harlow.

de Holan, P. M. and Phillips, N. (1997) 'Sun, Sand and Hard Currency', *Annals of Tourism Research,* Vol. 24(4), pp. 777–95.

Farchi, T. (1997) 'El Interior Apuesta al Público de Alto Nivel', *La Nación* (Buenos Aires) (16 March).

Farquharson, M. (1992) 'Tourism in Mexico: Luring Visitors and Investors', *Business Mexico,* pp. 37–8.

Freitag, T. G. (1994) 'Enclave Tourism Development: For Whom the Benefits Roll?', *Annals of Tourism Research,* Vol. 21(3), pp. 538–54.

Garcia, M. E. (1994) 'Barú: Una Ciudad Turística del Futuro', *El Tiempo* (Bogotá) (23 April).

Getino, O. (1990) *Turismo y Desarrollo en América Latina,* Editorial Limusa, México D.F.

Goodrich, J. (1993) 'Socialist Cuba: A Study of Health Tourism', *Journal of Travel Research,* Summer, pp. 36–41.

Gunn, C. A. (1994) *Tourism Planning: Basics, Concepts, Cases,* 3rd edition, Taylor & Francis, Washington D.C.

Hu, Y. and Brent Ritchie, J. R. (1993) 'Measuring Destination Attractiveness: A Contextual Approach', *Journal of Travel Research,* Vol. 32, pp. 25–34.

Inskeep, E. (1994) *National and Regional Tourism Planning: Methodologies and Case Studies,* Routledge, London.

Jesitus, J. (1993) 'Megaresort Expected to Boost Mexico's Tourism', *Hotel & Motel Management,* Vol. 208(2) (1 February).

Krohn, F. B. and O'Donnell, S. T. (1999) 'US Tourism Potential in a New Cuba', *Journal of Travel & Tourism Marketing,* Vol. 8(1), pp. 85–99.

Ludwick, J. (2000) 'City of Hope', *Latin America Press* (27 March).

Lumsdon, L. M. (1997) *Tourism Marketing,* International Thompson Business Press, London.

Lumsdon, L. M. and Swift, J. S. (1994) 'Latin American Tourism: The Dilemmas of the 21st Century' in A. V. Seaton (ed.), *Tourism: The State of the Art* (pp. 359–65), John Wiley, Chichester.

McIntosh, R. W., Goeldner, C. R. and Ritchie, J. R. B. (1995) *Tourism Principles, Practices, Philosophies,* John Wiley, New York.

Matley, I. (1992) 'Physical and Cultural Factors Influencing the Location of Tourism' in R. C. Mill and A. Morrison (eds), *The Tourism System* (pp. 239–61), Prentice Hall, Englewood Cliffs, NJ.

Perez-Lopez, J. (1994) *Cuba at a Crossroads: Politics and Economics After the Fourth Party,* University of Florida, Gainsville, Fla.

Poon, A. (1998) 'All Inclusive Resorts', *Travel & Tourism Analyst, 6,* Economist Intelligence Unit, London.

Reuters (1998) 'Cuban Official Calls Tourism Heart of the Economy', *News Wire 28* (February).

Riotur (1999) *Rio. Incomparable,* Prefeitura de Rio, Secretaria Especial de Turismo, Rio de Janeiro.

Salmas Chávaz, E. (1998) 'Turismo en Cuba, Desarollo, retos y perspectivas', *Estudios y Perspectivas en Turismo,* Vol. 7, pp. 151–64.

Schlüter, R. G. (1991) 'Latin American Tourism Supply: Facing the Extra Regional Market', *Tourism Management,* Vol. 12(3), pp. 221–8.

Schlüter, R. G. (1994) 'Tourism Development: A Latin American Perspective' in W. Theobald (ed.), *Global Tourism: The Next Decade* (pp. 246–60), Butterworth-Heinemann, Oxford.

Seaton, A. V. and Bennett, M. M. (1996) *Marketing Tourism Products,* International Thompson Business Press, London.

Travel & Tourism Intelligence (1999) 'Country Updates', The Economist Intelligence Unit, No. 1, January.

Wickers, D. (1989) 'Gems among the High Rises', *Sunday Times* (8 October).

CHAPTER 5

Nature-based Tourism

INTRODUCTION

The discussion about nature-based tourism in Latin America has, for the most part, focused on three countries: Brazil, Costa Rica and Ecuador (the Galapagos Islands). This is understandable, as each possesses numerous significant sites in terms of the world's bio-diversity and thus they have always been appealing to the scientific niche market. In this respect, each country has witnessed an increase in scientific investigation of their unique natural habitats and wildlife.

More significantly, in terms of tourism development, all three countries have emerged as pioneer eco-tourism destinations. They have received progressively greater numbers of visitors, arriving primarily to observe nature, while at the same time having an interest in conserving these rich habitats. It is questionable whether the balance between the conservation of nature and the commercial exploitation for tourism can be maintained, given the increasing recognition that all visitors, however benign, can have negative impacts on sensitive eco-systems (Tershy *et al.*, 1997; García-Falcon and Medina-Muñoz, 1999, p. 338). At the same time, well-respected conservationists such as the Costa Rican Mario Boza have campaigned for unified environmental protection throughout Latin America by proposing an 'Ecological Corridor of the Americas', from Alaska to the Tierra del Fuego, as the appeal of nature-based tourism has become more widely based.

The reader may be confused by the array of terms used to describe seemingly similar forms of tourism activity. These are listed below, in alphabetical order:

- adventure tourism
- alternative tourism
- eco-tourism
- new tourism

- responsible tourism
- sustainable tourism.

The term 'nature-based tourism' is used in this chapter to describe all forms of tourism offering in which the physiognomy of an area and its flora and fauna feature significantly. This can be sub-divided into adventure tourism and eco-tourism: the former makes good use of the natural features of a particular landscape, and is based on visitors' desire to develop their physical skills and test levels of skill, agility and endurance through activities such as white water rafting or pony trekking in the Andes. Eco-tourism relates to holidays or excursions that offer an opportunity to observe (but not disturb) nature at close quarters, as the prime focus of the tourism experience. In this respect, these terms describe types of tourism offerings. However, several terms such as 'alternative', 'new' and 'sustainable' tourism are very current in the tourism literature, and refer either to a set of principles which could be applied to tourism development, or to actual tourism offerings. In either case, they refer to both supplier and visitor behaviour, especially in connection with pristine or highly sensitive natural environments.

In terms of nature-based tourism, however, Latin America offers far more than the three core destinations mentioned previously; there are high Andean ranges, tropical rainforests, pampas and varied coastal regions to be found across the continent; many remain as major nature reserves, some are unique. It is this rich, diverse and often extensive natural resource which governments and tourism developers have sought to exploit in recent decades, with growing enthusiasm.

Nevertheless, the rationale advanced for the development of nature-orientated tourism is presented by governments as follows:

- It makes best use of the rich natural assets of the continent, which might otherwise be despoiled by other forms of economic development. Tourism development therefore affords some protection against exploitation by other sectors, such as mineral extraction or timber harvesting.
- While requiring some form of capital development, for example, in terms of basic infrastructure such as access roads and accommodation lodges, this is minimal in comparison to other forms of tourism, such as the building of integrated resorts.
- It facilitates the dispersion of visitors to very rural areas where other forms of tourism could not be developed easily; subsequently, visitor spend is directed to provincial and often isolated local economies.
- It meets the needs of a growing influential and wealthy international market sector. The diversity of nature offerings holds great appeal to a continually

widening niche market which would otherwise seek new experiences elsewhere in the world, mainly in Africa and Australasia.

The irony is that, whilst the nations of Latin America are host to many of the major eco-tourism destinations of the world, few have an explicit nature tourism or eco-tourism policy. According to a survey undertaken by the University of Idaho on behalf of the Organization of American States (OAS), only Cuba, the Dominican Republic, Honduras and Mexico have policy statements or policies directly referring to eco-tourism (Diamantis, 1999, p. 100).

Four Latin American countries – Brazil, Costa Rica, Mexico and the Dominican Republic – agreed to the Berlin Declaration on Biological Diversity and Sustainable Tourism. Other contributors and signatories to the United Nations International Conference of Environment Ministers included the Global Environment Facility, the World Tourism Organization (WTO) and the International Union for the Conservation of Nature and Natural Resources, as well as the United Nations Environment Programme. The Conference recognized that:

> achieving sustainable forms of tourism is the responsibility of all stakeholders involved, including governments at all levels, international organisations, the private sector, environmental groups and citizens both in tourism destination countries and countries of origin.
>
> (Berlin Declaration, 1997, p. 2)

Thus, in terms of a policy framework, for example that outlined by non governmental organizations such as the World Wide Fund for Nature (1992), or the Ecotourism Society (1993), there is a clear policy framework to guide stakeholders in the development of tourism in Latin America's remaining natural areas (Boo, 1993, pp. 23–4).

Herein lies the dilemma. Nature-based tourism, in theory, should offer both a low-impact and an environmentally sensitive form of tourism development which brings much-needed visitor spend to rural economies. This should, in turn, support conservation and the development of local culture. In practice, the fear is that, like all other forms of tourism, nature-based tourism has an impact on the environment which is yet to be assessed in the long term (Butler, 1991). As a consequence of poor management and weak control systems, it currently fails to provide sources of revenue which can be used to secure conservation, and very little money is devoted to protection measures for tourism landscapes (Healy, 1994; Tershy *et al.*, 1999). Of significant concern is that nature-based tourism has outgrown a niche market comprising scientists and specialist amateurs. According to some commentators, it is now 'the leading edge of mass tourism rather than an alternative' (Thomlinson and Getz, 1996, p. 185), whilst Wearing and Neil reinforce this notion by suggesting that it 'reflects a fundamental shift in the way human beings view and engage with nature' (1999, p. 1).

Thus there are concerns among conservation groups and in the academic literature that many unique habitats and sensitive environments will be irretrievably damaged as the process of developing nature-based tourism widens in Latin America to include ever greater numbers of visitors. The responsibility of all stakeholders cannot be guaranteed: for example, Agenda 21 has not been seen as an extensive mechanism to secure sustainable development, nor are there detailed plans for its implementation (Nelson, 1994, p. 254).

There is growing evidence to suggest that, for the most part, exactly the opposite is happening across Latin America. Without exception, most countries now promote nature-based tourism in one form or another – primarily to the North American market, but increasingly to European visitors. While Brazil, Costa Rica, Ecuador and Peru in particular have continued to emphasize nature tourism offerings, other countries have emerged as strong competitors. Argentina, Bolivia, Chile, Colombia, Guatemala and Venezuela have during the 1990s also developed nature-based tourism on a wider scale than previously. To a lesser extent Guatemala, Paraguay and Panama are also emerging as nature tourism destinations.

Even in the most marginal and isolated regions of Argentina there are calls for the development of eco-tourism to substitute for the changing patterns of agricultural production that require fewer workers (Reboratti, 1998). Whilst the main thrust of international demand is and will continue to be coastal-based tourism (primarily passive beach tourism), there is a discernible trend towards vacations which include activities, or where the visitor seeks greater exposure to indigenous people and natural features. In addition, the nature-based tourism market sector is estimated to be growing at a rate of 25–30 per cent in the USA (Pleumarom, 1994). Managing this demand will be one of the major challenges of tourism development in Latin America. The debate as to how this might be managed has been framed within a conservation ethic (Ryan and Grasse, 1991). The preservation of important natural zones such as the tropical rainforests has, however, been problematic. Several international interventions have been the subject of criticism, mainly on the grounds of ignoring the needs and wants of the local (especially indigenous) communities involved (McNeely, 1994; Cosgrove, 1995). This had led to a call for greater participation and ownership by the local communities in both conservation and complementary eco-tourism initiatives (Whitesell, 1996, p. 432). This point is reinforced by Silva in his study of sustainable development in tropical forests (Silva, 1994). This assumes a commitment to resourcing conservation initiatives from tourism. In many instances commentators report that the circular flow of resources is broken. The payback from visitors is, on the whole, sadly lacking, either in terms of revenues from visitors or through governmental support. Therefore, a fundamental question remains: to what extent should nature-based tourism be developed in the twenty-first century? This is ostensibly a political issue, and one which, despite the importance of the Rio Summit and Local Agenda 21, has been obfuscated by successive governments.

TOURISM TERMINOLOGY

The following section presents a critique (albeit limited) of the major terms or concepts presented by researchers over the past 20 years in relation to nature-based tourism in Latin America. The literature is replete with articles which feature alternative, eco-, responsible and sustainable tourism, terms that are sometimes used interchangeably. There are six key terms, described below.

Adventure Tourism

Adventure tourism is becoming increasingly popular in Latin America, and the associations responsible for bringing together specialist tour operators have become increasingly conscious of their role in the protection of sensitive landscapes. Fennell (1999, p. 42) quotes the Canadian Tourism Commission, which in 1995 defined adventure tourism as 'an outdoor leisure activity that takes place in an unusual, exotic, remote or wilderness destination, involves some form of unconventional means of transportation, and tends to be associated with low or high levels of activity'.

Adventure tourism is often associated with nature-based tourism because it uses the same natural resource base as eco-tourism. However, in terms of visitor motivation and activities pursued at the destination, there are fundamental differences. Adventure tourism is driven primarily by an element of risk, skill enhancement and team activity, whereas nature-based or eco-tourism focuses on the study of natural settings, wildlife and its conservation. Nor is one necessarily a sub-set of the other; they are essentially different forms of tourism activity, although, as suggested by Lumsdon and Swift (1998,

p. 167), visitors are increasingly seeking to carry out both while on holiday. There tends to be a distinction between 'soft' and 'hard' adventure when defining activities, but in reality there is a gradation of challenges based on the skills required and the level of risk involved.

Alternative Tourism

Alternative tourism is a term mostly used to describe the opposite of mass tourism (Wheeller, 1991; Butler, 1992, p. 31), and it is characterized by having a minimal impact on the environment, by being small scale and by being locally based. Wherever possible it stimulates both the local economy and cultural identity. In this context, it is often referred to as 'rural tourism', involving farms. It is an alternative to mass tourism, both in terms of scale and in the types of activities or pursuits engaged in by visitors:

> In essence, the traveller is preferred to the tourist, the individual to the group, the independent specialist operators are more acceptable than large firms, indigenous homely accommodation is preferred to multi-national hotel chains, etc. – basically 'small' versus 'mass'.
>
> (Wheeller, 1991, p. 91)

Eco-tourism

Eco-tourism (the most commonly used term in relation to Latin America) can be defined as a set of principles applied to nature-based tourism (Western, 1993). In this respect, Fennell describes it as:

> a sustainable form of natural resource-based tourism that focuses primarily on experiencing and learning about nature, and which is ethically managed to be low-impact, non-consumptive, and locally oriented (control, benefits, and scale). It typically occurs in natural areas, and should contribute to the conservation or preservation of such areas.
>
> (1999, p. 42)

There is a degree of confusion, however, as different authors refer to it in a number of ways. There is clearly a difference between eco-tourism as a defining set of principles and eco-tourism as a discrete tourism offering. Cater and Lowman see eco-tourism as a 'particular variant of alternative tourism. The attributes of ecological and socio-cultural integrity, responsibility and sustain-ability are qualities which may not, pertain to ecotourism as a product' (1994, p. 3). Whilst there is little dispute in the literature regarding the beneficial purpose of visitors studying the natural history of Latin America, the question remains concerning whether the integrity of significant eco-systems can be maintained, and the extent to which eco-tourism revenues are channelled to local residents, or used for conservation (Boo, 1990; Croall, 1995).

New Tourism

A less well-used term is 'new tourism'. It is used to describe new forms of customized tourism, which require active participation and skills development. It is usefully described by Mowforth and Munt as:

> combining a variety of 'activities' such as adventure, trekking, climbing, sketching and mountain biking. More significantly, on the other hand, it means the marriage of different, often intellectual, spheres of activity with tourism (that is, academic, anthropological, archaeological, ecological and scientific tourisms).

> (1998, p. 101)

In many respects, this is an apt description of nature-based tourism in Latin America, whereby visitors combine an educational or professional pursuit with differing degrees of adventure activity.

Responsible Tourism

The concept of responsible tourism assumes that the visitor is responsible or prudent in the way in which he or she consumes tourism; Wight, for example, considers that 'new consumers are beginning to translate their convictions into action' (1993, p. 39). There is an assumption, implicit in the definition, that the visitor is aware of the impact of his or her activities. This is questionable, given the very intangibility of the tourism offering. Thus, as the decision to travel is invariably made on the basis of imperfect information, it is often not until the visitor consumes a holiday at a particular destination that realism begins to modify a set of expectations.

Prosser (1994) questions the concept of visitor responsibility by arguing that the visitor is often far less altruistic than the literature suggests; he questions the degree of individual environmental responsibility in relation to the purchase of nature-based tourism. For example, the eco-tourist to Brazil trades the high level environmental impact associated with long haul jet travel for temporal involvement in the conservation of a particular habitat. Furthermore, it is only when a particular site reaches saturation that there will be a noticeable absence of wildlife, an unacceptable level of litter and detritus, increased peripheral commercialism and negative word of mouth by the visitor (Plog, 1994).

Sustainable Tourism

Sustainable tourism recognizes the need to consider environmental and social consequences of tourism development as well as economic impacts. It should, in theory, be an extension to the conceptual framework of sustainable development as defined in the Brundtland Report (1987, p. 8): 'a process of change in which the exploitation of resources, the direction of investments, the orientation of technological development, and institutional changes are made consistent with future as well as present needs'.

Another approach is to discuss eco-tourism as a sub-set of activity-based tourism. Adventure, exploration and eco-tourism holidays involve some form of activity or study; essentially they exploit or consume nature, if only as a backdrop for some form of adventure such as white water rafting or shark fishing. In terms of qualifying this wide definitional framework, Lumsdon and Swift (1998) list the characteristics of nature-based tourism in Costa Rica which includes supply sectors and host communities (see Box 5.A).

Box 5.A. Sustainable tourism in Costa Rica

It encourages consumption of natural landscapes to varying degrees of intensity; tends to be group based, drawn primarily from North European and North America markets, and invariably uses the services of a native guide(s), or one that has extensive knowledge of a locale; it involves small numbers in most cases, although the exception of cruise ship parties is a major and growing exception; it attracts well-educated, high income and 'adventurer-explorer' visitors; it offers as a main appeal a subtle mixture of education and entertainment; it is managed by small-scale specialist companies based mainly in generating countries. These companies tend to sub-contract to local tour operators at the host destination; it generally uses local accommodation facilities.

(Lumsdon and Swift, 1998, p. 157)

Within the context of Latin America, the term eco-tourism is more commonly used than the other terms are. It is important to describe a type of tourism offering that is promoted to the market by tour companies, destinations and government organizations. There is a growing consensus of opinion that eco-tourism is best applied to the wider framework of tourism development:

> Much as we may want to define ecotourism narrowly, in reality the principles applied to the mass market can do more good for conservation – and alleviate more harm – than a small elitist market. Eco tourism, accepted in this way, is shifting from a definition of small-scale nature tourism to a set of principles applicable to any nature related tourism.
>
> (Western, 1993, p. 10)

Thus, for many Latin American countries nature-based tourism is of vital importance in the development of the overall tourism offering, as it appeals to high spending long haul visitors. The next section reviews some of the major nature-based tourism offerings in Latin America.

NATURE-BASED TOURISM OFFERINGS

Introduction

The Latin American eco-system is remarkable for its enormity and diversity. Beyond the major urban centres are extensive nature reserves and areas often of unique scientific significance. It is only possible to summarize these in terms of simple outlines of developments in a number of countries. Collectively, they provide a mosaic of nature tourism offerings throughout the continent.

Argentina

The appeal of Argentina is its diversity of landscapes and wildlife habitats from antarctic physiognomy to tropical forests. Approximately 10 per cent of Argentina is identified as a national park or having reserve status, therefore there is some protection afforded to rare or endangered species and habitats. The best-known areas are in Patagonia – for example, the Tierra del Fuego National Park in the south of the country. The interest in whale watching and birdlife has become increasing important on the Valdez Peninsula, and a number of small-scale tour operators specialize in arranging whale watching trips. This contrasts with the rainforests in the north of the country – for example, the national park which includes Iguazú Falls.

Antarctica

The continent of Antarctica lies to the far south of Argentina and Chile, across the Drake Passage to the Antarctic Pensinsula and the Antarctic Circle. It has no indigenous population, although there is a small and transient scientific community. The extensive ice packs and extremely harsh climate have not in the past appealed to the tourism market, and until the 1950s it remained virtually untouched. However, in the past 30 years, Antarctica has attracted a growing number of nature-based cruises which set ashore passengers (some 4000 in 1975 (Erize, 1987, p. 134)) to observe the wildlife, particularly penguins, seals and humpback whales. The area has become increasingly important, not just as an element of more broad-based offerings, but as the prime focus of a number of specialist tour operators, which offer an opportunity to view wildlife such as sea lions, fur seals, penguins, Magellanic Woodpeckers, Austral Parakeets and eagles, at close quarters.

Access to this region is mainly by way of Ushuaia in Argentina, which accounts for over 90 per cent of all visitors. The remainder generally travel via Punta Arenas in Chile to the South Shetland and Elephant Islands by cruise ship (IFT, 1998). It is argued that the self-regulatory mechanisms and procedures adopted by tour operators and captains of cruise vessels in handling visitors (known as the 'Lindblad system') has worked well in recent decades, and environmental impacts have been evaluated as minimal (Stonehouse, 1994). There have been a number of studies at the most heavily visited locations, which are the South Orkney and South Shetland Islands, as well as the Antarctic Peninsula north of 67° 34′ south (Headland, 1994, p. 270). The studies have investigated the management of groups and the impacts on wildlife so that management plans and procedures can be updated to meet the growing number of visitors. However, a discussion continues as to the carrying capacity of this fragile environment in relation to tourism activities. Whilst the current level of demand (approximately 10,000 visitors per annum) is considered sustainable, there remains a question as to whether Antarctica could cope with a rising trend in visitor numbers (Hall and McArthur, 1993). Table 5.1. illustrates the rising levels of tourist demand for visits to this region.

The International Association of Antarctic Tour Operators (IAATO) is a private sector organization founded in 1991 'to advocate, promote and practice safe and environmentally responsible private-sector travel to the Antarctic'. The organization forecasts that Antarctica is likely to remain a specialized and expensive destination. However, given the very sensitive nature of the environment, detailed monitoring will be required constantly.

Table 5.1. Tourist arrivals in Antarctica, 1992–8

Period	Total	Visitor numbers Percentage change on previous year
1992–3	6704	–
1993–4	8016	+16.4
1994–5	8120	+1.3
1995–6	9367	+13.3
1996–7	7413	−26.4
1997–8	9604	+22.8

Source: IAATO (1999)

Bolivia

Until the early 1990s Bolivia was not known for its nature tourism, despite the great diversity between the high level *altiplano* and the richly tropical lowlands of the Amazonian basin. Bolivia now promotes what is described by the government tourism department, SENATUR, as ethno-eco-tourism, which reflects the importance of indigenous Andean populations within important natural surroundings, although this is fraught with difficulties, such as in the exploitation of the Madidi National Park:

> Next to Guyana, Bolivia is the poorest country in South America. Most of its people worry more about survival than the environment, and so its politicians, even the honest ones, face strong pressure to support policies that will provide immediate jobs and thus preserve votes, not wildlife.
>
> The best hope for Madidi's future may be in places such as Chalalán, Caquiahuara and Charque, where the inhabitants are learning to be partners in the area's future. If most of the park's residents protected the wildlife and forests and learn to manage tourism, Madidi will remain incomparable.
>
> (Kemper, 2000, p. 23)

One strategic aim is to build international appeal by developing 'circuit tourism' based on Lake Titicaca, which, at 12,000 ft above sea level, is the highest lake in the world. One major limitation is that visitors have to contend with the effects of high altitudes and this can be debilitating for some, so that trains carry oxygen especially for visitors. There are also concerns that many tour operators and hotels are using the term eco-tourism to market their holidays but in reality are failing to adopt environmental principles:

> According to tour operators some self-described 'ecological hotels' around Lake Titicaca dump untreated wastewater into the lake. In the tropical Chapare region near Cochabamba, an immense area of jungle has been cleared to build a golf course for a five-star 'ecological' hotel. Bolivia, has in fact, no environmental standards for hotels and 'ecohotel' is a self-imposed title.
>
> (Cesar, 1999, p. 3)

Brazil

Brazil has a worldwide reputation for nature tourism based on the extensive Amazon basin and its numerous tributaries. The gateway to this massive and unique tropical rainforest has traditionally been Manaus, situated at a confluence of two main arteries, the Amazon River (Rio Solimões) and the Rio Negro. Far from being a small-scale niche market, Manaus has witnessed considerable growth in visitors; there are now several large-scale hotels catering for the burgeoning market for nature tourism. One estimate of projected demand is that visitors will increase from approximately 50,000 per annum to over 150,000 per annum during the early years of the twenty-first century (Smith, 1991). One of the major concerns is that there is currently a lack of resources to manage the protected areas at a time of increased visitation, and a dearth of mechanisms to extract revenues from visitors:

> Although the large parks and protected areas provide the best opportunity to protect representative samples of intact Amazon ecosystems, they currently lack the infrastructure, personnel, and concessionaires necessary to receive and manage visitors. Without visitors it is difficult to generate revenues, build a constituency that knows these protected areas, and subsequently lends financial and political support to them.
>
> (Wallace and Pierce, 1996, p. 187)

Most visitors are encouraged to stay at eco-lodges, many of which are situated near to Manaus and which employ local guides to guide visitors to different locations, usually during a four-day stay in Amazonas. Less well known is a large territory in the south of Brazil known as Pantanal which is developing at a far slower pace with some incremental upgrading of infrastructure and accommodation during the 1990s.

Chile

Chile has a variety of special landscapes; in the north, for example, is the Atacama desert, which includes the Lauca National Park, situated along a large part of the border with Bolivia, and which contains a world-renowned water reserve – Lake Chungará (see Box 5.B).

Box 5.B. Lauca National Park, Chile

Lake Chungará, an impressive water reserve which forms part of the Lauca National Park, and which was designated a World Biosphere Reserve by UNESCO, is located in the far north at a height of 4,517 meters above sea level. It is the natural habitat for countless species of birds, including especially the pink flamingo, and a protected area for vicuñas, llamas, and alpacas
. . .

(SERNATUR, 1999, p. 3)

To the south there are the fjords and glaciers of Patagonia and Tierra del Fuego, areas of equally spectacular scenery and wildlife. There are over 80 natural parks and reserves, some of which have been designated as World Biosphere Reserves by UNESCO. To date there has been a relatively low level of exploitation of nature tourism in Chile, but this is likely to change in the coming decade because transport systems to remote areas are being improved.

Colombia

Colombia is an Andean country with a potential for developing nature tourism along the Amazon and its tributaries. This currently involves tropical forest exploration from Leticia, for example, in the south of the country. To a lesser extent, the delta areas of rivers which flow into the Pacific also offer opportunities although nature tourism is not developed in these regions. There are conservation issues but there is also the problem of terrorists and drug traffickers operating in wilderness areas, and thus being a potential or perceived danger to visitors, and in some cases a very real danger.

Ecuador

Ecuador is one of the main nature-based tourism centres of the world. Most of the 500,000 international tourist arrivals are primarily motivated by nature tourism, as Ecuador possesses a wide variety of landscapes, from the Andean mountains to tropical rainforests, wetlands and coastal ranges. It contains one of the most diverse ecological systems remaining in the world. Of international repute are the Galapagos Islands where an extensive range of mammals, birdlife and insects exist (see Box 5.C).

Box 5.C. The Galapagos Islands

The Galapagos National Park (Ecuador), created in 1959, was already an important ecotourism destination before the term 'ecotourism' was coined. The islands, whose name derives from the giant turtles called Galapagos, began to be massively visited in 1970 when the first cruise ship arrived. The first plan for the management of the park was prepared beiween 1973 and 1974, and established the carrying capacity of the park at 12,000 visitors a year. As this figure was soon exceeded, the master plan was revised in 1985 and the new limit was set at 25,000 visitors per year.

(Schlüter, 1994, p. 253)

Currently, short cruises on motor yachts carrying up to 20 people are popular ways of viewing the wildlife. Accommodation standards vary, and some tours have botanists or biologists on board to provide expert analysis of the flora and fauna encountered. It is increasingly recognized that the activities of nature-based tourists have an impact on different species (Burger and Gochfeld, 1993).

Nature tourism development has been substantial, and is currently seen by the Ecuadorian government as crucial for the survival of many local economies, especially those situated near to the national parks. Considerable investment has been made in certain areas, such as the environmentally friendly 'eco-lodge' complex in the Kapawi Ecolodge & Reserve Complex, situated in the heart of the Ecuadorian rainforest. But at what price for the environment? For example, one of the most popular locations, the Cotopaxi National Park, like an increasing number of nature-orientated destinations, has suffered from encroachment by lodging and other facilities which have been built in an unplanned way. This has occurred despite controls and codes of conduct which all suppliers have agreed to endorse in order to protect environmentally sensitive areas.

Another example is that of Rio Blanco, where the indigenous community of the Quechea are developing eco-tourism themselves as a way of reducing their reliance on forest clearance for the expansion of agriculture. The project is under local control and despite still remaining small scale, has already brought tangible benefits to the local community (Schaller, 1998, p. 2).

The level of tourism visitation is now becoming a major dilemma for conservationists (Kenchington, 1989); it is argued that if Ecuador opens up its economy to foreign investors and consequently more mainstream tourism operators, this would pose a major threat to its precious nature-based assets, which it has sought to safeguard in past decades. As is the case with Costa Rica, Ecuador faces a major dilemma in achieving a balance between conservation and the drive to increase foreign exchange revenue.

Mexico

Mexico's national protected areas are increasingly being promoted as eco-tourism or nature-based destinations for both the domestic and the foreign visitor; some sites, such as the Monarch Butterfly Reserve to the west of Mexico City, now receive increasing numbers of visitors. Other parks include the Cumbres de Ajusto and La Marquesa, Miguel Hidalgo y Costilla Parks, and the Sian Ka'an Reserve which is a wetlands and tropical forest reserve established through a United Nations programme in 1986. The development of eco-tourism, however, can also be partly explained by the interest of tour operators such as Ecogrupos de México, which are stimulating interest from the US market.

Paraguay

Paraguay, like Brazil and Argentina, possesses the Iguazú Falls which appeal to an international market. It has, however, been slower to develop its eco-tourism potential than elsewhere. Of particular importance is the Chaco region in the east of the country, which is both isolated and lacking in infrastructure. This lack of basic infrastructure holds back the development of nature-based tourism. There remains a continued interest by suppliers to offer cruises on the Paraguay and Parana rivers, and it is in areas such as this that nature tourism is likely to increase marginally. However, in comparison to its competitors, there is limited international appeal in Paraguay, other than the Falls.

Peru

Whilst Peru is best known for its Andean culture and in particular the Inca ruins at Machu Picchu, it also has an emergent nature tourism sector which focuses on the tropical forests and sierra landscapes of the Andes. There are a number of national parks and reserves which amount to over 10 per cent of landscape under conservation.

In recent years Peru has sought to promote its nature tourism base in association with cultural heritage. As part of an agreement with the European Commission's 'Integrated Programme of Support for Tourism Development', there has been an increasing focus on tourism activities which strengthen cultural identity, environmental protection and the participation of local residents. This has brought a range of new tourism offerings, including thermal baths, trekking and the opening up of the mountain and northern coastal areas. Promperú (the Peruvian Tourism organization) has produced a number of good quality booklets in 'The Traveller's Guide' series, one dealing with 'Wildlife Watching in Peru' and another with 'Nature and Protected Areas in Peru'. The latter lists the parks and reserves throughout the country (see Table 5.2).

This table indicates the increasing awareness of the Peruvian government that nature tourism is important to the tourism economy. However, the problems associated with tourism and sustained contact with wildlife have yet to be fully explored (Groom *et al.*, 1991).

Table 5.2. 'Nature and Protected Areas in Peru'

Area type	Area name	Department(s)
National park	Cuervo	Cajamarca
	Tingo María	Huánuco
	Manu	Cuzco and Madre de Díos
	Huascarán	Ancash
	Cerros de Amotope	Tumbes and Piura
	Río Abieso	San Martín
	Yanachaga-Chemillén	Pasco
	Bahuaja-Sonene	Puno and Madre de Díos
National reserve	Pampa Galeras-Bárbara D'Actulle	Ayacucho
	Junín	Junín and Pasco
	Paracas	Ica
	Lachay	Lima
	Pacaya-Samiria	Loreto
	Salinas y Aguada Blanca	Arequipa and Moquega
	Calipuy	La Libertad
	Titicaca	Puno
National sanctuary	Huayllay	Pasco
	Calipuy	La Libertad
	Lagunas de Mejía	Arequipa
	Ampay	Apurímac
	Manglares de Tumbes	Tumbes
	Tabacones-Namballe	Cajamarca
Historical sanctuary	Chacamarca	Junín
	Pampas de Ayacucho	Ayacucho
	Machu Picchu	Cuzco
Reserved zone	Manu	Cuzco and Madre de Díos
	Laquipampa	Lambayeque
	Apurímac	Apurímac
	Pantanos de Villa	Lima
	Tambopata-Candamo	Madre de Díos, and Puno
	Batán Grande	Lambayeque
	Tumbes	Tumbes
	Algarrobal El Moro	La Libertad
	Chancaybaños	Cajamarca
	Gueppi	Loreto
Game reserve	Sunchubamba	Cajamarca
	El Angolo	Piura
Communal reserve	Yánesha	Pasco
	Tamshiyacu-Tahuayo	Loreto
Protected areas	Aledaño Bocatoma Canal Nueva Imperial	Lima
	Puquio-Rosa	La Libertad

Area type	Area name	Department(s)
	Pui Pui	Junín
	San Matías-San Carlos	Pasco
	Alto Mayo	San Martín
	Pagaibamba	Cajamarca
National forest	Pastaza-Morona-Marañón	Loreto
	Mariscal Cáceres	San Martín
	Biabo-Cordillera Azul	Loreto, San Martín, and Ucayali
	Alexander von Humbolt	Ucayali and Huánuco

Source: Promperú (1999)

Venezuela

Venezuela has a wide range of nature tourism offerings which have not as yet been developed to the same extent as those of its neighbours. The rich eco-systems of the Amazon and Andes have traditionally been protected in Venezuela, perhaps more than in other countries, as approximately 22 per cent of land is either a national park or a reserve, which affords some degree of protection to wildlife. There has been the growth of river cruises in cooperation with Brazilian suppliers, seeking to capture the nature market. This is beginning to open up the country for nature-based tourism, but as yet it is best described as small scale and emergent.

Conclusion

In summary, nature-based tourism offerings of Latin American nations are of considerable importance, and to date have not been extensively exploited in the majority of countries. There remains a critical tension between, on the one hand, conservation, and on the other, increased tourism development which brings with it intrusion and potential degradation.

ADVENTURE/ACTIVITY TOURISM

Introduction

France describes adventure tourism as part physical challenge, part education and contact with nature (France, 1997). She considers that nature-based tourism is one form of this wider definition; it involves principally the study of flora and fauna. This raises the question as to the relationship between nature-based, eco- and adventure tourism. Those who argue that there is a strong degree of similarity between each form suggest that they attract similar market segments who consume the same natural resource base, especially wilderness or protected areas, and are managed or governed by almost identical principles and visitor codes of conduct.

'Hard' and 'Soft' Adventure Tourism

Those who argue that adventure tourism is different from the others refer to the motivation of the visitor. The nature-based visitor is attracted by the appeal of observing and recording nature at close quarters, and gaining access to sensitive or protected areas is essential to this. In contrast, the adventure tourist, whilst possibly appreciating the backdrop of an exotic landscape, is primarily motivated by the activity *per se*, the risk associated in participating and possibly the form of transport used, such as mountain biking, canoeing or trekking. Swarbrooke and Horner (1999) suggest that, in broad terms, activity or adventure tourism encompasses three major types of activity:

- using modes of transport to tour areas which require effort on the part of the tourist such as walking, cycling and riding
- participating in land-based sports such as golf and tennis
- taking part in water-based activities like diving and wind-surfing.

(1999:38)

These elements are integral to the experience. Hall (1992), for example, indicates that the activity is far more important to the adventure traveller than the natural setting. Nevertheless, tour operators select destinations because they offer both a base for an activity and pristine environments in which the activity can take place. It very much depends on the type of activity and whether it is hard or soft adventure, i.e. the gradation and level of stamina and skill required to participate and the level of risk to the person involved.

Summary

It would be difficult to highlight one country in which adventure tourism is more important than another. Given the wide range of physical landscapes and climates to be found across the continent, there are substantial opportunities throughout each country. The organization of adventure tourism falls within the realm of special interest tourism in the USA and is increasingly being offered in Europe, mainly hiking, biking, rafting or horseback riding. Thus, companies might offer horseback trekking across the Patagonian Andes, canoeing expeditions in Venezuela to the Angel Falls, or cycling in Cuba, most of which are of a duration between 14 and 28 days. (See Box 5.D.)

> **Box 5.D. 'Venezuelan Explorer'**
>
> Our adventurous itinerary covers an extraordinary range of scenery: we start by exploring the 'Paramo', the high altitude plains of the Andes, where we visit tranquil glacial lakes and indian villages, as well as biological stations devoted to the preservation of the condor and Andean bear. Descending from the mountains we enter the vast plains of the 'Llanos', a wetland region ranking on the scale of Brazil's 'Pantanal' ... in richness of wildlife. Flying deeper south to the Orinocco river ... we embark on an expedition into the deepest jungle, travelling by native canoe and sleeping in hammocks ... Travel is by internal flight, minibus, jeep, river boat and canoe. Will best suit those who don't mind some physical effort and a degree of roughing it.
>
> (Exodus, 1999, p. 69)

COSTA RICA: A FUSION OF MARKETS?

Introduction

Costa Rica is a prime example of nature tourism development; much of the literature refers to it as eco-tourism. It is one of the most diverse nature tourism destinations of the world and the most advanced eco-tourism destination in Latin America (Weaver, 1994). Situated on the Central American isthmus between Nicaragua and Panama, the country exhibits a range of climates and eco-systems and it has a rich bio-diversity, providing a habitat for 4 per cent of the global total of different species (Boza, 1988). A series of conservation measures adopted by the Costa Rican government has resulted in the establishment of protected areas, mainly designated as nature reserves and national parks. This accounts for approximately 11 per cent of the land space.

Costa Rica is an interesting example in many respects, as it is a country which has embraced nature-based tourism as a core offering, yet is in danger of damaging its rich natural diversity through the exploitation of other forms of tourism. The main question being asked is whether it can sustain such an intensive pattern of growth in international arrivals and at the same time conserve such large tracts of special landscape. Tourism has now reached what is often described as a secondary stage of development, or the early stage of mass tourism (Butler, 1980). However, Costa Rica's development has not followed a pattern envisaged in Butler's generalized framework.

There was a gradual development of infrastructure during the 1980s, and at this time there was some resistance to plan large-scale coastal resorts despite

Table 5.3. Costa Rica: International arrivals, 1985–98

Year	Number of arrivals	% change on previous year
1985	261,552	–
1986	260,840	−0.3
1987	277,861	6.5
1988	329,386	18.5
1989	375,951	14.1
1990	435,037	15.7
1991	504,649	16.0
1992	610,591	21.0
1993	684,005	12.0
1994	761,448	11.3
1995	784,610	3.0
1996	781,127	−0.4
1997	811,490	3.9
1998	943,000	16.2

Sources: ICT (1999) and WTO (1999)

the appeal of the coastline. This has strengthened the nature-adventure sector in relation to beach tourism, although the latter has always been an appeal of Costa Rica. The growth in international arrivals from the mid-1980s to the present day is illustrated in Table 5.3.

In previous decades, Costa Rica attracted a very specialized niche market of scientists and a number of nature enthusiasts, and in the 1980s this was stimulated partly by international cause groups who exposed the rapid destruction of tropical rainforests to a global media. This stimulated a tourism boom in Costa Rica in the latter half of the 1980s (O'Brien, 1997), and successive governments were keen to prolong the interest as there was intense pressure from world development organizations such as the World Bank and the IMF to improve the economy (Fields, 1988, p. 1493). The market also changed dramatically in the 1980s. Costa Rica began to attract a market that was interested in nature, adventure and also enjoyed beach resorts, rather than just more specialist eco-tourism holidays.

It is predicted that Costa Rica will soon reach 1 million visitor arrivals, and a Tourist Intensity Rate of 1:3 during the early 2000s. Furthermore, encouragement of major hotel chains in the mid-1990s, such as the arrival of the Marriott in San José and the rapid growth of an integrated resort at Papaguayo, are firm indicators of a mass tourism strategy, as are the increased number of charter flights from Europe. At the same time, there are also clear examples of how carrying capacities of specific reserves are being exceeded (Maldonado *et al.*, 1992).

Segmentation of the Market in Costa Rica

There has been only limited recognition by writers of the dynamic nature of the marketplace in Costa Rica (EIU, 1996). The traditional polarization of segment profiles (eco-tourist versus mass or beach tourist) is a mis-representation of the market. By far the largest increase in visitors to Costa Rica has been the 'participant eco-tourist' rather than the eco-nature specialist, i.e. the visitor who is seeking a mix of holiday experiences ranging from the beach to nature. For example, one of the main tour companies in Costa Rica offers an eight-day 'eco-adventure' tour which includes canoeing and mountain biking at Las Baulus Biological Reserve, snorkelling in Bahia Culbra, observation of wildlife at a Cloud Forest Reserve, rafting on the Corobici River and horseback riding at Guacalito Private Reserve.

The distinction between soft adventure and nature-based tourism is becoming less clear in terms of the packaging of holidays, with companies describing their offerings as 'eco-adventure tourism'. A study of Costa Rican tour operators in 1996 revealed that several companies were unable to distinguish between eco-tourism and adventure tourism, such as in the following comment from a new entrant to the market: 'Eco tourism is seen as a mixture of adventure and nature tourism, much of it is focused on and around National Parks. It is difficult to offer a definition and difficult to distinguish eco from adventure tourism' (Lumsdon and Swift, 1998, p. 163).

What is increasingly apparent is that visitors seeking soft adventure expect a quality of landscape similar to that which eco-tourists desire. Whereas the specialist eco-tourist is concerned with the detailed observation of nature over longer periods of time, the eco-adventure tourist consumes locations at a faster pace, generally in greater comfort and thus seeking more resources (Schlüter, 1994, p. 257).

During the 1990s many tour operators have re-positioned themselves to meet the needs of the market. Promotional material includes a selection of nature tourism images interspersed with soft adventure and sporting pursuits and/or the beach. The visitor no longer feels that they are making an eco-pilgrimage but are travelling to a sun, sand and adventure destination where there are also opportunities to enjoy nature tourism.

Thus there is a 'grey area' which divides the eco-tourist from those seeking adventure, or the 'beach' and 'adventure' segments. As Boyd and Butler observe:

> in reality, there is often very little difference in many respects between
> such day recreation activities such as birdwatching and month-long

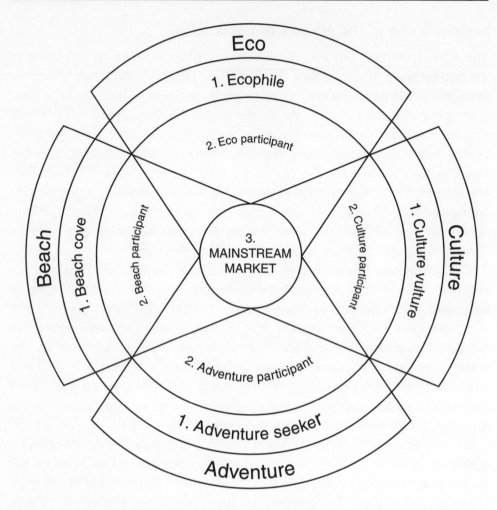

Figure 5.1. Costa Rica: The interrelationship of market segments
Source: Lumsdon and Swift (1998, p. 167)

ecotourism trips to observe birds, except the location where these activities take place, the length of time and the amount of expenditure involved.

(1996, p. 558)

Thus, the market is perhaps better represented as a series of segments, divided into levels, which reflect the intensity with which the visitor pursues the segment offering. Figure 5.1 points to the varying levels of interest and commitment. Level one refers to those visitors who are 'purist' in their pursuits; they have little or no interest in other offerings. The second level relates to those visitors who, whilst still located firmly within a particular segment, have other interests: this is likely to be the largest segment. Level three refers to those visitors who seek a multi-faceted holiday: this could well prove to be the market of the future.

Another factor is the duration of a visit. Increasing numbers of visitors want to be nature tourists for a day or, in the case of some cruise liner passengers, possibly for a half day only. They are far less interested or knowledgeable than specialist eco-tourists, desiring a taste of exotic plant or wildlife only. For example, one tour operator sells a combination tour including Poás Volcano and Braulio Carrillo National Parks, a boat trip on the Sarapiquí Jungle River and La Paz Waterfalls, stressing that they can all be visited on the same day.

There is, however, a danger of allowing this market to grow. It brings an increasing degree of intensity of visit which is difficult to manage and can lead to a deterioration of the environment. For example, there has been a sharp increase in the number of cruise liners calling at Puerto Caldera and Puerto Limon in the 1990s, rising from 74 embarkations in 1992 to 179 in 1994 with some 155,584 excursionists disembarking on day visits (ICT, 1995, p. 85), which has led some parks to regulate demand by time or day. Other strategies include charging a fee; Wearing and Neil (1999, p. 93) comment that the Santa Elena Rainforest Reserve receives some 7000 visitors annually and generates around US $40,000, much of which, in this case, is ploughed back into the local community.

The tour operator is a key element in managing demand levels. Despite the strong literature base on eco- or nature tourism markets (Cater and Lowman, 1994), there has been little analysis of the role of the supplier in the packaging of eco-tourism holidays (Higgins, 1996, p. 11). The Ecotourism Society and other organizations in the USA provide guidance for potential customers on how to select tour operators who are attempting to conserve the natural environment and sustain the well-being of local people at destinations. Beyond this, there is insufficient research about the way tour operators manage markets in this context. Yet the tour operator is a major facilitator of tourism development from niche to early mass markets, especially in emerging tourism economies (Jenkins, 1991).

Most tour operators are aware of the process of demand management in sensitive environments, but are less certain how the issue of market responsibility should be addressed, or by whom. The Lumsdon and Swift survey previously referred to verified the intense degree of competition and a lack of industry regulation in Costa Rica. This lack of regulation has led to a mushrooming of companies, with intense pressure on some operators to cut corners in order to compete. For example, in the mid-1980s there were less than 30 main tour operators offering nature tourism in Costa Rica; by the mid-

1990s numbers had grown to an estimated 155 tour operators and 13 tour wholesalers (INICEM, 1995).

There is also a reliance on the tour operator to be the custodian of the eco-tourism offering. The tour operator, for example, is expected to determine areas where the visitor could be taken, the duration of stay at sensitive sites, security matters, and the numbers of visitors to be taken at any given time. The Instituto Costarricense de Turisme (ICT) recognizes its role in the provision of a framework for the development of tourism but is primarily concerned with coordinating the promotion of Costa Rica to the market. There is an acceptance that suppliers will regulate the market themselves, ensuring that demand does not outstrip the capability of existing infrastructure.

However, the argument that tour operators can manage demand collectively and within a commercial framework is not proven. On the contrary, there is empirical evidence which suggests that local entrepreneurs will continue to exploit the potential of nature tourism to the full, rather than in a planned approach such as is envisaged in the principles of sustainable tourism. Brüggeman (1995), for example, suggests considerable evidence of tensions between owners of accommodation and custodians of conservation areas.

There are several tour operators that clearly exhibit distinct principles of conservation in their work, such as Horizontes Nature Tours, which has a distinctly ethical company philosophy. The type of approach adopted by companies such as Horizontes leads to low impact itineraries and high standards of service without compromising environmental principles; it would appear that such companies are, unfortunately, in the minority, as many tour operators do not exhibit this type of best practice. Many of the smaller, recent entrants are now targeting the participant eco-tourist by encouraging self-drive holidays and semi-packaged nature tourism breaks in lodges and hotels. This type of tourism impact is far less manageable.

The management of the parks and reserves envisages increasing problems in monitoring or controlling visitor impact, given the current predictions of demand and limited resource allocation. Thus, the arguments which suggest that tourism development in Costa Rica can be regulated by a partnership between government, tour operators and other businesses are suspect.

Summary

One of the major issues facing Costa Rica is whether or not it can hold true to the underlying principles of eco-tourism when coping with the pressures of a rapidly expanding and increasingly diversified market, which also happens to include an eco-tourism segment. The development of larger scale resorts such as Papagauyo might well exacerbate the situation in terms of volume and in terms of changing the nature of the visitor base from eco-specialist to eco-participant. Some argue that changes to date have already brought irreversible environmental impacts (Carriere, 1991). The increased market pressures from international developers and tour operators are likely to serve only to worsen these impacts.

The dilemmas faced by Costa Rica at the turn of the twenty-first century are similar to the issues that face nature tourism destinations throughout Latin America. It will become increasingly critical as sensitive environments are progressively despoiled through heavy visitation.

SUMMARY

The development of nature-based tourism offerings is likely to grow throughout Latin America. Not only is there sustained market demand from North America and Europe, but continued interest from the media and non governmental organizations. The latter have been important in establishing guidelines for the sustainable design and operation of tours which are targeted to nature-based tour companies (e.g. www.planeta. com); however, the level of compliance is questionable (Sirakaya, 1997, p. 34).

Furthermore, there is evidence to suggest that the efforts of non governmental organizations and the more environmentally conscious tour operators are being undermined. Some companies exhibit the very best practice, including the employment of local people, participating in scientific investigations and providing a percentage of their profits to local non-profit environmental conservation projects (Orams, 1995, p. 8). However, as the market widens, less scrupulous tour companies, driven by pricing considerations and short-term objectives, will become increasingly prolific in the market, displaying greater concern for eco-rhetoric than for eco-practice.

Similarly, whilst international organizations and Latin American governments have continued to support sustainable tourism development at a policy level, there is little evidence to link this to funding for nature-based or conservation projects on a major scale; eco-tourism projects are, if anything, generally thought to be a poor investment (Travel & Tourism Analyst, 1998, p. 80).

The level of resources available to manage and monitor existing nature reserves and biosphere sites is deemed inadequate by many commentators (Kaimowitz, 1996, p. 446). Poaching, degradation of landscapes, threats to indigenous communities and intense visitor pressures at key locations remain constant threats to the nature tourism offering in Latin America. Despite the efforts of progressive tour companies, non-governmental organizations and the scientific community, the prospects for the preservation of significant habitats through tourism development remain limited unless and until effective management controls are introduced, and linkages between visitor revenues and conservation measures are more clearly defined and implemented at a local level.

REFERENCES

Berlin Declaration (1997) *Conference Declaration,* International Conference of Environment Ministers on Biodiversity and Tourism, Berlin, 6–8 March, 1997.

Boo, E. (1990) *Ecotourism: The Potentials and Pitfalls (Vol. 1),* World Wide Fund for Nature, Washington D.C.

Boo, E. (1993) 'Ecotourism Planning For Protected Areas' in K. Linndberg and D. E. Hawkins (eds), *Ecotourism: A Guide For Planners and Managers,* Ecotourism Society, North Bennington, Vt.

Boyd, S. and Butler, R. W. (1996) 'Managing Ecotourism: An Opportunity Spectrum Approach', *Tourism Management,* Vol. 17(8), pp. 556–568.

Boza, M. A. (1988) *Costa Rica National Parks,* Editorial Heliconia, Fundación Neotropica, San José.

Brüggeman, J. (1995) 'In Search of Green Paradise' in N. Häusler, C. Kamp, P. Müller-Rockstroh, W. Scholz and B. E. Schulz (eds), *Retracing the Track of Tourism* (pp. 253–76), Verlag für Entwicklungspolitik Breitenback GmbH, Saabrücken.

Bruntland Report (1987) *Our Common Future,* World Commission on the Environment and Development (Tokyo Declaration, 27 February 1987), Oxford University Press, Oxford.

Burger, J. and Gochfeld, M. (1993) 'Tourism and Short-Term Behavioural Responses of Nesting, Masked, Red-Footed, and Blue-Footed Boobies in the Galapagos', *Environmental Conservation,* Vol. 20, pp. 255–9.

Butler, R. W. (1980) 'The Concept of a Tourism Area Cycle of Evolution', *Canadian Geographer,* Vol. 24(1), pp. 5–12.

Butler, R. W. (1991) 'Tourism, Environment and Sustainable Development', *Environmental Conservation,* Vol. 18(2), pp. 201–9.

Butler, R. W. (1992) 'Alternative Tourism: The Thin Edge of the Wedge' in V. L. Smith and W. R. Eadington (eds), *Tourism Alternatives* (pp. 34–46), University of Pennsylvania Press, Philadelphia, Pa.

Carriere, J. (1991) 'The Crisis in Costa Rica: An Ecological Perspective' in D. Goodman and M. Redclift (eds), *Environment and Development in Latin America: The Politics of Sustainability* (pp. 184–204), Manchester University Press, Manchester.

Cater, E. and Lowman, G. (eds) (1994) *Ecotourism: A Sustainable Option?* John Wiley, Chichester.

Cesar, M. (1999) 'The Myth of "Ecotourism" ', *Latin America Press,* Vol. 13 (September).

Cosgrove, D. (1995) 'Habitable Earth: Wilderness, Empire and Race in America' in D. Rothenberg (ed.), *Wild Ideas* (pp. 26–41), University of Minnesota Press, Minneapolis.

Croall, J. (1995) *Preserve or Destroy: Tourism and the Environment,* Cabouste Gulben Klan Foundation, London.

Diamantis, D. (1999) 'Green Strategies for Tourism Worldwide', *Travel & Tourism Analyst,* Vol. 4 (pp. 89–112), Economist Intelligence Unit, London.

Ecotourism Society (1993) *Ecotourism: A Guide for Planners and Managers,* Ecotourism Society, North Bennington, Vt.

EIU (1996) 'Costa Rica: Travel and Tourism Intelligence', *International Tourism Reports (No. 3)*, Economist Intelligence Unit, London.

Erize, F. (1987) 'The Impact of Tourism on the Antarctic Environment', *Environment International*, Vol. 13(1) pp. 133–6.

Exodus (1999) *Exodus: Discovery and Adventure, 2000–2001*, Exodus Travels Ltd, London.

Fennell, D. A. (1999) *Ecotourism: An Introduction*, Routledge, London.

Fields, G. (1988) 'Employment and Economic Growth in Costa Rica', *World Development*, Vol. 16(12), pp. 1493–509.

France, L. (ed.) (1997) *Sustainable Tourism*, Earthscan, London.

García-Falcón, J. M and Medina-Muñoz, D. (1999) 'Sustainable Tourism Development in Islands: A Case Study of Gran Canaria', *Business Strategies and the Environment*, Vol. 8, pp. 336–57.

Groom, M. J., Podolsk, R. D. and Munn, C. A. (1991) 'Tourism as a Sustained Use of Wildlife: A Case Study of Madre Dios, Southeastern Peru' in J. G. Robinson and K. H. Redford (eds), *Neotropic Wildlife Use and Conservation* (pp. 393–415), University of Chicago Press, Chicago.

Hall, C. M. (1992) 'Adventure, Sport and Health Tourism' in B. Weiler and C. M. Hall (eds), *Special Interest Tourism* (pp. 393–415), Belhaven Press, London.

Hall, C. M. and McArthur, S. (1993) 'Ecotourism in Antarctica and Adjacent Sub-Arctic Islands: Development Impacts and Management', *Tourism Management*, Vol. 14, May, pp. 177–82.

Headland, R. K. (1994) 'Historical Development of Antarctic Tourism', *Annals of Tourism Research*, Vol. 21(2), pp. 269–90.

Healy, R. G. (1994) 'The "Common Pool" Problem in Tourism Landscapes', *Annals of Tourism Research*, Vol. 21(3), pp. 596–611.

Higgins, B. R. (1996) 'The Global Structure of the Nature Tourism Industry: Ecotourism, Tour Operators and Local Businesses', *Journal of Travel Research*, Vol. 35(2), pp. 11–17.

IAATO (1999) 'Antarctic Tourists – Ship and Land Based', International Association of Antarctic Tour Operators (@ http://www. iaato.org/ship and land based.html).

ICT (1995) Data supplied by the Instituto Costarricense de Turismo, San José.

ICT (1999) Data supplied by the Instituto Costarricense de Turismo, San José.

IFT (1998) *Report on Antarctic Tourism Through Ushuaia, 1997–1998*, Instituto Fuegino de Turismo, xxiiATCM/1Pii6, Ushuaia.

INICEM (1995) *Costa Rica: Datos e Indicadores Basicos*, INICEM, San José.

Jenkins, C. L. (1991) 'Tourism Policies in Developing Countries' in S. Medlik (ed.), *Managing Tourism* (pp. 269–78), Butterworth-Heinemann, Oxford.

Kaimowitz, D. (1996) 'The Political Economy of Environmental Policy Reform in Latin America', *Development & Change*, Vol. 27(1), pp. 433–52.

Kemper, S. (2000) 'Madidi: Will Bolivia Drown its New National Park?', *National Geographic*, March, pp. 2–23.

Kenchington, L. A. (1989) 'Tourism in the Galapagos Islands: The Dilemma of Conservation', *Environmental Conservation*, Vol. 16, pp. 227–36.

Lumsdon, L. M. and Swift, J. S. (1998) 'Ecotourism at a Crossroads: The Case of Costa Rica', *Journal of Sustainable Tourism*, Vol. 6(2), pp. 155–72.

McNeely, J. A. (1994) 'Protected areas for the 21st century: working to provide benefits to society', *Biodiversity and conservation*, Vol. 3(5), pp. 390–405.

Maldonado, T., Hurtado de Mendoza, L. and Saborio, O. (1992) *Análisis de Capacidad de Carga para Visitación en las Areas Silvestres de Costa Rica*, Fundación Neotrópica, San José.

Mowforth, M. and Munt, I. (1998) *Tourism and Sustainability*, Routledge, London.

Nelson, J. G. (1994) 'The Spread of Ecotourism. Some Planning Implications', *Environmental Conservation*, Vol. 21(3), pp. 248–55.

O'Brien, P. J. (1997) 'Tourism, Sustainable Development and Participation', paper presented to the *Environment Matters Conference,* Glasgow, (29 April–2 May 1997).

Orams, M. B. (1995) 'Towards a More Desirable Form of Ecotourism', *Tourism Management,* Vol. 16(1), pp. 3–8.

Pleumarom, A. (1994) 'The Political Economy of Tourism', *The Ecologist,* Vol. 24(4), pp. 142–8.

Plog, S. C. (1994) 'Leisure Travel: An Extraordinary Industry Facing Superordinary Problems' in W. Theobald (ed.), *Global Tourism: The Next Decade* (pp. 40–54), Butterworth-Heinemann, Oxford.

Promperú (1999) *The Traveller's Guide to Nature and Protected Areas in Peru,* Promperú, Lima.

Prosser, R. (1994) 'Societal Change and Growth in Alternative Tourism' in P. Cater and G. Lowman (eds), *Ecotourism: A Sustainable Option?* (pp. 19–37), John Wiley, Chichester.

Reboratti, C. (1998) *El Alto Bermejo: Realidades y Conflictos,* Editorial La Colmera, Buenos Aires.

Ryan, C. and Grasse, T. (1991) 'Marketing Ecotourism: Attracting the Elusive Ecotourist' in T. Whelan (ed.), *Nature Tourism: Managing for the Environment* (pp. 89–104), Island Press, Washington D.C.

Schaller, A. (1998) 'The Case of Rio Blanco, Ecuador', website published paper, University of Minnesota, Minn.

Schlüter, R. G. (1994) 'Tourism Development: A Latin American Perspective' in W. Theobald (ed.), *Global Tourism: The Next Decade* (pp. 246–60), Butterworth-Heinemann, Oxford.

SERNATUR (1999) *Atacama Desert: The Driest Desert on the Planet,* SERNATUR, Santiago de Chile.

Silva, E. (1994) 'Thinking Politically About Sustainable Development in Tropical Forests of Latin America', *Development & Change,* Vol. 25, pp. 697–721.

Sirakaya, E. (1997) 'Assessment of Factors Affecting Conformance Behaviour of Ecotour Operators with Industry Guidelines', *Tourism Analysis,* Vol. 2, pp. 17–35.

Smith, G. (1991) 'A New Species of Tourists', *Americas,* Vol. 42(6), pp. 17–20.

Stonehouse, B. (1994) 'Ecotourism in Antarctica' in E. Cater and G. Lowman (eds), *Ecotourism: A Sustainable Option?* (pp. 195–212), John Wiley, Chichester.

Swarbrooke, J. and Horner, S. (1999) *Consumer Behaviour in Tourism,* Butterworth-Heinemann, Oxford.

Tershy, B. R., Breese, D. and Croll, D. A. (1997) 'Human Perturbations and Conservation Strategies on San Pedro Martín Island, Islas de Golfo de California Reserve', *Environmental Conservation,* Vol. 24(3), pp. 261–70.

Tershy, B. R., Bourillon, L., Metzler, L. and Barnes, J. (1999) 'A Survey of Ecotourism on Islands in Northwestern Mexico', *Environmental Conservation,* Vol. 26(3), pp. 212–17.

Thomlinson, E. and Getz, D. (1996) 'The Question of Scale of Ecotourism. Case Study of Two Small Ecotour Operators in the Mundo Maya Region of Central America', *Journal of Sustainable Tourism,* Vol. 4(4), pp. 183–200.

Travel & Tourism Analyst (1998) 'The World Bank Corporation and Tourism', No. 5, *Travel & Tourism Intelligence,* London.

Wallace, G. N. and Pierce, S. M. (1996) 'An Evaluation of Ecotourism in Amazonas, Brazil', *Annals of Tourism Research,* Vol. 23(4), pp. 843–74.

Wearing, S. and Neil, J. (1999) *Ecotourism: Impacts, Potentials and Possibilities,* Butterworth-Heinemann, Oxford.

Weaver, D. (1994) 'Ecotourism in the Caribbean Basin' in E. Cater and G. Lowman (eds), *Ecotourism: A Sustainable Option?* (pp. 159–77), John Wiley, Chichester.

Western, D. (1993) 'Defining Ecotourism' in K. Lindberg and D. Hawkins (eds), *Ecotourism: A Guide for Planners and Managers* (pp. 7–11), The Ecotourism Society, North Bennington, Vt.

Wheeller, B. (1991) 'Tourism's Troubled Times: Responsible Tourism is Not the Answer', *Tourism Management*, June, pp. 91–6.

Whitesell, E. A. (1996) 'Local Struggles Over Rain-Forest Conservation in Alaska and Amazonia', *The Geographical Review*, Vol. 86(3), pp. 414–36.

Wight, P. (1993) 'Ecotourism: Ethics or Eco-Sell?', *Journal of Travel Research*, Vol. 31(3), pp. 3–9.

World Wide Fund for Nature (1992) 'Beyond The Green Horizon', a discussion paper on Principles for Sustainable Tourism, Tourism Concern and WWF, London.

WTO (1999) Data supplied by Division of Economics Market Research, World Tourism Organization, Madrid.

CHAPTER 6

Cultural Tourism

INTRODUCTION

Whilst anthropologists and archaeologists have been studying civilizations (both past and present) for some 200 years, it is only within the last 30–40 years that culture has become a focus of interest and entertainment for the tourist. According to Middleton, cultural attractions comprise: 'history and folklore, religion and art, theatre, music, dance and other entertainment, and museums; some of these may be developed into special events, festivals and pageants' (1994, p. 87).

Cultural tourism in Latin America can be divided into two basic categories: contemporary and historical. Whilst this is an arbitrary division, it does, nevertheless, reflect the basic distinction between the 'old' (pre-Columbian) civilizations and the 'new' (post-Conquest) civilizations of Latin America.

CONTEMPORARY CULTURE

Introduction

The study of contemporary indigenous peoples, their civilizations, customs and way of life is one of the fastest growing branches of tourism, and according to Walle has: 'become a major source of revenue for regions which support it. Developing countries ... often benefit by showcasing indigenous societies as part of a cultural tourism strategy' (1996, p. 874).

Swarbrooke and Horner suggest that, broadly speaking, contemporary culture encompasses four main elements of the tourism market:

- visits to heritage attractions and destinations, and attendance at traditional festivals;
- holidays motivated by a desire to sample national, regional or local food and wine;

- watching traditional sporting events and taking part in local leisure activities;
- visiting workplaces whether they be farms, craft centres or factories.

(1999, pp. 36–7)

There is a great degree of overlap between categorizations. For example, whilst 'sampling of food and wine' might be regarded as the principal reason to visit a particular destination, it could equally be viewed as an integral part of the 'traditional festivals' segment. Furthermore, it is possible to add 'local communities and their way of life' to the 'heritage attractions and destinations' segment. Nevertheless, the categorization provides a useful framework with which to examine in detail the cultural tourism offerings of the region.

Heritage Attractions and Destinations

The heritage attractions of most Latin American nations reflect the historical dominance of various cultural groups at different stages of the region's development, from the Conquest to the present day. In general, heritage comprises the cultural 'history' of a people or nation, and can be sub-divided into many areas. The key areas (in terms of Latin American tourism) are: museums, indigenous communities and their way of life, festivals/carnivals, architecture, handicrafts/local industries, language, music and dance.

Contact with local communities can give the visitor a heightened appreciation of the many cultural elements of these communities, their daily life and agricultural or artisanal output (Ritchie and Zins, 1978, p. 257; Healy, 1994, p. 140; Reisinger, 1994, p. 744). However, in the initial stages of the development of tourism in rural communities, as many of them had been relatively isolated from outside cultural attitudes, they could not readily understand the motivation of tourists. Van den Berghe, writing about ethnic tourism promotion in Mexico, claims that: 'It took some time for local mestizos to realize that foreign tourists had come to see "living Mayas" rather than the colonial town, and to understand why tourists should find Indians interesting' (1995, p. 580).

Most countries have established (or are in the process of establishing) some form of ethnic or indigenous tourism, which is promoted to an international audience. In Peru, for instance, the Department of Puno is marketed by FOPTUR (the Peruvian tourism authority) as 'Peru's Folkloric Capital', with an emphasis on the Aymaran and Quechuan communities that live around Lake Titicaca. A similar approach has been taken by IPAT (the Instituto Panameño de Turismo), the Panamanian government tourist bureau, which has sought to develop the Darien region on the border with Colombia as a national park, where visitors can come into contact with the various Choco Indian communities that live in the region.

The marketing of cultural objects to visitors has become increasingly important in Central America, particularly in Guatemala (Moreno and Littrell, 1996, p. 138). The Instituto Guatemalteco de Turísmo (Guatemalan Institute of Tourism) includes a similar programme of development in its strategic plan: 'Sustainable Tourism Development To The Year 2005'. The Institute outlines seven major tourism experiences that are being developed for the twenty-first century, one of which, the 'Highland Indian Communities', features contact with the local communities, an opportunity to purchase artisanal works in the local open air markets, and to see folkdances, rituals and processions. The Guatemalan authorities view this form of tourism as increasingly in demand (see Box 6.A), but equally recognize the dangers of contamination of a remote people.

Box 6.A. Highland Indian Communities of Guatemala

This product is what the tourist is increasingly looking for: contact with the local communities, which in this particular case are represented by those ethno-linguistic communities that are descended from the Mayan culture, and some of which speak 'Quiché', 'Cakchiquel', 'Mam', 'Ixil', 'Uspanteco', 'Tz'utujil' and 'Pocomam'. There is also the opportunity to gain a deeper understanding of Guatemalan history, through the religious and cultural costumes ...

(INGUAT, 1995)

The major fear of several researchers is that indigenous communities will succumb to the contamination and a consequent loss of identity as a result of their contact with visitors from outside the community. The issue of indigenous communities is of wider concern than a mere discussion of the benefits and disbenefits from tourism development (Sofield, 1993, p. 730). Another perspective is that they become 'fossilized', a living museum, that exists solely for the entertainment of the tourist, and hence raising the question of 'authenticity' and commodization (Cohen, 1988, p. 371; Silver, 1993, p. 308). The issue was graphically described by *The Economist* well over a decade ago:

Fifty years ago Aldous Huxley's 'Brave New World' drew a grisly picture of the Pueblo Indians' sacred dances on the way to becoming a tourist sight. He set the scene some centuries into the future. He was too kind: it was true by the 1950s.

(1989, p. 22)

Festivals and carnivals are amongst the most important expressions of a nation's cultural heritage, and bring together other cultural elements, such as music, dance, food and drink. In Latin America they generally have their origins in religious or historical events such as a Saint's Day, or the country's independence from Spain or Portugal. For example, there are some twelve fixed-date religious festivals, commemorating Saints' Days, Christmas Day, The Assumption, Epiphany, All Souls' Day and many others. In addition, many countries have moveable holidays, such as Easter week ('*Semana Santa*'), generally held sometime between March and April, and '*Corpus Christi*', which is usually sometime in May or June.

Political/historical-inspired holidays vary greatly from country to country and, as such, are perhaps more indicative of a specific national heritage. In Mexico, for instance, there are six national holidays a year dedicated to the celebration of political events: Constitution Day, 5 February; Independence Day, 16 September; Mexican National Day, 12 October; and the Anniversary of the Revolution, 20 November. Other holidays are held for the birth of Juárez (23 March) and the Battle of Puebla (5 May).

There has been a conscious effort to incorporate the more important festivals into tourist itineraries wherever possible. Some such as the famous Carnival in Rio de Janeiro are now considered tourist attractions in their own right, attracting global media attention (Bedding, 1998). According to the Brazilian government (EMBRATUR, 1998, pp. 17–22), Rio is the city most visited by foreign tourists, with some 557,188 foreign visitors in 1997. On average, they stayed ten days in the city, spending some US $224.72 per day on accommodation and subsistence, a total of US $2,247.20 per visit per person. Indeed, major international tour operators such as 'Journey Latin America' specifically focus on the carnival as a major selling point in their tours of Brazil. (See Box 6.B.)

Box 6.B. 'Rio de Janeiro'

Carnival: 13–17 February 1999. At the height of the southern summer, when temperatures are likely to soar to 40° C, Rio, Salvador and Recife celebrate this once-religious festival of excess before Lent. For four days prior to Ash Wednesday Brazilians let go – over-eating, over-drinking, overdressing, underdressing: over-indulgence in just about everything that is considered better in moderation for the rest of the year. Once a year is enough – once a lifetime is a must!

(Journey Latin America, 1998, p. 9)

Apart from Rio, other major carnival destinations in Brazil are Salvador and Recife, and some specialist tour operators promote the 'Brazilian Carnival Experience' as a distinct package, or as extensions to their main packages.

The architectural heritage is largely a product of colonial Spanish or Portuguese influence; whilst it provides a spectacular backdrop to many tours, it is less likely to form the main focus of the tour itself. Most countries retain examples of colonial architecture, in varying states of repair; in Colombia, for instance, the most spectacular examples are to be found in the La Candelaría district of Bogota, at Villa de Leyva, some three hours from the capital, and in the colonial walled city of Cartagena on the Caribbean coast, which was declared a 'World Heritage' site by UNESCO in 1985. Guarding the city approaches is the fortress of San Felipe de Barajas, which is the best preserved example of a Spanish colonial fortress anywhere in the Americas. As a consequence of its Caribbean location, Cartagena is frequently included in cruise itineraries and its colonial heritage is the main promotional theme.

In Mexico, Guanajuato, San Miguel de Allende and Querétaro are near perfect examples of colonial towns, particularly Guanajuato, where the opulence of its past based on the mining of silver is still very much in evidence (Harvey, 1997; Brunton, 1998; Elms, 1998). On the Caribbean coast of Mexico lies the city of Vera Cruz, with its magnificent colonnaded central square and the fortress of San Juan de Ulua, which guarded this important seaport and point of exit for most of the Aztec gold shipped to Spain.

In Panama, the IPAT launched a 'Hispanic Heritage' product in 1992, to coincide with the 500th anniversary of the arrival of the Spanish in the Americas. Much of the emphasis was on the architectural heritage of 'Old Panama' and 'Colonial Panama', the original parts of the capital city; despite the fact that only just over half of the original buildings remain, those that do are: 'in perfect condition, and easily accessible to tourists on foot' (IPAT, 1992). Other examples of the colonial heritage are the fortified city of San Felipe de Portobello and the fortifications at San Lorenzo el Real de Chagres. In Paraguay, the major colonial attractions are the seven Jesuit 'missions' founded between 1609 and 1706, two of which (the Jesús de Tavarangue and the Santísima Trinidad del Paraná), were declared 'World Heritage' sites by UNESCO in 1993.

By contrast, in some countries there appears to be a more fragmented, less developed approach to marketing the colonial past: for example, in Venezuela the Corporación Mérideña de Turísmo (the Mérida District Tourist Corporation) promotes what they refer to as the 'Colonial Route to the South', which purports to link most of the major colonial towns in this region of the country.

In some countries, little has been done to preserve or renovate existing buildings. In Cuba, for instance, years of neglect have turned what was once the jewel in the Spanish crown into a dilapidated, run-down shadow of its former self. Old Havana was declared a 'World Heritage' site by UNESCO in 1982, but this seems to have done little to halt the deterioration of much of the colonial infrastructure (Fletcher, 1996).

In conclusion, there is a wide range of heritage attractions and traditional festivals, many of which are, as yet, relatively underexploited. In this respect, the 'heritage' presents a similar dilemma to that of eco-tourism: how to develop the full tourism potential of these areas without changing their basic nature, and how to prevent structural damage as a consequence of increased visitor numbers.

National, Regional or Local Cuisine

Whilst most Latin American republics have specialist dishes, not many can boast worldwide recognition; only Mexico can justifiably claim this distinction, as Mexican food has been introduced to much of the world, largely through the marketing activities of food processing companies, working in conjunction with major supermarket chains (Pilcher, 1998). By the late 1990s, *tomales, burritos, nachos* and *enchiladas* had become nearly as familiar as *spaghetti* and *pizza*.

Argentinian cuisine is less well known outside the country, and the secret of its success appears to lie in the consumption of great quantities of all types of meat, the use of an abundance of fresh, simple ingredients and locally produced wine. The 1994 Argentinian Tourist Authority campaign 'Argentina: Land of Six Continents' actively sought to emphasize the *asado* (barbeque) as an essential cultural ingredient of the 'Pampas' region around Buenos Aires. (See Box 6.C.)

Box 6.C. The Argentinian 'asado'

The traditional Argentinean 'asado' is the centrepiece of a culinary heritage which has been shaped by many influences. It has been defined as 'a ritual of time, contemplation and taste'. The basic ingredients are, of course, meat cooked over a quebracho or carob fire ... try it 'a la cruz' or spit roast, country style, or even easier barbecued. Ask for 'asado de tira', 'churrasco', 'matambre', 'bife de lomo o de chorizo', 'achuras y chinchulinas' and 'sazónelo con chimichurri.'

(Secretaría de Turismo de la Nación, 1994)

Ironically, whilst Mexican cuisine probably has a greater worldwide reputation, it is the Argentinian *asado* that tends to feature in the holiday brochures and other promotional literature, generally as the highpoint of a visit to an *estancia*, or working ranch.

Traditional Sporting Events/Leisure Activities

In Latin America, those sporting activities that feature as destination attractions are predominately those that can be pursued almost anywhere in the world: golf, hunting, game fishing, pony trekking, in addition to the numerous watersports such as 'white water rafting'. Of these, game fishing is a segment that is assuming greater importance, particularly in Cuba and other countries with Caribbean coastlines. Cuba is particularly determined to heighten its tourism profile in those areas in which it has a natural advantage – beaches and the sea.

Prisma, the Cuban tourist magazine and promotional organ of the Cuban tourism authority, recently emphasized the country's modern marine tourism offering, referring to the Trans-Caribbean regatta from Martinique and the other regattas from Havana to the Cayman Islands and to Florida. Other activities of international importance have been based at the town of Cienfuegos, such as the 'Formula Tunel T-1 Speedboat Races' and similar events held since the late 1990s. Cienfuegos is being developed principally as a 'colonial' coastal city, with a variety of natural land- and water-based attractions. (See Box 6.D.)

Box 6.D. Cienfuegos: An attractive coastal city

Little keys, highly valuable historical landscapes, a fishing village built on stilts on one of the shores, and the variety of birds that have their habitats here are marvellous sights for anyone who ventures out into the gentle waters of the bay.

Going out past the bay and into the Caribbean, visitors can discover the beauty of three marvellous beaches … Just 15 minutes sail brings visitors to the special wealth contained on the sea floor. There are over thirty places to go scuba diving where it is possible to view underwater valleys covered by one of the most populated reefs in the area.

(Destino Cuba, 1998)

At the same time, the memory of Cuba's most famous deep-sea fisherman, Ernest Hemingway, is evoked to maximum benefit by the authorities: 'Cuba will never forget Hemingway and he had a special spot in his heart for this island and its fishers, to which he bequeathed his 1954 Nobel Prize' (Prisma, 1999, p. 56).

In Venezuela, for example, VIASA (Venezuelan Airlines) in cooperation with 'Tandem' (a local specialist tour operator), have targeted the Spanish market with two luxury tailor-made packages for the game fishing enthusiast. Box 6.E shows what the package includes.

Box 6.E. Game fishing in the Venezuelan Caribbean

- Return air ticket, tourist class.
- Transfers, airport – hotel – airport.
- Four nights' accommodation at the Hotel Sheraton Macuto.
- Three days fishing on board our 36 ft. cruiser: fully-crewed, and rods, bait and accessories all provided.
- Refrigeration facilities and sandwiches provided for the duration of the fishing trip.
- Two nights, full board, at the Hoturvensa de Canaima camp.
- A forty-five minute sightseeing flight over Angel Falls, and a trip by launch in Lake Canaima.

(VIASA, 1995)

To talk of 'traditional' activities in the historical sense is perhaps somewhat misleading, as very few are 'native' to the region. 'Leisure activities' (including spectator sports) still largely comprise events similar to those found throughout much of the world, such as football, which is particularly popular in Brazil and Argentina. Exceptions include the bullfight (culturally a preserve of the 'Latin' nations), which is highly regarded in Colombia, Mexico, Peru and Venezuela. To this it is possible to add the 'rodeo', polo and horse racing in Argentina and Uruguay. Nevertheless, most of these events are generally regarded only as 'day excursions' or similar by most operators, who generally sub-contract to local travel agents. It is highly unlikely that, by themselves, they could ever constitute the major motivation for visiting a particular country or area.

Local 'leisure activities' which do constitute attractions unique to the countries and regions of Latin America are the traditional regional dances and music; they are often grouped under the 'folklore' label, and provide a representation of ethnic, racial and social identities (Mendoza, 1998, p. 165). The variation is considerable:

> Folk music varies from country to country: while quiet cowboy songs typify Argentina and Venezuela, Brazilian music is usually stormy and rhythmic. Music and dance in the Andean countries draw on Indian sources; typical musical instruments are the *charango*, the drum, and the reed flute.
>
> (Shichor, 1993, p. 21)

Of these, a number are known internationally; they include the *tango* in Argentina, the *bambuco* in Colombia, and the famous *mariachi* music of Mexico.

Buenos Aires appears particularly fortunate in this respect; not only does the city have a wealth of most forms of entertainment, but it is home to a unique musical phenomena, the world renowned dance, 'the tango' (see Box 6.F).

Box 6.F. 'The tango'

The tango is something of a paradox in Buenos Aires: it is both everywhere and nowhere. Visitors who have their hearts set on spending every night in dark, glamorous clubs enthralled by local couples dramatically re-enacting the tango's primitive ritual are likely to be disappointed. On the other hand, those who are attentive to the city's more muted melodies that suddenly break through a surface of urban sound to reveal its soul, will hear tango in taxis, cafés, and floating out of upstairs windows.

Bordellos played a major role in launching the tango. Brothels and rough-and-tumble cafés attracted Argentina's predominantly male immigrants. There men escaped their loneliness and poverty, spending evenings listening to the bawdy lyrics of the early anonymous 'tanguistas' and dancing among themselves.

(Evans, 1996, p. 161)

An entire folklore industry has been built around the tango, Argentina's 'most deeply rooted music' (Jacobson, 1998), and the cafés and bars where it is performed, including the Caminito street in the *La Boca* quarter of Buenos Aires' docklands area, have a place assured in the guide books. As a recent travelogue report in *The Times* claimed:

> But even if true Buenos Aires tango has become a mix of memory and instant folklore, it still provides wonderful outings for visitors and Argentinians alike: for me, one of the real purposes in visiting BA, maybe even one of the 'meanings' of the city.

(Hopkins, 1998)

Farms, Craft Centres or Factories

Agricultural and rural craft tourism is another rapidly developing sector, and lends itself to many of the destination offerings in Latin America. Full day excursions and short breaks to working ranches are popular in Argentina; the whole *Gaucho* experience mimics that of the 'Dude Ranches' in the USA. Visitors to an *estancia* can see the daily work, can ride on horseback, or simply relax. The highlight of the excursion is usually the huge *gaucho*-style barbecue in the open air. For example, the Spanish company Ambassador Tours, offers a 14-day (two-country) tour covering Buenos Aires, San Gará, Posadas and Rio de Janeiro, of which two days are devoted to a visit to the Estancia San Gara, one hour from Buenos Aires (see Box 6.G).

Box 6.G. A working ranch in Argentina

Day 6: A country-style breakfast is followed by an expedition on horseback (or by wagon) to the small islands in the nearby marshland, where you can appreciate the unspoiled scenery and wildlife. After a picnic lunch, we return to the ranch by late afternoon. Before the evening meal, we sample 'pastelitos', the traditional pasties from this region, while preparations are made for the 'asado', the traditional 'gaucho' barbecue. Local wine and music accompany the meal ...

Day 7: Breakfast is followed by a demonstration of horsemanship skills, such as lassooing, and breaking in wild horses. This is followed by lunch on the patio, where the National Geographic Institute has filmed the life and costumes of the contemporary 'Gauchos' ...

(Ambassador Tours, 1993)

In Colombia, it is the coffee farms (*fincas*) that generally constitute the major tourist attraction. There are coffee harvests throughout most of the year, depending on the region, so trips around working coffee farms are relatively easy to find, and in the district of Manizales, for instance, the regional Coffee Growers Association has developed a package that looks in detail at the life of the growers themselves. Independent tour operators package the coffee experience in many different ways, including the use of the plantation *haciendas* (estate houses) as a base from which to go horse riding, walking, or visiting the local mountain villages (ECOLATINA, 1998).

The other major coffee producer, Costa Rica, has also sought to incorporate aspects of its commercial coffee production into tourist itineraries; by contrast with Colombia, the Costa Rican approach seems to focus on the provision of day excursions. Another example of tourism demand stimulating small-scale enterprise is the Sarchí in the Central Valley of Costa Rica, where unemployed agricultural workers have turned to artisan crafts. According to Pérez Sánz, this illustrates another dimension to the local economy, where an agglomeration of small organizations have combined to develop 'the cradle of Costa Rican crafts' (1998, p. 171). Empirical research conducted by Van den Berghe (1994) in Crístobal, Chiapas (Mexico), supports the view that craft and ethnic folkloric tourism can be of benefit to local communities which both are isolated and have been marginalized within the national process of economic development. Van den Berghe recognizes the importance of the participation of locals in the process of tourism development.

HISTORICAL CULTURE

Introduction

Whilst the various elements that comprise the cultural tourism offering are unlikely, by themselves, to constitute a major appeal to visit a particular Latin American country, archaeological tourism is more significant. The ruins left by the pre-Columbian civilizations of The Americas provide the interested tourist with sights equalled only by those of ancient Egypt. Indeed, FOPTUR (the Peruvian tourist board) promotes the archaeological remains at Tucume, to the north of the country as: 'Túcume: Valley of Pyramids'.

The three most well known of these pre-Columbian civilizations are the Aztecs (Mexico), the Incas (Peru, Bolivia, Chile) and the Mayas (Mexico, Guatemala, Honduras). What is undoubtedly the most fascinating aspect of these empires for the modern-day tourist is the archaeological legacy left by these people: temples, statues and cities scattered throughout the continent attract a wide range of visitors including the professional scientist, amateur tourist-archaeologist, cultural historian and day excursionist. In addition, many of these ruins have lain 'undiscovered' for centuries, all of which adds to their mystique and attraction. For example, the Mayan temple at Palenque, in the State of Chiapas, was only 'discovered' deep in the jungle in 1947 by the archaeologist Alberto Ruz Lhullier.

This air of mystery and challenge and the sheer enormity of some of the more famous sites, such as the ruined city of Teotihuacán, undoubtedly goes some way to explaining the popularity of the remains left by these ancient civilizations. The other site which provokes such emotions is Easter Island, 3700 kilometres from the Chilean coast. This island, home to the mysterious 'Giant Heads' (*Moaias*), is described by SERNATUR (the Chilean National Tourism Service) as:

> a real open air museum of more than 160 square kilometers, whose mysteries and geographical features make it ideal for tourism. It can be toured by car, on a motorbike, on horseback, by bicycle, and even on foot ... Many different areas of the island are impregnated with an atmosphere of mystery and legend. This is especially true of the caves and caverns, where the silence conceals surprising archaeological treasures.
>
> (SERNATUR, 1994)

In order to examine the tourist potential of these archaeological remains, the following analysis is divided into two sections: the civilizations of Central

America (Mexico, Guatemala and Honduras), followed by those cultures that flourished in South America – in Peru, Bolivia and Chile.

The Civilizations of Central America

The first civilization of Mexico were the *Olmecs*, who are remembered, amongst other things, for their huge pieces of monumental art, particularly large carved stone heads. Other important tribes were the *Aztecs* (a fierce warrior race), the *Toltecs* (also builders of cities and statues), the *Zapotecs* (whose capital was the fortified city of *Monte Albán*), and perhaps of greatest significance in view of the subsequent tourism potential, the *Mayas*.

Pre-dating all these civilizations, however, was the city state of Teotihuacán, which was built around the time of the birth of Christ, and which was revered by the *Aztecs* as the place where the Gods created the sun and the moon. When the Spanish arrived in the central valley of Mexico, they found that the city had been unaccountably abandoned some 750 years earlier. It is the awe-inspiring size and majesty of Teotihuacán that explains its fascination for visitors: at the height of its power (AD 1 to 150), it is estimated to have covered some 20 square kilometres, and supported a population of between 25,000 and 30,000 inhabitants (García Valadés, 1975, p. 7).

The *Aztec* Empire encompassed most of what is today Mexico, and at its height was probably the most powerful civilization in Central America. In reality, the *Aztec* Empire was based on an alliance between the city states of Tenochtitlán (the home of the *Mexica* people and centre of the empire), Texcoco and Tacuba. In a deliberate attempt to subjugate the *Aztecs*, the Spanish *Conquistadores* destroyed the city of Tenochtitlán and founded Mexico City on the ruins. This means that throughout the entire modern city, the tourist can experience first hand the remains of various buildings.

The other major attractions of Mexico City, in terms of archaeological interest, are the many excellent museums throughout the city: the National Anthropology Museum is one of the largest and most important in the country and very well worth a visit. It has 12 galleries on the first floor, housing the most impressive archaeological pieces from pre-Columbian civilizations, including the famous 'Sunstone', the *Aztec* Calendar. The Great Temple Museum, built to house the artefacts unearthed during the 1978–82 excavation of the *Aztec* Great Temple, is an architectural achievement in its own right: the rooms were built to resemble the ruins of the original temples, and preserve the remains in an appropriately solemn atmosphere. Other museums which contain exhibits from the pre-Columbia era are the National Art Museum and the Diego Rivera 'Anahuacalli' Museum. Whilst each state has its own museums, some of the more spectacular collections outside Mexico City are to be found in the State of Tabasco.

Another museum of note is the Gold Museum in Bogotá (see Box 6.H).

Box 6.H. The Bogotá Gold Museum

an enormous collection of over 23,000 pre-Columbian items gathered together by the Bank of the Republic once the wise decision had been taken to stop melting down objects that were unearthed ... It is recognised as the most important museum of goldwork in all Spanish America, although a number of Colombian collections failed to find a home here ... The museum has several travelling displays, and also branches in Cartagena, Calí, Santa Marta and Armenia ...

(Jaramillo Panesso, 1993, p. 45)

Entrance to the Museum is by lift, restricting the number of visitors on each occasion. Visitors are led into a darkened room, and when the lift doors have been secured, the room is illuminated, giving the visitor the full impact of the exhibits. Armed guards are stationed at various points around the room, adding to the air of mystique and danger which pervades the Museum, all of which is ironically appropriate when one considers the bloody history behind many of the exhibits.

Without doubt, though, the most numerous remains are those left behind by the Mayan civilization – the best of which are to be found in the Yucatán Peninsula to the south of Mexico and in various sites in Guatemala and Honduras. Major tourism developments began in the Yucatán in the early 1970s, with the establishment of Cancún and Isla Mujeres as beach destinations. Whilst the local inhabitants were aware of the historic ruins in the region, such as the magnificent temple at Chichén Itzá, the majority of tourists visiting the area were not. The author Frederic Raphael claims that when a friend of his visited Cozumel in 1950, it was so undiscovered by tourists that he was referred to as *el turista* (*the* tourist) (Raphael, 1996).

Gradually, however, interest developed and the archaeological potential of this area as a tourist attraction has been recognized by the tourism authorities. By the late 1970s, the Secretaría de Turísmo was emphasizing the archaeological attractions of Yucatán (along with the sites of Teotihuacán and Tula to the north) as examples of the diversity of attractions to be found throughout the country (Secretaría de Turísmo, 1978). It also formed part of a long-term strategy on the part of the Mexican government to disperse visitors away from the more popular destinations, such as Mexico City and Acapulco.

Since these early attempts, the archaeological tourism industry in the

Yucatán Peninsula has increased in sophistication; there are now day packages from Mérida to Palenque, which include airflights, tours of the pyramids and additional excursions to Villahermosa and Oaxaca. The official Tourist Guide issued by COTEY (the promotional arm of the Dirección de Turísmo del Estado de Yucatán (the Yucatán State Tourist Authority)), describes the Chichén Itzá site in some detail, showing the level of development of tourist facilities. The changes have been considerable; the area has achieved international fame and recognition and, as such, is now promoted to tourists as much for its archaeological sites as for its beaches. For example, a 1996–7 brochure, produced by specialist tour operator 'Exodus', offered a 16-day 'Yucatán Adventure' which combined the archaeological and cultural attractions of the region, with those of beach tourism (see Box 6.I).

Box 6.I. 'Yucatan Adventure'

The jungles, beaches, highlands and colonial towns of Mexico's Yucatan peninsular [*sic*], and the majestic ruins of the Mayas.

The Yucatan peninsular is without doubt the most interesting part of Mexico. It has a beautiful coastline, with miles of clean sandy beaches fringing pleasantly warm seas. There are interesting colonial towns such as Merida, from the Spanish era, while inland are great stretches of tropical jungle which give way in the south to attractive highland country. This is the home of the Tzotzel people, the nearest descendants of the Mayas, the remains of whose enigmatic civilisation are one of the greatest attractions of the Yucatan. Their vast and fascinating ruins, massive pyramidal temples peeping out of the jungle, provide the final focal point of a trip which is rich in natural and human interest.

(Exodus, 1996)

The Civilizations of South America

Whilst there were a number of important civilizations in Central America, to the south of the Continent, the *Inca* Empire was significantly more important than any other in the region. The Empire – which covered most of present-day Chile, Bolivia and Peru – had a communications infrastructure far in advance of that of any other pre-Columbian civilization. The main cities, such as Cochabamba, Machu Picchu, Cuzco and Ayacucha, were connected by a series of tracks (footpaths) that crossed the length and breadth of the region, connecting the extremities of the *Inca* world.

There were six tribes settled in this region prior to the emergence of the *Incas*: the *Chavín*, the *Mochica*, the *Paracas*, the *Nazca*, the *Tiahuanaco* and the *Chimú*. Many artefacts from these various civilizations remain, despite the fact that the *Incas* deliberately tried to obliterate all evidence of cultures which preceded their own. One of the great archaeological mysteries of the area is the history of the famous Lines of Nazca:

> The greatest mystery of the Inca-Nazca culture is the vast network of 'lines', a fantastic assembly of rectangles and squares that have been etched into the sand and waste gravel. Outsized birds, spiders, whales, and surrealistic figures are also present. These lines, some running for miles in length, have remained in a good state of preservation ... These lines are approximately fifteen hundred years old.
>
> (Von Hagen, 1961, p. 26)

Ironically, the lines on the plain of Nazca first came to worldwide prominence in 1969, but not as a consequence of archaeological interest, nor as a result of promotion from the Peruvian tourist authorities, but through the theories put forward in a controversial book *Chariots of the Gods?* written by Swiss hotelier Eric Von Däniken. His theories linking these constructions to extra-terrestrial space travellers led to widened interest in something that had, until then, been studied only by archaeologists. The tourist potential of this area is now well established: FOPTUR (the Peruvian Tourist Board) devotes half the space in its publicity leaflets about the *Nazca* region to the lines. (See Box 6.J.)

Box 6.J. The Lines of Nazca

Nasca: Mysteries and Adventure.

This is Nasca, a unique place due to the mysteries of its marvellous lines and figures, drawn with spectacular perfection, by the gods ... by aliens ... by giants ... or by ordinary people? The beauty and magnitude of the lines must be observed from above.

The drawings and their meaning are even more mysterious than their origin. It is not even known how long it took to create them, nor how the creators were able to measure them with such perfection, since there were no aircraft in those days. This mystery inspires many theories.

In terms of science, these lines have a series of characteristics potentially aimed at astronomy or agriculture. Or perhaps they were created to direct extraterrestrials, as the lines are related to the earth's magnetic field, the horoscope, and many other mysteries, which in the final years of the 20th century have not yet been deciphered.

(FOPTUR, 1993)

The other unexplained mystery is that of *Tiahuanaco*:

> Like all the pre-Inca cultures, it has left us only unexplained mysteries. The remains of what must have been the greatest ceremonial centre in all the Andes are still to be seen on the Altiplano in Bolivia, near Lake Titicaca at an altitude of 12,500 feet.
>
> (Von Hagen, 1961, pp. 27–8)

As to the origins of the *Incas* themselves, their records tell us that they emerged from the Lake Titicaca region and from there migrated north to the valley of Cuzco, where they founded their capital. Their evolution in the Cuzco valley has been confirmed by archaeologists. From this point, they began the colonization of the entire region, becoming the dominant power in the process. Whilst there are many similarities between the rise of the *Inca* and *Aztec* Empires, the great difference between the two cultures lay in the way in which they asserted control over other tribes in the region. Whilst the *Aztecs* conquered neighbouring peoples and killed and enslaved them, the *Incas* tended to use their military might to assimilate local tribes, and incorporate them into the Empire. This explains the need for the superb communications network, as it was clearly required to keep control over all parts of the Empire.

Following the arrival of the Spanish, the *Inca* civilization was subjected to a campaign of premeditated destruction, similar to that which befell the peoples of Central America. Consequently, many cities were completely or partially destroyed and new cities built on their ruins, in many cases incorporating original foundations and stones. Others became forgotten in the jungle, and were only rediscovered centuries later: such as Machu Picchu, the fabled 'lost city' of the *Incas*, which remained hidden until 1911. Evidence of the *Inca* past can be seen today, even in the capitals of Lima (Peru) and Sucre (Bolivia), and the *de facto* capital of Bolivia, La Paz. New discoveries are still being made, such as the tomb of The Great Lord of Sipan, which was discovered in 1988, and according to contemporary reports is as important as 'the discovery in 1922 of King Tutankhamen's burial place in Egypt' (Hayes, 1988).

Unlike the *Nazca* region, Machu Picchu has been a well-known tourist attraction ever since the early 1950s. The city was rediscovered by Hiram Bingham in 1911, and subsequently became a prime site of interest for many of the world's archaeologists and scientists. By the 1970s, the tourism industry (of which Machu Picchu is the jewel) had become so important to the Peruvian economy that foreign earnings were equivalent to those earned from the export of zinc and fishmeal (Strong, 1992, p. 198).

The importance of the tourism industry, and the Machu Picchu site in particular, was underlined by the fact that the *Sendero Luminoso* terrorist group (which operated a campaign of terror and violence in this and other inland areas between 1980 and 1992) specifically targeted the area; they bombed the tourist train in June 1986, killing 7 foreign tourists, and wounding 40 more.

Consequently, the numbers of visitors to Machu Picchu fell, and by 1992 had reached an all-time low of 65,000 (Coster, 1997). Since the capture of the guerrilla leader Anibal Gúzman, in the same year, the numbers of inbound visitors to Peru has increased steadily and the city remains the major destination for foreign visitors (Euromonitor, 1994, p. 144). The Peruvian Tourist Authority has devoted considerable attention to promoting the site, as it represents a unique destination offering; there is now direct rail access from Cuzco to the Puente Ruinas station by the river in Urubamba Canyon, directly below the ruins. The journey takes four hours and, on arrival at the station, visitors can catch a minibus for the 20-minute drive up the steep roadway to the hotel. From here it is a relatively short walk to the centre of the ruins. Estimates vary, but the most recent suggest that up to 300,000 tourists visit the site every year (Hide, 1999). There is, however, increasing concern regarding the growth in visitor numbers and the management problems associated with conserving the site. For example, there are currently plans to erect a cable car to the summit, which is the subject of deep controversy.

The net result is, unfortunately, increasing environmental degradation, specifically in terms of litter and the erosion of footpaths, and in some instances, damage to the buildings themselves. Recent claims by locals maintained that of the 150 tour companies using the *Inca* Trail, only 13 have signed up to an association that promises to adopt good eco-minded practices (Hide, 1999). The authorities, however, have begun to adopt some measures towards conservation; for example, it is prohibited to take bottled water to Machu Picchu, presumably to reduce the number of empty plastic bottles discarded by visitors.

SUMMARY

Whilst cultural tourism has grown considerably in importance in the 1990s, it is unlikely in itself to form a main attraction for the mass market. Even the domestic market, for whom the cultural tourism experience is more easily accessible, may be reluctant converts, as an interest in their indigenous heritage is not something that has traditionally appealed to most Latin American middle classes as a holiday pastime. However, such attitudes are changing, albeit slowly; it is likely that interest will grow, especially if cultural tourism is assimilated into an increasing commitment to cultural diversity. For example, Chile is preparing a new policy for promoting culture, following a programme of consultation in districts and regions regarding artistic expression and the preservation and protection of the country's 'cultural, ecological and genetic patrimony' (Canihuate, 2000, p. 4).

Archaeological tourism has always been popular, and forms a unique attraction in its own right. The main problem stems directly from its very popularity: namely, a heavy demand level, all following the same well-worn areas. Partly, this is a consequence of over-promotion and increasingly easy access. The sheer numbers of visitors to the more popular sites such as Machu Picchu or Teotihuacán are bringing discernible impacts and, if this continues, governments and non governmental organizations will be forced to address the question of preservation, not only of the architectural sites themselves, but of the surrounding eco-system.

REFERENCES

Ambassador Tours (1993) *Ambassador Tours: Descubra el Mundo (mayo '93–junio '94)*, Ambassador Tours, Barcelona.

Bedding, J. (1998) 'When the Slums Get to Samba', *Daily Telegraph* (21 February).

Brunton, J. (1998) 'Dream Cities in Mexico's Colonial Crown', *The Times* (26 December).

Canihaute, G. (2000) 'Cultural Bill of Rights', *Latin America Press* (6 March).

Cohen, E. (1988) 'Authenticity and Commoditization in Tourism', *Annals of Tourism Research*, Vol. 15(3), pp. 371–86.

Coster, G. (1997) 'Flying Saucers? Perfectly Believable in Peru', *Daily Telegraph* (8 February).

Destino Cuba (1998) 'Cienfuegos: An Attractive Coastal City', *Destino Cuba (Revista Profesional de Turismo)*, No. 6 (April–June), pp. 12–17.

ECOLATINA (1998) *Exploring COLOMBIA: Its Land, People, Heritage & Culture*, ECOLATINA Ltd, Richmond.

The Economist (1989) 'Third World Tourism: Visitors Are Good For You', *The Economist*, Vol. 310(7593), pp. 21–4.

Elms, R. (1998) 'Ore Inspired', *Sunday Times* (25 January).

EMBRATUR (1998) *Anuário Estatístico EMBRATUR, Vol. 25 (1998)*, Instituto Brasileiro de Turísmo – EMBRATUR, Brasília, D.F.

Euromonitor (1994) *Travel and Tourism in Latin America*, Euromonitor, London.

Evans, J. (1996) 'Tango' in K. Wheaton (ed.), *Insight Guides: Buenos Aires*, (pp. 161–71), APA Publications, London.

Exodus (1996) *Exodus Discovery Holidays, 1996–1997*, Exodus Travels Ltd, London.

Fletcher, P. (1996) 'Old Havana Seeking a New Look', *Financial Times* (31 August).

FOPTUR (1993) *The Nasca Lines*, FOPTUR (Peruvian Tourist Board), Lima.

García Valadés, A. (1975) *Teotihuacan: La Ciudad y Sus Monumentos*, Distribución Cultural Especializada, S.A., Mexico D.F.

Harvey, S. (1997) 'Where the Local Museum is Beyond the Grave', *Daily Telegraph* (18 January).

Hayes, M. (1988) 'Peru Tomb "A Rival to Tutankhamen"', *Daily Telegraph* (7 October).

Healy, R. G. (1994) '"Tourist Merchandise" as a Means of Generating Local Benefits from Ecotourism', *Journal of Sustainable Tourism*, Vol. 2(3), pp. 137–51.

Hide, S. (1999) 'Inca City "In Danger"', *Daily Telegraph* (13 March).

Hopkins, A. (1998) 'The Most Fun You Can Have Dressed', *The Times* (5 December).

INGUAT (1995) *Guatemala: Desarollo Turístico Sustenable Hacía El Año 2005*, Instituto Guatemalteco de Turísmo (INGUAT), Guatemala, C.A.

IPAT (1992) *Panamá: Herencia Hispánica*, Instituto Panameño de Turísmo, Panama.

Jacobson, P. (1998) 'His Smoke Still Gets in Their Eyes', *Daily Telegraph* (19 September).

Jaramillo Panesso, R. (1993) *Colombia (2.da Edición)*, Editorial Norma, S.A., Santafé de Bogotá.

Journey Latin America (1998) *Bespoke Holiday Journeys 1998/1999*, Journey Latin America, London.

Mendoza, Z. S. (1998) 'Defining Folklore: Mestizo and Indigenous Identities on the Move', *Bulletin of Latin American Research*, Vol. 17(2), pp. 165–83.

Middleton, V. T. C. (1994) *Marketing in Travel and Tourism*, 2nd edition, Butterworth-Heinemann, Oxford.

Moreno, J. M. and Littrell, M. A. (1996) 'Marketing Culture to Tourists: Interpreting and Translating Textile Traditions in Antigua, Guatemala' in M. Robinson, N. Evans and P. Callaghan (eds), *Tourism and Culture* (pp. 138–44), University of Northumbria Press, Newcastle-upon-Tyne.

Pérez Sánz, J. P. (1998) 'The New Faces of Informality in Central America', *Journal of Latin American Studies*, Vol. 30(1), pp. 157–79.

Pilcher, J. M. (1998) *Que Vivan los Tomales!: Food and the Making of Mexican Identity*, University of New Mexico Press, Albuquerque, N. Mex.

Prisma (1999) 'Hemingway's Seas', *Prisma del Turismo en Cuba*, Año 293, p. 56.

Raphael, F. (1996) 'Stony Silence', *Daily Telegraph* (18 January).

Reisinger, Y. (1994) 'Social Contact Between Tourists and Hosts of Different Cultural Backgrounds' in A. V. Seaton (ed.), *Tourism: The State of the Art* (pp. 743–54), John Wiley, Chichester.

Ritchie, J. R. B. and Zins, M. (1978) 'Culture as a Determinant of the Attractiveness of a Tourist Region', *Annals of Tourism Research*, Vol. 5(2), pp. 252–67.

Secretaría de Turísmo (1978) *Welcome to Mexico*, Secretaría de Turísmo, Consejo Nacional de Turísmo, Mexico D.F.

Secretaría de Turismo de la Nación (1994) *La Pampa, Land of the Gaucho*, Secretaría de Turismo de la Nación, Buenos Aires.

SERNATUR (1994) *Easter Island*, Servicio Nacional de Turismo – Chile, Santiago de Chile.

Shichor, M. (1993) *Bolivia and Peru*, Inbal Travel Information Ltd, Tel Aviv.

Silver, I. (1993) 'Marketing Authenticity in Third World Countries', *Annals of Tourism Research*, Vol. 20(2), pp. 302–18.

Sofield, T. (1993) 'Indigenous Tourism Development', *Annals of Tourism Research*, Vol. 20, pp. 729–50.

Strong, S. (1992) *Shining Path: The World's Deadliest Revolutionary Force*, HarperCollins, London.

Swarbrooke, J. and Horner, S. (1999) *Consumer Behaviour in Tourism*, Butterworth-Heinemann, Oxford.

Van den Berghe, P. (1994) *The Quest for the Other: Ethnic Tourism in San Cristobal, Mexico*, University of Washington Press, Seattle.

Van den Berghe, P. (1995) 'Marketing Mayas: Ethnic Tourism Promotion in Mexico', *Annals of Tourism Research*, Vol. 22(3), pp. 568–88.

VIASA (1995) *Vacaciones y Pesca En El Caribe Venezolano*, Viasa, Caracas.

Von Hagen, V. W. (1961) *Realm of the Incas*, The New American Library, Inc., New York.

Walle, A. H. (1996) 'Habits of Thought and Cultural Tourism', *Annals of Tourism Research*, Vol. 23(4), pp. 874–90.

CHAPTER 7

Urban Tourism

INTRODUCTION

In Latin American countries, cities have always been attractive to the visitor, not only because of their wide range of attractions and facilities, but also because of their atmosphere – a mix of culture, history and shopping, all to be found within a relatively compact central zone. In this respect, the tourism authorities have an advantage, as the city centre has traditionally been the main arena for social and cultural events (Ward, 1993, p. 1131). City tourism authorities target a wide range of international visitors, such as organized groups, individual leisure travellers, business travellers, young explorers, conference delegates, attendees at trade fairs and other events, and those who use the city as a convenient stop-over point in a longer journey. At a domestic level, business travellers tend to dominate, followed by those visiting friends and relatives.

It is possible to analyse urban tourism in Latin America, using two essentially physical components suggested by Middleton (1994, p. 86): (1) destination attractions and environment; (2) destination facilities and services.

The analysis focuses on tourism, but at the same time is cognizant of a number of salient aspects of urban tourism development in a changing global economy: such as private versus public investment, trends of migration (Drakakis-Smith, 1995, p. 666), industrialization, poverty and housing conditions, and the inadequacy of the basic infrastructure to support fast-growing populations (Portes *et al.*, 1997). In Lima, for example, it was estimated that during the period of rapid growth in tourism in the 1980s, only 7 per cent of the population living in the peripheral squatter zones had access to drinking water considered fit for human consumption (Rondinelli, 1986). This is characteristic of many Latin American cities. Approximately two-thirds of the 20 million residents of Mexico City live in poor housing with inadequate water, sewage and basic facilities. The situation is summarized by Angotti thus: 'The Latin American Metropolis is characterised by mass poverty and environmental pollution on a scale generally unparalled in the North' (1996, p. 12).

Given the magnitude of these trends, it is difficult to operationalize tourism management concepts such as the destination life cycle as a planning tool, certainly not in the short term (Butler, 1980; Brownlie, 1985).

GATEWAY AND CAPITAL CITIES

Of particular relevance to Latin American urban tourism is the issue of 'gateway cities': a gateway city (generally, but not exclusively, the capital city) is the major point of entry to a country for most international visitors, and acts as a conduit through which visitors are dispersed to other parts of the country (Lumsdon and Swift, 1993, p. 2). Unfortunately, in many instances, cities act as a closed door rather than a gateway, as many visitors spend much of their time (and money) in the city itself and restrict their exploration of the rest of the country to day excursions from the city. This has the undesirable effect of reinforcing the economic disparities that usually exist between the urban conurbations and the remainder of the country.

The majority of gateway cities are capitals: they tend to be the first port of call for most visitors, and provide typical examples of both the tourism opportunities and the problems faced by many large urban conglomerations in Latin America. If a gateway city is one that acts as a channel or focus for tourist activity to the interior of the country, then many of the large cities in Latin America could be considered gateway cities (see Table 7.1).

Gateway cities offer a first (and sometimes lasting impression) of a region or state for the visitor; the perception of a country may be heavily dependent on what happens to the visitor on arrival. Furthermore, gateway cities offer a potential in their own right for short breaks and specialist holidays within the intra-Latin American market. If cities retain or develop intrinsic components of interest for the visitor, they have the potential to maintain or grow market share against other city-based destinations. The business sector, above all, looks for a tourism appeal and facilities to attract wider investment (Kotler *et al.*, 1993).

The appeal of the gateway cities of Latin America to the visitor lies not only in their cultural richness but also in the lifestyle of the population and in the many and varied styles of architecture found within them. For most cities, visitors are comparatively less important to the economy of the

Table 7.1. Main gateway cities in Latin America

Country	Main Gateway Cities
Argentina	Buenos Aires, Mendoza, Rosario
Bolivia	La Paz
Brazil	Río de Janeiro, São Paulo, Florianópolis, Salvador, Foz do Igaçu, Porto Alegre, Recife
Chile	Santiage de Chile, Valparaiso, Puerto Montt
Colombia	Santafé de Bogotá, Barranquilla, Cartagena de las Indias,
Costa Rica	San José, Limón
Cuba	La Habana
Dominican Republic	Santo Domingo
Ecuador	Quito, Guayaquil, Baltra (Galapagos)
El Salvador	San Salvador
Guatemala	Guatemala C.A., Puerto Barrios
Honduras	Tegulcigalpa
Mexico	México D.F., Veracruz, Mérida, Cancún, Tijuana, Acapulco
Nicaragua	Managua
Panama	Ciudad Panamá, Colón
Paraguay	Asunción
Peru	Lima
Uruguay	Montevideo
Venezuela	Caracas, San Cristobál

city than they are to a traditional mountain or seaside resort. This in turn means that, rather than adapting to the needs of the visitor (such as in a resort area), visitors are more likely to have to adapt to the way of life of the city and, in the process, make a more direct contribution to the central economy of the city through their use of hotels, restaurants, public transport, etc.

The basic issue for most of the major gateway cities of Latin America is how they can enhance their current position and gain from tourism growth without overloading the tourism and city infrastructure. This is particularly difficult given that, in most cities, core functional activities are undertaken by a mix of municipal authorities and private enterprise (Wöber, 1997, p. 3).

Buenos Aires clearly exhibits the potential and problems typical of many gateway cities. The Argentinian tourist authorities wish to develop the city both as a tourist destination in its own right and as a gateway to the rest of Argentina. In recent years they have presented a promotional campaign: 'Argentina: The Land of Six Continents' (see Box 7.A).

Ironically, the very success in promoting Buenos Aires as a destination in its own right could be to the detriment of other parts of the country. First, the

---

Box 7.A. Buenos Aires: Destination and gateway city

Built along the Río de la Plata, Buenos Aires is South America's most elegant city – bustling capital by day, ablaze with entertainment by night. Theatres and museums, parks and boulevards, shops and hotels, and a wide choice of restaurants in which to sample the world-famous Argentinian beef.

A modern and dynamic city, rubbing shoulders with the Buenos Aires of old-fashioned cafes and nostalgic tango bars. For the European, Buenos Aires is the cosmopolitan gateway to the great outdoors.

(Secretaría de Turismo de la Nación, 1994)

---

distance of Buenos Aires from other destinations is a major barrier to development; the vast *pampas* which separate the capital from the North West (the region around Salta), the North East (the province of Missiones and the spectacular Igazú Falls on the border with Brazil and Paraguay) and the South (Tierra del Fuego), constitute a considerable barrier to travel. To travel to Salta, for example, requires a coach journey of over 20 hours; this is the cheapest way to travel, as the railway system is now severely truncated, and air travel is expensive. In reality, it may sometimes be easier (and cheaper) to access many of the interior destinations from neighbouring countries such as Chile, Brazil and Paraguay, rather than from Buenos Aires.

DESTINATION ATTRACTIONS AND CITYSCAPE

According to Middleton (1994, p. 87), the overall portfolio of a city destination offered to the visitor can be divided into four types of attraction: (1) natural attractions, (2) built attractions, (3) cultural attractions and (4) social attractions. Cultural and social attractions have already been introduced in Chapter 6 ('Cultural Tourism'), and will not, therefore, be the subject of detailed discussion here, other than to point out that they are of particular importance in terms of urban tourism (Hardoy, 1982, p. 19).

Natural Attractions

According to Middleton, these comprise: 'landscape, seascape, beaches, climate and other geographical features' (1994, p. 86). Within the context of urban tourism, as opposed to beach tourism (previously discussed in Chapter 4), each cityscape offers particular geographical features, such as Rio de Janeiro, featured in Box 7.B.

Box 7.B. Rio de Janeiro

Río is a really beautiful city. The combination of Guanabara Bay, with its famous Ipanema and Copacabana beaches, its bare granite hills topped with vegetation, seafront walks and the lively locals, cannot fail to impress any visitor. The beaches stretch in a seemingly unending succession towards the south ...

But Río is also famous for its nightlife, which includes the restaurants: barbecued meat and seafood are the local speciality. Also, don't miss the spectacular shows ... including Samba shows and some showing the Carnival costumes.

(Mundiclass, 1995)

Those towns or cities that base their appeal on natural attractions (other than beaches) tend to be in the more remote areas of the continent, and focus on areas of unspoilt natural beauty where the visitor can appreciate the beauty and tranquillity of their surroundings. For example, the coastal town of Ushuaia in the Southeast of Argentina is a destination that owes its popularity to the magnificence of its scenery, or alternatively Bariloche, the key town in the Argentinian 'Lake District'. 'Eurotur', an Argentinian tour operator based in Buenos Aires, offers a four-day package based in Ushuaia, with excursions to points of interest around the town. Trips include a cruise along the Beagle Channel, a visit to the Tierra del Fuego National Park, and a trip to the 'Hidden Lake' high in the mountains (Eurotur, 1996).

San José, the capital of Costa Rica, gives the visitor access to exceptional landscape, within some 30 minutes' drive from the city centre. In this respect, the major advantage the city has over many other capitals is that spectacular scenery is in such near proximity, and the city can be used as a base from which to offer a series of day excursions to a variety of climates, views and natural phenomena (Lumsdon and Swift, 1998, p. 155); one tour operator offers a series of day excursions to the 'Arenal' and Irazú volcanoes, the hot springs at Tabacón, the 'Tilarán' mountain range and the 'Carara' Biological Reserve.

Built Attractions

These include:

> buildings and tourism infrastructure, including historic and modern architecture, monuments, promenades, parks and gardens, convention centres, marinas, ski slopes, industrial archaeology, managed visitor attractions generally, golf courses, speciality shops and themed retail areas.
>
> (Middleton, 1994, pp. 86–7)

Many of the historical (colonial) architectural attractions have already been the subject of discussion in Chapter 6; the Spanish colonial authorities imposed a basic model of development in the late sixteenth century, and this has been used to shape the urban structure of many Latin American cities (Dickenson, 1994, p. 13). In recent decades there has been a commitment on the part of city authorities to restore or upgrade access to historic monuments. For example, in Lima there is at the time of writing an ongoing public-private sector initiative to restore a significant collection of sculptures in the city's *Presbítero Maestro* Cemetery (Fraser, 2000, p. 4).

Modern architecture, by contrast, is perhaps not as well appreciated, particularly as many modern buildings lack the charm, elegance and ambience of the colonial constructions. It is difficult, therefore, to identify many cities in which modern architecture can truly be cited as a tourist attraction. There are, however, some exceptions, such as the spectacular buildings in Brasília. The city was founded in 1956 by President Kubitschek, in a deliberate attempt to move the *locus* of power away from Río de Janeiro and to open up the central plateau region. Brasília, described as a 'futuristic city' (Poppino, 1973, p. 39), was built principally to house the Brazilian government, the civil service and the foreign embassies (Holston, 1989). The climate is monotonously oppressive most of the year round, and under windy conditions everything becomes covered with a fine layer of red dust from the reddish-coloured earth on which the city is built.

Thus, it is unlikely that architecture alone would be sufficient to entice many tourists to the Brazilian capital; this is reflected by the almost total absence of packages which include the city, even *en passant* to other destinations. In spite of (or perhaps because of) these inherent disadvantages, the Brazilian tourism authorities attempted to promote the city as the 'Gateway to the Mystical World' in 1996. However, despite their efforts and those of the 500 cults and religious sects that have made the city their home (Eads, 1996), Brasília still lacks charisma.

The other facilities discussed by Middleton can be grouped into four categories: (1) civic attractions (parks and gardens, monuments), (2) sporting attractions (marinas, golf courses, ski slopes), (3) business tourism (conventions), and (4) retail tourism (speciality shops and themed retail areas). Of these, civic attractions, whilst undoubtedly providing added interest for the visitor, are unlikely to be the major reason for their visit, although Latin American cities are renowned for their squares and parks.

Sporting attractions are becoming increasingly important, if only for a specialist market (see the previous chapter, 'Cultural Tourism'). Many Latin

American destinations are developing sporting complexes, particularly in the Caribbean. Winter sports (particularly skiing) and off-shore watersports, such as yachting and sea-fishing, also form part of the overall attractions of Latin American cities.

Business tourism, in particular promoting a city as an attractive venue for a conference or convention, is one of the fastest-growing segments of urban tourism. Many cities are increasingly seeking to position themselves as 'conference centres' within a regional context; Bogota, for example, stresses the variety of high-class hotels, with purpose-built conference centres, in addition to the museums, art galleries and various cultural attractions throughout the city (Guía Publicaciones Ltda, 1994). However, the conference market is one which increasingly focuses on global markets:

> While there is a strong element of regionalization in the international conference market, this coexists with a growing tendency to globalization. For example, the American Law Association has held its conference in London, and there are increasing numbers of truly world conferences, such as the Rio 'Earth Summit'.
>
> (Shaw and Williams, 1994, p. 39)

Buenos Aires is also targeting the business market at a regional level, but with an appeal to a global market; in this respect the city has many advantages in relation to other venues, as it can offer attractive architecture, parks and gardens, and shops equal to those of major northern hemisphere cities. Buenos Aires is, however, a relatively expensive location, in addition to being at a considerable distance for most European and North American delegates. Partially in an attempt to counter the high prices in Buenos Aires, the Argentinian authorities brought in a 'tax free' scheme in 1992, which allowed tourists to reclaim the cost of the VAT paid on goods on departing the country.

Many of the Mexican and Caribbean destinations have the added advantage of being closer and cheaper to their main markets. In May 1998, for example, there were three tourism conventions held in Cuba. One was for PARLATINO (the Latin American Parliamentary Tourism Commission), which was held in the modern purpose-built conference facilities at the resort town of Varadero.

In terms of specialist retailing there is considerable variety. For example, Bogota has a virtual world monopoly on the sale of emeralds, whilst Buenos Aires is the place to go for silver and semi-precious stones such as lapis lazuli. In leather goods, such as handbags, clothing and footwear, Buenos Aires,

Bogotá, Montevideo, Caracas and Asunción offer high quality, but Ascunción is the city that maintains a reputation of the best value for money, as rates of tax are low. This attracts a substantial number of short break coaching holidays from neighbouring countries.

Designer clothing and other up-market branded goods are to be found in the Calle Florida in Buenos Aires and the centre of Bogota. Other purchases tend to fall into the 'handicrafts' category, and in this respect, the best cities are Cuzco, Lima and Puno (Peru), Caracas (Venezuela), Asunción (Paraguay), La Paz and Tarabuco (Bolivia), Cartagena, Bogota, Medellin, Villa de Leyva and Calí (Colombia), Mexico City, Puebla and Guanajuato (Mexico), Salvador, Rio de Janeiro, Bahía and Recife (Brazil). Peru, Bolivia, Colombia, Chile and (northern) Argentina tend to specialize in clothing and rugs, handbags, etc. made from llama or alpaca wool, musical instruments, and semi-precious metals made into jewellery. Leather goods, including jackets, handbags and footwear, are to be found in Argentina, Uruguay, Colombia, Venezuela, Mexico and Paraguay. Paraguay is also famous for its intricate lacework, which is usually sold as tablecloths or shawls. Peru, Bolivia, Chile, Colombia and Venezuela all specialize in reproductions of pre-Columbian artefacts, in particular ceremonial knives and statues. Similar reproductions are on sale throughout most of Central America, particularly in Mexico, which is also famous for its silver.

Whilst shopping is not the principal reason for most European or North American visitors coming to Latin America, it is important in terms of the sale of souvenirs. In their tour of Bolivia, 'Journey Latin America' take most of one day out of a four-day tour to visit the market at Tarabuco (see Box 7.C).

Box 7.C. Tarabuco Market, Bolivia

Day 3: Short dusty drive to Tarabuco, where the market is held in the central square of this picturesque village; the inhabitants still wear their traditional 'ponchos' and head-dress, and this is considered by many to be the most photogenic market in South America.

(Journey Latin America, 1998)

DESTINATION FACILITIES AND SERVICES

Facilities and services are an unusual element in the whole tourist experience, because whilst they do not feature as the main attraction of a destination, they do nevertheless add (or detract) from the overall tourism experience. Poor or inadequate levels of service can create a lasting impression in the mind of the visitor, even to the extent of undermining the pleasure gained from the destination attractions. As Kotler *et al.* have observed, it is necessary to combine all, attractions and services, to ensure success: 'The ability to concentrate attractions, facilities, and services in a convenient, accessible location is essential to create a strong destination pull' (1993, pp. 656–7).

Facilities and services can be sub-divided into: (1) accommodation units, (2) eating establishments (restaurants, bars, cafés) and (3) transport at the destination. As the provision of transportation (both within a destination and to/from a destination) forms the major element of the city's (or country's) infrastructure, it is proposed to examine transportation in conjunction with the other factors under the broad heading of 'Supporting Infrastructure'.

Accommodation

Accommodation units, according to Middleton's definition (1994, p. 87), comprise hotels, holiday villages, apartments, villas, campsites, caravan parks, hostels, condominiums, farms and guesthouses. Within towns and cities, hotels, hostels, apartments and condominiums are the most common; in Latin America, guesthouses are very rare, and very few urban areas have camping or caravan sites. Holiday villages and villas tend to be located in integrated sites, and farmhouses are not usually an option at all.

The basic problem with much of the accommodation supply in Latin America is that it caters for the top and the bottom ends of the market, with comparatively little in between. A 1996 research study undertaken by the Dirección General de Turismo de Buenos Aires revealed the distribution of hotels in the Argentinian capital as is shown in Table 7.2. Assuming that the 5-star and 4-star hotels are geared towards the top end of the market, and the 3-star and 2-star towards the middle (with 1-star and the *pensiones* catering for budget travellers), then the disparity in bed numbers becomes even more apparent: 5- and 4-star (top of the market): 13,993; 3- and 2-star (mid-range) 9077; 1-star and *pensiones* (bottom): 14,281.

Table 7.2. Hotel and hostel accommodation: Buenos Aires, 1996

Category	Rating	Number of establishments	Rooms	Places/sleeps
Hotels	5-star	10	2,742	5,596
	4-star	36	4,110	8,397
	3-star	32	2,579	5,448
	2-star	36	1,784	3,629
	1-star	30	1,140	2,317
	Sub-total	144	12,355	25,387
Hostels	Grade A	106	3,349	6,630
(pensiones)	Grade B	95	2,615	5,334
	Sub-total	201	5,964	11,964
	Grand total	345	18,319	37,351

Source: Dirección General de Turismo de la Ciudad de Buenos Aires (1996, p. 9)

At the top end, the international chains proliferate, fuelled largely by the demand from senior business executives. In Mexico, for example, there are chains such as the 'Radisson' (Monterrey), the 'Hyatt' and the 'Holiday Inn' (Villahermosa) and the 'Camino Real' (Mexico City). In 1992, two new US $40 million 5-star hotels opened in Buenos Aires, the Park Hyatt Buenos Aires and the Caesar Park Buenos Aires. The 'Sheraton' group has the 'Sheraton Hotel & Towers' in the city and, according to McDermott and McDermott, demand for such hotels in the Argentinian capital remained buoyant throughout the 1990s, principally due to the business market:

> The city swarms with international C.E.O.'s, their lawyers, accountants and researchers – business travellers on expense accounts who can afford to pay for the best accommodations that Buenos Aires has to offer.
>
> The nine five-star hotel properties in the city forecast between 60 percent to 80 percent of their occupancy to stem from business travel in 1993, the bulk of which is expected to originate in North America.
>
> (1993, p. 6)

Very much targeted at the middle-range executive are some of the national chains, such as the Colombian 'Hoteles Dann' group, which has four hotels in Santafé de Bogotá and another three in other parts of the country. Similarly, the 'Empresa Hotelera Panamericana S.A.' group in Chile has hotels in Santiago de Chile, Viña del Mar, Arica and Concepción, and a joint venture in Paraguay. The 'Husa Hotels' chain (also in Chile) has two hotels in Santiago de Chile, and others in Algarrobo, Viña del Mar, Puerto Varas and San Felipe.

What all of these have in common is that they are still basically business-oriented hotels, and their range of services reflects this emphasis.

Many countries have sought foreign capital investment, and to this end have engaged in joint ventures with international hotel chains in order to improve the capacity in city destinations. For example, in Nicaragua the government has agreed a ten-year moratorium on taxes and import duties on hotel supplies and tourism-related services; neighbouring Panama launched a programme to increase hotel capacity by over 9000 rooms by the end of 1998, by giving priority to planning applications for hotels (Lumsdon and Swift, 1996).

The lowest end of the market is equally well catered for, at least in terms of quantity, if not quality. However, as the tourist profile changes away from 'backpackers' towards a more 'middle-class, middle-age, middle-income' visitor, it is increasingly likely that the cheaper hotels and hostels (*pensiones*) will no longer be acceptable. The demand in the future will be for hotels in the mid-price range, the typical 3-star hotel, with fewer 'business-oriented' facilities, but better levels of service and good value for money. As Swarbrooke and Horner point out: 'The tourism organisations targeting this group must offer exciting destinations but with the added benefits of good value for money discounts, reliability of service and reassurance about safety' (1999, p. 224).

Hospitality: Food & Beverage

King defines commercial hospitality as:

> a specific kind of relationship between individuals – a host and a guest. In this relationship, the host understands what would give pleasure to the guest and enhance his or her comfort and well-being, and delivers it generously and flawlessly in face to face interactions, with deference, tactfulness and the process of social ritual. The objective is to enhance guest satisfaction and develop repeat business.
>
> (1995, p. 231)

The wide variety of restaurants and cafés to be found in most cities is largely a consequence of cultural attitudes. The 'Hispanic' heritage of most Latin American countries (see Chapter 1), manifests itself in people's social patterns; many city dwellers in Latin America not only frequent restaurants during the week, but in cities such as Buenos Aires it is common for the entire family to have their Sunday lunch out. Thus, the supply of restaurants is driven by a continually high level of demand.

The real challenge to established eating patterns has been the introduction of fast-food establishments, mostly targeted at the 15–25 age groups. In

Colombia, for example, McDonald's opened its first outlets in Bogota in July 1995, followed by branches in Baranquilla, Calí, Medellín and Cartagena in 1996. According to Pedro Medina Lara, Managing Director of McDonald's (Colombia), the country was targeted because:

> In the first place, Colombia is the second most populous country in South America, which gives a wide potential market; on the other hand, the Colombian market has certain interesting characteristics for our business: for example, the Colombians love fast food, and this whole sector is ripe for further development.
>
> (Portafolio, 1995)

From a relatively slow start, these restaurants appear to be rapidly gaining market share, generally at the expense of cafés; Italian food is also making inroads into the market, largely in the form of 'Pizza' establishments. In Argentina, however, probably as a consequence of the large Italian population (see Chapter 1), Italian restaurants have been established for many years, and many are of a high quality.

Supporting Infrastructure

Just as accommodation and subsistence are essential ingredients of the tourism experience, transport is 'an integral part of tourism' (Page, 1999, p. 1). The key modes of travel and a discussion on transport as a component sector have been reviewed in Chapter 3.

The basic transport infrastructure of any destination includes roads, airports, railways, seaports and marinas. In addition, there are other elements that are of importance to the tourist and business visitor alike, such as banking and money exchange facilities, communications and the provision of specific tourism-related services, such as travel agencies and ground handlers. The provision of an adequate infrastructure at the destination may greatly enhance or detract from the overall holiday experience.

The three factors that determine the level of accessibility of a destination are: (1) the infrastructure, (2) the equipment and operational factors and (3) government regulations. As the composition, equipment and operational factors involved in the establishment and maintenance of a city's infrastructure are likely to be influenced by the third factor (government regulations), these will not be considered separately. Furthermore, in a Latin American context, government regulations tend to apply only to those who cannot afford to buy immunity.

The major concern is really directed towards the provision of adequate, affordable, reliable, clean and pollution-reducing forms of public transport, for both the resident population and the visitor (Wright, 1992). With the exception of Heraty (1989), there has, however, been relatively little research undertaken on the provision of transport within destinations in developing countries.

Aside from the planning and privatization issue there is the question of what services the visitor can expect. Within the major cities there is a great deal of variation. Looking solely at the capital cities, a major difference in terms of transportation is the provision of an underground system. Santiago de Chile has an excellent underground system. The Mexico City underground, though older, is also efficient, serving most parts of the city. In Buenos Aires, the underground system is in need of renovation, some of the carriages dating back to the 1950s. An 'Action Plan' for the 1990s, published by the Buenos Aires Tourist Authority in 1993, identified tourist transport as lacking in both availability and quality. Other areas singled out for special action included the regeneration and development of the San Telmo area of the city – a favourite tourist destination, but one that has suffered recently as a consequence of increased visitor numbers and a lack of investment in infrastructure. Plans were formulated to pedestrianize certain streets, to conserve street facades of buildings of architectural interest, to recondition the San Telmo market and to instal a tram system. In general terms, the Action Plan called for a categorization of the city's hotels, a reorganization of the transportation system to make more stops at places of touristic interest, greater control over taxis, and a register of officially approved city guides, under the auspices of the Tourist Authority (Subsecretaría de Turismo, 1993).

Whilst the underground systems represent the best and most efficient mover of people in terms of urban transport, they are only available in a minority of cities: costs and environmental considerations (such as earthquakes) have precluded their construction in most cities, which means that most people are forced to travel by public bus or private car. The thousands of workers who migrate daily into city centres from the outlying shanty towns have no option but to use these poor quality buses, as they cannot generally afford to live nearer the city centres, nor can they afford their own car (Gilbert, 1995). The level of pollution caused by an increasing number of cars and buses, especially the older vehicles, has brought a very poor level of air quality to many Latin American cities: 'Mexico City is the most polluted major city in the world, mainly as a result of vehicle emissions, and the smog is both sickening its inhabitants and eating away at its colonial buildings with acidic grime' (Coe, 1993, p. 46).

In addition to pollution, the proliferation of buses and private vehicles leads to serious problems of traffic congestion, particularly in cities such as Caracas, Mexico City, São Paulo, Lima and Bogota. In Bogota the problems centre largely around inner-city transportation, and the resulting pollution and congestion. The Colombian press regularly carries articles on congestion on major streets such as Carrera 13; the question of congestion and transportation within the capital was a major area of debate during the 1994 presidential elections. The latest idea is for a raised track system (*'el metro'*), such as already exists in the city of Medellín (Editorial, 1994).

In many countries, travel by public transport other than on the underground is not advised by tour companies and tourism authorities: one of the exceptions being Santiago de Chile, where the bus fleet is both relatively modern and clean. Thus, in many cases, taxis and bespoke minibuses provide the mainstay of tourism transport in Latin American cities, alongside walking, but the latter is only encouraged in identifiably secure zones.

OTHER TOURISM SERVICES

Most Latin American cities possess a city organization responsible primarily for promoting the city's image, visitor attractions and facilities. In some cases they provide additional tourism services, such as booking accommodation, events organization, trade support and publicity distribution (Morrison *et al.*, 1995). The rest of this chapter discusses two aspects: sustainability and promotion imagery.

SUSTAINABILITY IN THE URBAN ENVIRONMENT

The appeal of urban tourism to those responsible for the economic development of an urban area is understandable; visitors contribute revenue to the local economy and in the process they become the catalyst for an enhancement of facilities that have the potential to be used by both resident and visitor alike. Unfortunately, there are also dis-benefits; hence the issue of sustainability is as appropriate in the urban as it is in the rural environment (Drakakis-Smith, 1995). Ensuring that the city does not reach (or even exceed) its carrying capacity is, for example, one of the critical factors in achieving long-term success in the visitor market and maintaining the goodwill of the host community.

The problem is compounded in many Latin American cities by the growing numbers of rural dwellers seeking refuge in periphery hillside shanty towns (Goethert, 1991, p. 58; Drakakis-Smith, 1995, p. 667). The migratory populations of recent decades have stretched the infrastructure of many cities to their limits (Lloyd-Sherlock, 1997). There is a continued contest for space by different groups, but especially the displaced poor (Viviescas, 1985; Jones, 1994). Overlaying this is the growth in visitor numbers and thus tourism has contributed to the negative impacts so often cited in the media and guide books: crime, prostitution, dilution of local cultures and inflation. The result has been a wave of media and travel writer comments which project a negative image of the gateway cities, based on a degree of reality.

Atkinson has suggested that there are three major hurdles in terms of achieving sustainability in Third World cities: (1) the research focus on problems of water supply, drainage, sanitation, etc., generally at the expense of other, wider or longer term issues; (2) a lack of financial and managerial resources; and (3) the inability of governments to agree within themselves (or with sources of funding) on the best approach to achieving sustainability (1994, p. 100). Certainly within most Latin American cities these problems are familiar, in particular the lack of financial and managerial resources. Within this context it is difficult to assess the extent to which tourism development exacerbates or alleviates the problems associated with city development, which in many respects still reflect a deep-rooted polarization.

City Imagery

The imagery of a city is viewed by a number of researchers as one of the most important issues faced by tourism organizations (Wahab et al., 1976). The authors examined the way that various Latin American cities were perceived by UK tour operators specializing in Latin American destinations; they were approached for their opinions on the overall image of key Latin American cities. Their responses were formed on the basis of feedback from customers, personal observations of the respondent and the experiences of colleagues. The authors contacted 15 randomly-selected UK-based tour operators who offered holidays in Latin America; they were approached initially by telephone, and surveyed by means of a postal questionnaire. Some face-to-face interviews were also carried out. Executives responsible for Latin American destinations were asked to comment about the tourism potential of the major cities, using the following criteria (derived from discussions with travel executives at the World Travel Market, in London):

- Accommodation
- Shows/night life
- Street cleanliness
- Public transport
- Level of pollution

- Historical attractions
- Cost of living
- Museums/galleries
- Level of street crime
- Theatres/cinemas

- Architecture
- Festivals/fairs
- Restaurants/cafés

Respondents were asked to rank cities against each of these criteria, with a score of one indicating very poor (unacceptable standards/conditions) and five indicating very good. The best and worst aspects are summarized in Table 7.3. It is important to recognize the limitations of this type of qualitative research, but nevertheless it does provide an insight into how destinations might be developed or improved, and the possible strengths and weaknesses of various cities in terms of the tourism offering. For example, Buenos Aires, which is one of the most favourably rated city destinations in Latin America, scores highly on the provision of parks and gardens, shows/nightlife, restaurants/cafés and accommodation, yet is at the same time considered a very expensive city, almost prohibitively so in the opinion of some respondents. The cost of living in the capital is bemoaned by the *Porteños* (inhabitants of Buenos Aires), for whom high prices are reminiscent of the period of rampant inflation of the 1980s. Price emerged as a distinct advantage for regional tourism, with coastal resorts generally scoring highly, and promoting heavily discounted hotel accommodation (Aznarez, 1994). In contrast to Buenos Aires, Brasília ranks poorly on most aspects apart from architecture. One respondent summed up the city as: 'Soulless, dull; you go there to work, not to play. Good modern architecture though'.

Factors such as the level of street crime, the degree of street cleanliness and the level and type of pollution within the city were important in forming negative images (see also Chapter 8). Many tour operators considered that some cities have much still to do in terms of these factors for the visitor. For example, in terms of street crime levels, major gateway cities such as Bogota, Caracas, Lima and Rio de Janeiro rank very poorly.

It is interesting to note that, despite a negative press, some cities still retain an historical-cultural offering that visitors find attractive. One respondent described Rio as 'dirty and dangerous but having a heart and soul of its own!'. He also commented that Lima was 'dirty and dangerous but without a heart and soul of its own!'.

In terms of pollution, São Paulo, Bogota, Mexico City and Guayaquil score equally poorly. Indeed, one respondent said: 'Mexico City is disgusting!

Without doubt the worst place I have ever visited in the world, in terms of pollution.' Whilst another summed up Guayaquil as: 'polluted – one of the least attractive cities for tourists'.

Table 7.3. Tour operator assessments of various Latin American cities

Criteria of assessment	Best cities	Worst cities
Parks & gardens	Buenos Aires	Bahía, Caracas, Ciudad Bolívar
Public transport	Mendoza, São Paulo, Arequipa, Río de Janeiro	La Habana
Restaurants and cafés	Buenos Aires, Mendoza, Salta, Santiago de Chile, São Paulo	Manaus, Antofagasta, Maracaibo, Ciudad Bolívar
Festivals & fairs	Río de Janeiro, Bahía, Buenos Aires, Salta, Mendoza, La Habana, Cartagena de las Indias, Arequipa.	Brasília
Nightlife/shows	Rio de Janeiro, Bahía, Buenos Aires, La Habana	Brasília, Asunción
Historical attractions	Bahía, La Habana, Cuzco, Arequipa, Guatemala City, Cartagena de las Indias	Brasília
Accommodation	São Paulo, Buenos Aires, Cartagena de las Indias, Santiago de Chile	Baltra, Veracruz, Asunción
Museums, galleries, etc.	Buenos Aires, Mexico City, Santafé de Bogotá, Calí, Cartagena de las Indias	Brasília, Asunción, Caracas, Antofagasta
Architecture	Brasília, Bahía, Buenos Aires, Guanajuato	Arica, Valdivia, Cancún
Pollution	(low levels of) La Paz	(high levels of) Mexico City, Santafé de Bogotá
Street crime	(low levels of) Salta, Mendoza, Antofagasta, Arica, Valdivia, Veracruz	(high levels of) Bahía, Santafé de Bogotá, Río de Janeiro
Cost of living	(low) Ascunción, Ciudad Bolívar	(high) Buenos Aires, Santiago de Chile

SUMMARY

The crises facing many Latin American cities are those experienced throughout the developing world: migration from the rural hinterland into already crowded areas; a lack of core infrastructure; and social and economic problems associated with under-employment and unemployment. Given the significant changes occurring in urban conurbations in response to increasing globalization, sectoral changes towards services and international electronic communications, the management of structural change will become increasingly important (Beaverstock *et al.*, 2000, p. 132). In this context, many Latin American cities may continue to opt for a pattern of development more commonly associated with North America: an urban enclave approach, in which tourism quarters are developed separately from the rest of the city. This might have social consequences, such as in the historic neighbourhood of San Felipe (Panama City), where there are plans to displace over 600 low income families (Boyd, 1999, p. 2). A major concern is that tourism-related projects such as this might destroy the very appeal of the city – that which makes Rio de Janeiro so different from Buenos Aires or Cuzco.

At present, there would appear to be a marginal improvement of image on the one hand, and a gradual worsening of infrastructure on the other. Assessment of trends in the market environment suggests that gateway cities into Latin America will continue to gain in the short term, but in the longer term, integrated resorts will assume greater importance, possibly becoming gateways in their own right. Airlines and tour operators have already begun the process, with the introduction of direct flights to resorts such as Cancún and Cartagena.

The fortunes of other city destinations are likely to fluctuate as in the past, but there is unlikely to be any significant level of growth; there is already evidence to suggest that multi-centre holidays are offering fewer nights in cities, at the expense of eco-destinations and adventure destinations. If city tourism is to realize its potential in Latin America, there will have to be a far more cohesive and responsive plan to improve the quality of life in central zones (Violich and Daughters, 1987) and to market the diversity and richness of cities to a market which currently appears to lack interest in this type of vacation.

REFERENCES

Angotti, T. (1996) 'Latin American Urbanization and Planning: Inequality and Unsustainability in North and South', *Latin American Perspectives*, Issue 91, Vol. 23(4), pp. 12–34.

Atkinson, A. (1994) 'The Contribution of Cities to Sustainability', *Third World Planning Review*, Vol. 16(2), pp. 97–101.

Aznarez, J. C. (1994) 'Una Tentación: la Costa con sus Descuentos', *La Nación* (Buenos Aires) (26 March).

Beaverstock, J. V., Smith, R. G. and Taylor, P. J. (2000) 'World-City Network: A New Meta-geography?', *Annals of the Association of American Geographers*, Vol. 90(1), pp. 123–34.

Boyd, S. (1999) 'Tourism Searching for Ethics Under the Sun', *Financial Times* (13 September).

Brownlie, D. (1985) 'Strategic Marketing Concepts and Models', *Journal of Marketing Management*, Vol. 1, pp. 157–94.

Butler, R. (1980) 'The Concept of a Tourist Area Cycle of Evolution: Implications for Management of Resources', *Canadian Geographer*, Vol. 24, pp. 5–12.

Coe, A. (1993) *Mexico*, The Guidebook Company Ltd, Hong Kong.

Dickenson, J. (1994) 'The Future of the Past in the Latin American City: The Case of Brazil', *Bulletin of Latin American Research*, Vol. 13(1), pp. 13–25.

Dirección General de Turismo de la Ciudad de Buenos Aires (1996) *Características de la Oferta y Demanda Turística de la Ciudad de Buenos Aires (Año 1996)*, Dirección General de Turismo de la Ciudad de Buenos Aires, Buenos Aires.

Drakakis-Smith, D. (1995) 'Third World Cities: Sustainable Urban Development', *Urban Studies*, Vol. 32(4–5), pp. 659–77.

Eads, B. (1996) 'Gathering Nuts', *Daily Telegraph* (6 July).

Editorial (1994) 'Un Metro para Bogotá: Kilómetros de Acciones', *El Tiempo* (Bogota) (23 April).

Eurotur (1996) *Argentina: Regular & Special Tours*, Eurotour: Empresa de Viajes y Turismo, Buenos Aires.

Fraser, B. (2000) 'Keeping Heritage Alive', *Latin America Press* (6 March).

Gilbert, A. (1995) 'Debt, Poverty and the Latin American City', *Geography*, Vol. 80(349), pp. 323–33.

Goethert, R. (1991) 'Lessons from Squatters in Latin America: Housing on Hillsides for Low-Income Groups', *Regional Development Dialogue*, Vol. 12(2), pp. 57–75.

Guía Publicaciones Ltda (1994) *La Guía de Bogotá: Año 20 (124)*, Guía Publicaciones Ltda, Santafé de Bogotá.

Hardoy, J. (1982) 'The Building of Latin American Cities' in A. Gilbert (ed.), *Urbanisation in Contemporary Latin America* (pp. 19–34), John Wiley, New York.

Heraty, M. J. (1989) 'Tourism Transport – Implications for Developing Countries', *Tourism Management*, Vol. 10(4), pp. 288–92.

Holston, J. (1989) *The Modernist City: An Anthropological Critique of Brasilia*, University of Chicago Press, Chicago.

Jones, G. (1994) 'Latin American Cities as Contested Space: A Manifesto', *Bulletin of Latin American Research*, Vol. 13(1), pp. 1–12.

Journey Latin America (1998) *Journey Latin America, Bespoke Holiday Journeys 1998–1999*, Journey Latin America, London.

King, C. A. (1995) 'What is Hospitality?', *International Journal of Hospitality Management*, Vol. 14(3/4), pp. 219–34.

Kotler, P., Haider, D. M. and Rein, I. (1993) *Marketing Places: Attracting Investment, Industry, and Tourism to Cities, States and Nations*, The Free Press, New York.

Lloyd-Sherlock, P. (1997) *Old Age and Urban Poverty in the Developing World: The Shanty Towns of Buenos Aires*, Macmillan, London.

Lumsdon, L. M. and Swift, J. S. (1993) 'The Development of Tourism in Latin American Gateway Cities' (paper presented to the 7th General Conference of EADI (European Association of Development Research and Training Institutes): *Transformation and Development: Eastern Europe and the South*, Berlin, 15–18 September 1993.

Lumsdon, L. M. and Swift, J. S. (1996) 'The Influence of Human Security Issues on Competitiveness in Long Haul Tourism: Evidence From Latin America' (paper presented to the 8th General Conference of EADI (European Association of Development Research and Training Institutes): *Globalisation, Competitiveness and Human Security: Challenges for Development and Institutional Change*, Vienna, 11–14 September 1996.

Lumsdon, L. M. and Swift, J. S. (1998) 'Ecotourism at a Crossroads: The Case of Costa Rica', *Journal of Sustainable Tourism*, Vol. 6(2), pp. 155–72.

McDermott, J. and McDermott, B. (1993) 'Buenos Aires Builds Hotel Supply', *Hotel & Motel Management*, Vol. 208(5), pp. 6 and 58.

Middleton, V. T. C. (1994) *Marketing in Travel and Tourism*, 2nd edition, Butterworth-Heinemann, Oxford.

Morrison, A. M., Braunlich, C. G., Kamaruddin, N. and Cai, L. A. (1995) 'National Tourism Offices in North America: An Analysis', *Tourism Management*, Vol. 16(8), pp. 605–17.

Mundiclass (1995) *Mundidestinos: 1995–1996*, Mundiclass, S.A., Madrid.

Page, S. (1999) *Transport and Tourism*, Longman, Harlow.

Poppino, R. E. (1973) *Brazil: The Land and People*, 2nd edition, Oxford University Press, New York.

Portafolio (1995) 'McDonald's Traerá sus Propias Hambugesas', *Portafolio* (Bogota) (29 May).

Portes, A., Dore-Cabral, C. and Landolt, P. (eds) (1997) *The Urban Caribbean: Transition to the New Global Economy*, The Johns Hopkins University Press, Baltimore.

Rondinelli, D. (1986) 'Increasing the Access of the Poor to Urban Services' in D. Rondinelli and G. Cheena (eds), *Urban Services in Developing Countries* (pp. 78–89), Macmillan, London.

Secretaría de Turismo de la Nación (1994) *Argentina: The Land of Six Continents*, Secretaría de Turismo de la Nación, Buenos Aires.

Shaw. G. and Williams, A. M. (1994) *Critical Issues in Tourism: A Geographical Perspective*, Basil Blackwell, Oxford.

Subsecretaría de Turismo (1993) *Plan de Acción: Buenos Aires*, Subsecretaría de Turismo, Buenos Aires.

Swarbrooke, J. and Horner, S. (1999) *Consumer Behaviour in Tourism*, Butterworth-Heinemann, Oxford.

Violich, F. and Daughters, E. (1987) *Urban Planning for Latin America: The Challenge of Metropolitan Growth*, Gunn and Hain, Boston, Mass.

Viviescas, F. (1985) 'La Negación del Espacio Colectivo o de Control de la Ciudad Latinoamericano', *Cuadernos Cuidad y Sociedad*, Vol. 9, pp. 43–58.

Wahab, S., Crampon, L. J. and Rothfield, L. M. (1976) *Tourism Marketing. A Destination-Oriented Programme for the Marketing of International Tourism*, Tourism Press, London.

Ward, P. M. (1993) 'The Latin American Inner City: Differences of Degree or of Kind?', *Environment and Planning*, A 25, pp. 1131–60.

Wöber, K. (1997) 'Local Tourism Organisations' in J. A. Mazanec (ed.), *European Cities in International City Tourism Analysis and Strategy*, Pinter, London.

Wright, C. L. (1992) *Fast Wheels Slow Traffic: Urban Transport Choices*, Temple University Press, Philadelphia.

PART III

Major Issues in Tourism Development

CHAPTER 8

Tourism: Image and Reality

INTRODUCTION

Hart and Stapleton define image as a composite 'mental picture formed by people about an organization or its products' (1987, p. 102). In marketing, and especially in the marketing of a tourist destination, image is of vital importance: the composite 'mental picture' developed by potential visitors is an influential factor in their purchase decision.

For Middleton, image is 'one of five components in the overall tourism product and ... a vital element within the augmented product' (1994, p. 91). Furthermore, he advises that image is: 'an essential objective of destination marketing to sustain, alter, or develop images in order to influence prospective buyer's expectations' (1994, p. 88).

Image enhancement (and by extension, visitor perception) should be key components of any tourism marketing strategy. Ashworth and Goodall (1988, p. 218) stress the importance of information about the destination within the consumer decision-making process. Thus commentators have highlighted the need for tourism authorities and private sector organizations to supply appropriate information. Failure to do this will leave the potential visitor with an information vacuum which, at the very least, offers no positive images and inducements to visit. At worst, this vacuum will be filled by other, negative information, which in many respects is reflective of Latin America in the 1980s and 1990s. At the first meeting of Experts on Tourist Safety and Security convened by the WTO in Madrid, in April 1994, the issue of media coverage was examined in detail, and the conclusion reached is shown in Box 8.A.

Box 8.A. The media and tourist safety and security

the media have a key role in identifying emerging problems and in contributing to public awareness. The local partnerships should make a special effort to work together with the media in the development and promotion of successful measures to enhance safety and security, and to insist on accurate, balanced and responsible media coverage.

(WTO, 1994, p. 2)

A positive image of a destination will help to generate a positive attitude towards it; the process is complex, and whilst one stage does not always lead to another, image is an integral influence on the formation of attitude, which, in turn, can be decisive in consumer purchase decisions.

Lea (1988) views image as a process that can be examined both from the point of view of the tourist and from the perspective of those involved in developing destination marketing strategies. However, as Rushton and Carson (1985) point out, the creation of an image for an intangible (such as a holiday destination) is more difficult and generally requires a more sophisticated approach than that of image creation for a tangible product.

Seaton (1990) refers to 'representation' as part of the image building of destinations and suggests that it can 'help to shape the tourism experience itself – people go looking for what they expect to find'; in this he is supported by Muller (1991). Working on the premise presented by Seaton, what the visitor expects to find should be clearly indicated, visible and detailed by the image maker; in terms of promotion, the desired image should be presented (to the target market) in an attractive form, which is easy to understand and unambiguous. Research by Gilbert and Houghton (1990) suggests that the 'initial visual impact' of brochure material is extremely important, whilst Rao *et al.* (1992) found that although US outward travellers used a 'myriad of information sources', the print media was still the most influential.

According to Chisnall, attitudes are acquired or modified by influences from any or all of four sources, which he lists as: 'information exposure, group membership, environment, and want satisfaction' (1995, p. 84). In terms of tourism marketing, information exposure is achieved through brochures, television advertising, travel programmes, press reports and personal selling. Group membership can be influential in terms of group dynamics and opinion leaders: in practical terms, certain destinations are considered 'in' (trendy or *de rigeur*) or 'out' (*passe*) and, depending on the degree of influence exerted on individual consumers by concepts such as social class and reference groups, these can be of greater or lesser importance. Group dynamics are very important in certain markets – for instance, they are the basis on which many of the 'club'-type holiday packages are based. The environment is the existing environment of the consumer, and the way this is interpreted is through the cultural and social filter of an individual's background. 'Want satisfaction' is a culmination of many varied factors, such as individual traits and those other factors already mentioned. As Chisnall observes: 'Consumption habits, which are part of the behaviour patterns of individuals, are deeply affected by the prevailing culture of the society in which people live' (1995, p. 108).

The manipulation of image by those involved in selling a destination is an important ingredient of the promotional mix, and its potential value as a means of gaining and maintaining a competitive advantage has become increasingly apparent. Image exerts a powerful influence on consumer purchase decisions in general, but in particular, on the purchase of intangibles such as holidays. Some intangibles may carry a high level of financial and emotional risk, such as an expensive foreign holiday, that the individual has looked forward to all year. Consequently, consumers are likely to become more sensitive to all sources of information relating to their prospective holiday destination; this increases the overall information input and, at least in theory, enables them to reduce the degree of risk involved in the final purchase decision. A holiday is a high-risk purchase (in terms of both financial and personal risk), which means that consumers are more likely actively to seek information to decrease this element of risk.

Personal experience is probably the single most important source of information; the problem, therefore, is two-fold: how to get the visitor to a certain destination in the first place, and secondly, how to ensure that the visitor is likely to return. As Seaton points out: 'You can't test-drive a holiday, or try on a new airline schedule. This means that the role of promotion is critical. Promotion must generate desire and acceptance in the absence of more tangible kinds of evidence' (1989, p. 337). This view is supported by Papadopoulos, who feels that visitors choose destinations 'as much (if not more) on image as on "hard information"' (1993, p. 30). Gartner notes the frequency with which touristic images are based 'more on perceptions than reality' (1993, p. 196) and suggests that whilst we may indeed 'attribute meanings to things', this in no way implies the accuracy or otherwise of the meanings attributed. This is an important consideration, as consumer perceptions may be based on inaccurate or biased information, yet they still contribute to image development and, consequently, towards attitude formation.

IMAGES OF LATIN AMERICA

Introduction

Ironically, although most Latin American nations have sought to encourage tourism as a means of stimulating economic growth (Lumsdon and Swift, 1993), in some instances economic growth has stimulated tourism development – Argentina and Chile being cases in point. This is a consequence of many factors, not least of which is the image of the destination under consideration. Economic growth (in theory) encourages an increase in prosperity, leading to increased standards of living and better public services; these help put visitors at ease:

> Tourists expect a destination to be safe and clean, and they want to feel welcome and at ease. But clean, safe and friendly communities exist only if the local citizens care about them. And local citizens only care about their communities if the community demonstrates care for its citizens.
>
> (Haywood, 1990, p. 201)

In contrast, whilst it may take little time to create a negative image of a destination (and hence influence attitudes towards that destination), it usually takes considerably longer to change that image. Nor is it simply a question of one piece of positive information cancelling out one piece of negative information; as Haywood has observed: 'Bad news (negative information) can change attitudes ... Yet good news (positive information) alone will not reverse this perception' (*ibid.*, 1991, pp. 47–8).

Whilst many positive images of Latin America are actively promoted, negative images are, as already intimated, more powerful, and have a relatively more significant impact on the consumer buying decision process. Therefore it is proposed to concentrate on an analysis of *negative* images associated with Latin America: unfortunately, it is the negative images that apparently have the potential to exert an unduly powerful influence on destination choice.

The reasons why negative images should have such a powerful influence are many and varied; Seaton (1989) feels that their importance lies in their role as reinforcers of perceived risk. In this respect, those factors that are connected with personal safety are of paramount importance. Other reasons may be linked to issues of political conviction (the excesses of extremist governments) or a sense of moral outrage engendered by human rights abuses, corruption and poverty.

All these are brought to the attention of potential visitors through the constant drip of negative publicity about Latin America (Sönmez and Graefe, 1998), which has the effect of keeping Latin America firmly in the public eye, but for all the wrong reasons. Constant message reinforcement is a classic advertising strategy, used in the creation and maintenance of associations in a transformational advertising campaign. It is particularly effective when the intended target has little or no personal experience of the issue under discussion:

> Transformational advertising is more likely to work when a consumer cannot make quality judgements for himself or herself and needs advertising to help interpret the product or use experience, because the situation is open to multiple interpretations. This is more likely in service situations ...
>
> (Aaker *et al.*, 1992, p. 231)

Moreover, it is arguable that these images may be considerably more effective because they are *not* advertisements and are therefore perceived as having a high degree of objectivity and source credibility. In this respect, the warning (issued by the British Foreign Office in January 1999) to British citizens contemplating travelling to Colombia must have seemed particularly ominous (see Box 8.B).

Box 8.B. Travel to Colombia

Violence and kidnapping are serious problems in urban Colombia. In rural areas there is a risk of being caught up in guerrilla or paramilitary attacks, or opportunistic kidnapping. The border area with Panama and the Uraba region of Antioquia are especially high risk, as are other areas outside government control. Visitors should not stray away from major urban areas or from established tourist routes and should be aware that even these can become dangerous, usually without warning. It is often safer to travel by air than to risk a road journey. Road travel after dark is extremely dangerous. Visitors should consult the British Embassy in Bogota ... and the local authorities before finalising their travel plans.

(Statement by H.M. Foreign Office, January 1999)

It was, however, felt that not all the negative images of Latin America are of equal importance. Some, such as the levels of corruption amongst officials, were thought by themselves not to be likely to deter visitors from a particular destination, although they clearly contributed towards an overall negative picture of that destination in the mind of the consumer. By contrast, reports of attacks on tourists *are* highly likely to deter visitors. It was decided therefore to concentrate on those three areas that have the potential for engendering the greatest negative image in the mind of the consumer: visitor safety, tourism infrastructure and socio-economic factors.

Visitor Safety

With the exception of those people who actively seek vacations that offer a controlled element of danger or risk, such as activity or adventure holidays, personal risk is probably the single most important factor in the creation of a negative destination image. Furthermore, it is true to say that most visitors also wish to avoid exposure to any form of inconvenience that may interrupt their planned period of enjoyment and relaxation.

Petty crime, such as theft from persons, is the negative aspect that is most likely to affect the visitor, as this can happen in every country; and in developing countries 'rich' foreign tourists present particularly attractive targets. Whilst some destinations have levels of petty crime no higher than those found in comparable European or US cities, some areas are considerably more dangerous. The level of street crime was a particular problem in Peru and presented the authorities with the classic dilemma: should they warn visitors and put them on their guard (whilst at the same time putting off potential visitors), or should they pretend the problem does not exist?

Tourism in Brazil has suffered greatly over the past decade, as a direct consequence of the increasing levels of violent crime in cities such as Rio de Janeiro and São Paulo. Rio has been particularly badly hit, and in December 1992 the city was forced to take the unusual step of forming a 'Tourist Police Force': this was made up of 475 officers whose task it was to patrol the city and beaches in an attempt to reduce the levels of violent crime against tourists. By February of the following year, these measures were having some (albeit limited) success: 'The number of daily incidents involving tourists (mainly muggings) has dropped from nine to six. Yet there has still been a total of 266 assaults or thefts in the past couple of weeks' (Vanvolsem, 1993). Despite such efforts, *The Economist* argued that street violence in the city was responsible for the decline in visitor numbers; hotel occupancy rates reached an all-time low of 60 per cent in the period December 1993 to March 1994 (*The Economist*, 1995).

Ironically, a reputation as a safe destination can sometimes be problematic. Costa Rica, for example, is considered to be one of the safest destinations in Latin America; however, this relatively high level of visitor safety in San José has begun to have a negative effect. In a survey undertaken by Lumsdon and Swift (1998), tour operators reported that tourism-related crime had increased, generally in terms of petty crime, and mostly in the capital, San José. One major tour operator felt that the country's peaceful reputation had the drawback of making tourists overconfident and failing to take even the most basic of safety precautions. In response to the changing situation, the Instituto Costarricense de Turismo (the Costa Rican Tourist Institute) now issues visitors with what it calls a 'security passport', which details eight simple guidelines for personal security.

Street crime appears inevitably to follow tourism. The latest destination to play host to an influx of tourists is Cuba, and a recent report in the *Daily Telegraph* noted an increase in street crime.

> Since Cuba has opened up to mass tourism in the early Nineties, street crime has risen steadily. Pickpocketing, mugging and bag snatching are all common-place, particularly in Havana, where the government says 80 per cent of all crime takes place.
>
> (Behan and Walker, 1999)

Tour operators increasingly take the issue seriously and issue safety advice with their brochures. It could be argued that such advice may well deter potential visitors from visiting the destination in question; whilst this may be the case, it is also just as likely that those operators who wish to maintain a long-term presence in the region understand that it is better to lose a sale than to lose a customer. Typical of the advice given by the more sensitive operators is that offered by Bales Tours in their 'Tour Notes' accompanying their 'Magic of Brazil – Rio and Igazù Falls Trip' (see Box 8.C).

Box 8.C. Personal security in Brazil

There is a certain risk of theft of personal possessions in parts of many South American countries, particularly in those cities where there is high unemployment and raging inflation coupled with poor wages and living conditions. To reduce any risk we advise you to take the following sensible precautions:

Do not bring valuable items with you. Good jewellery and expensive watches should not be worn outside your hotel. It is also important not to leave cash, travellers' cheques or other items of value in your room when you are not present. The hotel provides safety deposit boxes which can be used for your travellers' cheques, passports, documents and valuables.

(Bales Tours, 1995)

Whilst warfare (both civil and external), *coups d'etat*, terrorist attacks and the kidnapping of foreigners all happen with far less frequency than do incidents of street crime, they tend to have a higher news profile, especially in the foreign press. Consequently, they are more likely to create a negative impression on potential visitors (Sönmez and Graefe, 1998), even though street crime presents the most common form of actual crime likely to be suffered by tourists. Peru is a good example of a destination that has suffered as a consequence of guerrilla activity, specifically the war waged against the Maoist guerrilla group *Sendero Luminoso*. The widespread violence generated by this group has had the effect of encouraging tourists to avoid Peru altogether, with consequent negative economic effects on the economy. The number of foreign visitors coming to Peru fell to 272,000 in 1991, from 334,000 only some two years earlier in 1989 (WTO, 1996). The greatest fall in foreign visitor numbers has been in those coming from the USA: according to one report, in the city of Cuzco alone, inbound tourism fell by more than 130,000 visitors in 1992, and 43 of the area's 128 hotels had been forced into closure by 1993 (Speer, 1993).

Even Mexico, long considered the model for Latin American stability, is not immune from guerrilla activity and civil unrest: as recently as January 1994 there was a peasant uprising in the State of Chiapas. As the *Financial Times* correspondent pointed out: 'Whilst the military threat of the rebels is negligible, the uprising comes at a time when the government is keen to project Mexico as a peaceful and stable country ... The insurrection offers a very different image ...' (Fraser, 1994). The problems did not end there, however, as the assassination of a senior member of the government took place in October of the same year, and mob violence erupted in the State of Tabasco the following year; all of which threatened to upset the 'safe' image that Mexico had hitherto enjoyed.

A major war against another country tends to have a significant impact on all aspects of the economies of the participant nations. Tourism tends to be one of the hardest hit sectors, with many visitors cancelling planned visits altogether, or taking their planned holiday at another destination. The Falklands War of 1982 effectively isolated Argentina from much of the world; El Salvador suffered similarly as a consequence of the civil war. More recently, a territorial war broke out between Ecuador and Peru in January 1995; as fighting took place in the Amazonas region, it had a severe effect on Ecuador's eco-tourism offering, with many tourists going instead either to Costa Rica, or, ironically, to the major Peruvian eco-tourism areas which are to the south of the country, far away from the areas of military activity.

Terrorism is a far greater threat to Latin American tourism destinations, principally because the whole *raison d'être* of the terrorist is the creation of a negative image and, according to Halperin, the desire 'to demonstrate that his opponents are powerless to protect themselves and the general public. He need not physically destroy his enemy; he needs only to destroy the enemy's authority or morale' (1976, p. 7). It is this challenge to the establishment, demonstrated through random acts of violence, theft or sabotage, that provides the principal focus for terrorist activity (Ryan, 1993); if they can be perpetrated against foreign tourists, then the terrorist objectives can be realized without running the risk of alienating the resident population (Richter and Waugh, 1991, p. 325).

The country that has the dubious distinction of being the most violent, with the highest level of both guerrilla activity and drug-related violence (plus high levels of street crime), is Colombia. The country in general, and Bogotá in particular, has long suffered from a violent reputation.

> Violence is a fact of life in Colombia; it has been so throughout the country's 175-year history. The Spanish word *violencia* is even used to refer to a particularly bloody period in Colombia history in which an estimated 200,000 people lost their lives – *La Violencia*.
>
> (Boudon, 1996, p. 279)

Ignoring the lower-profile levels of street crime in the country, and concentrating only on the high-profile incidents such as guerrilla activity, kidnapping and the excesses of the Colombian drug barons, an analysis of the period 1980–99 reveals the extent of the problem. There has been at least one major incident every year during this period. In February 1980, guerrillas from the M-19 group seized control of the Embassy of the Dominican Republic in Bogotá, holding over 20 diplomats from various countries hostage. In April 1984 the Colombian Justice Minister, Rodrigo Lara Bonilla, was assassinated by drug barons, and President Betancourt extended the existing 'State of Siege' to cover the entire country.

Guerrilla activity increased throughout 1985, spreading from the rural areas to the cities; in November 1985 around 20 guerrillas stormed the Supreme Court building in Bogotá, holding over 100 employees hostage, including the President of the Supreme Court. The late 1980s saw the blurring of the distinction between organized crime (the drug barons, or *narcotraficantes*) and the more politically motivated guerrilla activity. *The Economist* (1993) noted, many guerrilla factions were 'now in business for the money' and, as such, had become increasingly involved in the drugs trade.

There was an escalation of random violence, increasingly targeted at the tourist industry, with bomb attacks at the Cartagena Hilton in September 1989. It was claimed by the then Minister of Economic Development that as a direct consequence of this and other attacks, three Caribbean tour companies had removed Cartagena from their itineraries, and 'thousands of Canadian tourists had cancelled regular weekly charters to the city' (Quinn, 1989). The civil war continues to present Colombia with an underlying threat of violence and insecurity. The situation was summed up in a Euromonitor report, which suggested that Colombia suffered from 'street crime and violence, as well as an international image associated with drug trafficking and human rights abuse, factors that collectively point to a bleak future for the international holiday market' (1994, p. 95).

Abuses of human rights is another area which generates negative images; the violent excesses inflicted by government troops on the local populations and the activities of the para-military death squads are, unfortunately, familiar in stories in many countries, particularly Argentina, Brazil, Bolivia, Chile, Guatemala, Honduras and Paraguay (Scarpaci and Frazier, 1993). Well-meaning attempts to bring the perpetrators of such crimes to justice have generally only served to reinforce the negative images and to remind people of these shameful periods in their nation's history. An official Chilean investigation into the extent of the crimes committed under the Pinochet regime produced a 19,000-page report, which claims that 'more than 2,300 people were executed for political reasons, died whilst being tortured, or simply disappeared' (Crawford, 1991).

Natural disasters also play their part in reinforcing the negative image of Latin America as a dangerous part of the world: disasters such as the Mexican earthquake of 1985, for which official estimates were 4000 dead, although because many shanty towns around Mexico City were destroyed (for which population records are non-existent), unofficial estimates have put the loss of life at just under 10,000 (O'Shaunessy, 1985). Much of Latin America suffers from volcanic activity, such as that which caused a mudslide to descend on the Colombian town of Armero in November 1985, killing some 25,000 people.

The 'El Niño' storms of 1997–8 were disastrous for much of Latin America and the Caribbean, with extreme weather conditions leading to a loss of life and widespread destruction of property and infrastructure. Estimates suggested that around 1000 people lost their lives throughout the region, with some 600,000 more being made homeless. In Colombia, floods caused an estimated US $3 billion's worth of damage, whilst the drought in Central America is thought to have lost Guatemala around 10 per cent of its grain harvest, and Costa Rica 30 per cent of its coffee harvest (*The Economist*, 1998). Hurricane Mitch, which swept through much of Central America and the Caribbean in October 1998, is estimated to have caused millions of dollars' worth of damage to the already poor infrastructure throughout the region. Honduras was particularly badly hit, at what was traditionally its high season period, with companies reporting 100 per cent cancellations until January of the following year (Box, 1999). More recently, the disastrous mud slides and flooding that hit Venezuela in December 1999 caused thousands of deaths, and widespread destruction of property with disruption of communications.

Other natural disasters, whilst not as damaging in terms of loss of life, or economic destruction, may still have an effect on the tourism potential. For example, the Galapagos Islands suffered extensive environmental damage when fires swept through the main islands in April 1994. The Minister of Tourism assured the media that there was no danger to human life, but all tourist flights to the islands were suspended, with obvious loss of revenue (Laurence, 1994).

Another consideration for visitors to Latin America is the threat posed by disease and dangerous animals or insects. Disease presents by far the greatest danger and is of concern, not just to those directly at risk (the tourist), but to the medical services of both host and market nations. The numbers of long haul tourists contracting malaria is growing, due to the increasing numbers of tourists from the developed world visiting destinations in the developing world (see Box 8.D).

Box 8.D. Malaria cases in Latin America (1995)

Malaria cases (per 100,000 people)

Country	Reported cases
Nicaragua	1525.6
Honduras	1022.1
Peru	804.5
Bolivia	617.8
Brazil	350.2
Guatemala	236.0
Ecuador	155.0
Colombia	126.4
Venezuela	73.4
El Salvador	58.1
Panama	27.3
Paraguay	18.1
Mexico	7.9
Argentina	3.0

(United Nations Development Programme, 1998)

The *Financial Times* regularly carries a column of advice on disease contraction prevention aimed at business travellers; however, it would appear that in many cases, pre-trip immunization is not as effective as avoiding the risk of exposure. One column, for example, suggested that cholera vaccines provide 'only negligible protection': a somewhat alarming statement when one considers the extent of the latest cholera outbreak that began in Peru in 1991 and claimed at least 1000 victims (Hargreaves and Timmons, 1991). The disease subsequently spread to Bolivia, Ecuador, southern Colombia, northern Argentina and northern Chile.

Some destinations present greater risks than do others, and the type of holiday can also determine the level and type of risk to which the visitor is exposed. The eco-adventure segment presents the greatest potential for injury or disease contraction. Apart from those risks usually associated with watersports and mountaineering, there are risks from the resident flora and fauna: in addition to the malarial mosquitos already referred to, there are poisonous snakes, scorpions, sharks, jellyfish, spiders, frogs and plants. Certain rivers hold real dangers from piranha, anacondas and caimans (a type of crocodile found in South America). Most of these sources of danger are relatively well known and as their habitats are identifiable, they are usually easily avoided; by contrast, the source of diseases such as chagas or bilharzia are invisible to the naked eye and are therefore more dangerous. In view of the increasing popularity of eco-adventure holidays, tourists are increasingly likely to visit more remote areas, where these diseases are still relatively common.

It must be pointed out, however, that the actual threat posed by the challenges of the landscape to the majority of tourists is very slight, far less than their actual contribution to the popular image of Latin America as a dangerous, disease-ridden continent.

Tourism Infrastructure

The infrastructure of the host country also has the potential to contribute to the formation of a negative image. Whilst poor facilities may not be life-threatening, they can detract from the overall visitor enjoyment of the experience. Under extreme conditions, however, factors such as hotel and restaurant cleanliness can become serious health hazards, as 'Airtours' obviously decided with regard to four of the hotels they used in the Dominican Republic. (See Box 8.E.)

Box 8.E. Health issues in the Dominican Republic

Thousands of sunseekers had their travel plans thrown into doubt today after health fears forced Airtours to cross four hotels off its list.

The Rossendale-based company says the hotels, in the Dominican Republic, fail to meet their 'stringent health and safety inspections.' Hundreds of customers are suing the company after becoming ill on the island ... The axed hotels are the Cayo Levantado, Gran Bahia, La Esplanada, and Punta Garza. Airtours said today that it will continue to use another 12 hotels on the island ... Tour operator Inspirations dropped the island altogether from its programme last year over health and hygiene standards.

(Salter, 1998)

Issues of public hygiene, transport and communications, and pollution can be decisive in influencing visitor perceptions of a particular destination, usually in relation to specific cities and towns. Furthermore, certain cities have justifiably poor reputations in terms of both air and noise pollution; in this respect the worst five are probably Bogota, Caracas, Lima, Mexico City and São Paulo, where air pollution is a direct consequence of too many outdated and badly maintained motor vehicles. However, the un-regulated industrial waste disposal is increasingly polluting the land around major cities and, in some instances, the rivers that flow through these cities. One report on the Tiete (which flows through São Paulo), noted that the river

has turned into one of the world's biggest cesspools. The stretch running through the industrial area of the city ceased to support any life in the 1950s. A sickly stench exudes from the Tiete's waters, which are used as an open sewer for São Paulo's domestic waste.

(Griffith, 1991)

Unfortunately such pollution is no longer confined to the industrial areas of large cities, but has encroached into those areas specifically dedicated to tourism. Acapulco in Mexico has seen a fall in international arrivals over the last decade, a consequence, according to Denton (1993, p. 15), of the 'tarnished image' of the city, where sewage was dumped along the bay, and the streets remained unswept. Such activities do more than merely degrade the environment; they can ultimately compromise visitor safety, as they can lead to hepatitis or, more immediately, encourage shark attack. Sharks are known to be attracted to human waste, and the Shark Research Panel of the US Navy's Office of Naval Research offers the somewhat understated advice to 'use discretion in terms of putting human waste into the water', especially in waters where sharks are known to be active (Baldridge, 1976, p. 270).

Socio-economic Factors

Whilst socio-economic considerations alone are unlikely to deter visitors to a specific destination, taken *en bloc* they contribute to the overall destination image and, therefore, can be considered as elements of attitude formation. Factors such as the level of inflation and exchange rates, by contrast, *are* important in their own right in influencing destination choice. In terms of intra-regional tourism, exchange rates and levels of inflation play a vital role in influencing cross-border tourism flows, as most international tourism to Latin America originates in neighbouring countries. Such a reliance on so few markets means that the bulk of tourist revenues are dependent on exchange rates and other fiscal considerations; the major banking crisis in Venezuela in 1994, and Venezuelan inflation reaching 52.6 per cent in 1995 (Gámez, 1994), meant that Colombian hoteliers were reluctant to accept payment by credit cards issued by Venezuelan banks.

Corruption

Another issue that is regularly highlighted by the media, and which is likely to contribute to the overall negative image of Latin America, is that of corruption. Corruption has historically been a problem throughout the region. Recent events have kept the issue at the forefront of public opinion, with the impeachment of President Fernando Collor de Mello in Brazil for corrupt practices in 1992, the bribery scandals that rocked Argentina, and touched President Carlos Menem in 1992–3 (Barham, 1993), and the drive against corruption in the Mexican police force in 1993 (Fraser and Conger, 1993), which continued throughout the 1990s. In terms of world corruption comparisons, Brazil and Mexico rank fifteenth and seventeenth respectively (Jamieson, 1997).

NEGATIVE IMAGE AND VISITOR NUMBERS

The basic premise is that it is the generally negative image associated with most Latin American destinations that prevents them assuming greater importance in terms of world markets. It is accepted by researchers that there are positive relationships between political instability and low (or negative) economic growth in developing countries. A study by Gyimah-Brempong and Muñoz de Camacho (1998) on the effects of political instability on capital formation and economic growth, confirmed the work of earlier researchers in this area.

With regard to Colombia, Yunis claims that:

> From 1965 onwards, a spectacular development of tourism had taken place and the flow of tourists grew very rapidly until 1982, when a peak was reached with over 1.2 mn visitors. But then the image of the country started to deteriorate, due to guerrilla activities in some locations and to the illegal operations and violent actions of various drug traffic cartels.
>
> (1994, p. 120)

The existence of a statistically significant correlation between negative destination image and declining numbers of incoming tourists is difficult to prove: there are factors other than image that serve to reduce incoming visitor numbers, such as competition from other destinations and economic considerations (in both the market and the destination countries). Furthermore, what may be viewed as constituting an unnaturally high risk in one market may be of relatively little consequence in another. For example, it is likely that negative image factors have the greatest influence on visitor numbers from Europe or North America. High levels of street violence may well deter a potential visitor from Europe, but are likely to have less impact on a potential visitor from another Latin American republic, for whom street violence may be a relatively familiar (if unwelcome) aspect of their own country. In other words, the impact of negative news items is likely to depend as much on the audience to whom they are directed, as on the images they contain.

Having accepted these provisos, it was nevertheless decided to test the assertion made by Yunis and compare numbers of incoming tourists to Colombia on a yearly basis with the years for which 'negative' reports about the country appeared in the international press and therefore would be likely to have been seen by potential visitors. The period chosen was that between 1974 (when the guerrilla problem was widely assumed to have been solved) and 1997 (see Tables 8.1 and 8.2). In general terms, there appears to have

Table 8.1. The formation of negative image: Colombia, 1974–95

Year	Incidents which were reported in the international press
1974	In terms of international image, this was a very good year, with the government accepting the surrender of some 200 guerrillas from the ELN (National Liberation Army).
1976	A 'State of Siege' was declared, the 13th since 1944.
1980	In February, guerrillas from the M19 (19th of May) group broke into the Embassy of the Dominican Republic in Bogota, and took the Embassy staff and Ambassadors from 14 other countries hostage.
1984	The Colombia Justice Minister was assassinated by *narcotraficantes* (drug cartels), in April.
1985	(i) Outbreaks of civil unrest, instigated by M19, in the urban slums of Bogotá.
	(ii) In November, members of the ELN stormed the Supreme Court of Bogota, forcing the Police and Army into a bloody shootout in which all the guerrillas were killed.
	(iii) Also in November, over 20,000 people were feared dead after the village of Armero was hit by a landslide of mud and rocks, after the eruption of a volcano.
1986	The Spanish daily *Ya* reported that 20,000 soldiers, police and secret police had been mobilized by the Colombian authorities for the protection of the Pope during his forthcoming visit to the country.

Year	Incidents which were reported in the international press
1987	(i) In January, British Foreign Secretary Sir Geoffrey Howe on a visit to Cartagena, promised Colombia equipment and training to help combat drug-trafficking: the activities of Colombian drug cartels in the UK had been the subject of newspaper speculation for over two months.
	(ii) Over 200 people were killed when a landslide hit Medellín, in September.
1988	(i) In January, a State of Emergency was declared in Medellín, 'amid fears of a complete breakdown of law and order. Violence has flared and is mounting between warring drug gangs and political groups' (Taylor, 1988).
	(ii) The same month, the Colombian Attorney General was kidnapped and murdered by drug traffickers.
	(iii) Between September 1987 and February 1988, there were six staff kidnapped and murdered from the University of Antioquia.
	(iv) Reports suggested that some 600 people had been killed in the run-up to the local elections on 13 March (O'Shaunessy, 1988).
	(v) Riots and clashes with police following the kidnapping of a senior politician left over 100 dead in Bogota in June.
1989	(i) In August, paramilitary and police units arrested 10,000 people, mostly in Bogota and Medellín, in what was the largest ever purge of suspected drug gang members.
	(ii) By September, the war against the drug barons had intensified, and the USA had sent military advisers to offer assistance, in addition to the DEA officials who had already been there for some time (McGreal, 1989); in the same month, President Bush formally offered to send US forces to Colombia to fight the drug cartels (Brodie and Davies, 1989).
1990	Drug gangs assaulted the headquarters of the Medellín police force in May; estimates put drug-related murders at around 50 a day (Wearne, 1990).
1992	A 'State of Emergency' was declared in November.
1993	In January a series of bomb explosions rocked Bogota, killing 20 people; this was followed by further bombs in February, killing and injuring more people, including guests at the prestigious Intercontinental-Tequendama hotel.
1994	(i) In March it was reported that: 'at least 10 congressional candidates have been killed, kidnapped or injured during the campaign. One sociologist calculates that elections in more than half Colombia's municipalities are affected by guerrilla violence' (Kendall, 1994).
	(ii) After numerous complaints and illnesses amongst tourists, 'First Choice' holidays dropped the Colombian island of San Andres from their list of destinations; a report, in the *Sunday Times* spoke of: 'drug barons, excreta-contaminated swamps and endemic dysentery' (Harlow, 1994).

Year	Incidents which were reported in the international press
1995	(i) An article in **The European** claimed that Colombia had the highest rate of kidnapping in the world between 1989 and 1995: at 1768 it was nearly as much as the combined totals for all other countries (Verchère, 1995).
	(ii) In August the government declared a 'State of Emergency', following the deaths of 24 people in massacres in the north-western region of Uraba, and the widespread destruction inflicted on the town of Miraflores, when it was attacked by a force of some 500 guerrillas of the ELN.

Table 8.2. Colombia: Foreign tourist arrivals, 1972–97

Year	Number of foreign tourists	Change on previous year	
		Number	Percentage
1972	229,111	+ 31,608	+ 16.0
1973	274,846	+ 45,735	+ 20.0
1974	362,917	+ 88,071	+ 32.0
1975	443,264	+ 80,347	+ 22.1
1976	522,135	+ 78,871	+ 17.8
1977	708,618	+ 186,483	+ 35.7
1978	826,276	+ 117,658	+ 16.6
1979	1,116,777	+ 290,501	+ 35.2
1980	1,227,666	+ 110,889	+ 9.9
1981	1,059,630	− 168,036	− 13.7
1982	1,082,442	+ 22,812	+ 2.1
1983	506,833	− 575,609	− 53.2
1984	715,277	+ 208,444	+ 41.1
1985	784,023	+ 68,746	+ 9.6
1986	732,200	− 51,823	− 6.6
1987	541,268	− 190,932	− 26.1
1988	828,903	+ 287,635	+ 53.1
1989	732,982	− 95,921	− 11.6
1990	812,796	+ 79,814	+ 10.9
1991	856,862	+ 44,066	+ 5.4
1992	1,076,000	+ 219,138	+ 25.6
1993	1,047,000	− 29,000	− 2.7
1994	1,016,000	− 31,000	− 3.0
1995	1,310,000	+ 294,000	+ 28.9
1996	1,253,000	− 57,000	− 4.4
1997	1,193,000	− 60,000	− 4.8

Source: CNT (1994) and WTO (1998)

been relatively little (of a negative nature) reported in the international press prior to 1980, when the ELN attacked the Dominican Republic Embassy. Interestingly, the first year in which numbers of incoming tourists fell was 1981, the year following this highly publicized incident.

Whilst incoming tourist numbers had risen steadily up to the early 1970s, the seven years between 1973 and 1980 saw a dramatic increase of some 346.6 per cent, from 274,846 (1973) to 1,227,666 (1980). 1980 was the watershed point, as since then the overall pattern of incoming visitor numbers has been highly erratic, with a series of 'ups' and 'downs' characterizing the new trends. For example, by 1983 incoming visitor numbers had fallen to just over 500,000; by 1984 they had increased by around 41 per cent, followed by a much smaller increase in 1985. Numbers fell in 1986, this time by over 51,000 (some 6 per cent), and this was followed by an even greater fall in 1987 of nearly 91,000. Since 1988 visitor numbers have continued to fluctuate between the highest registered increase (over 50 per cent in 1988), to the greatest decline of over 95,000 (26 per cent) the following year. In view of the increased number of internationally reported incidents throughout this period, the evidence would tend to support the claim made previously by Yunis and suggest that an increasingly negative press has had a long-term, cumulative affect on the attractiveness of Colombia as a tourist destination.

SUMMARY

In conclusion, the importance of image as an influencer of consumer attitude must be taken into consideration by those hoping to promote destinations. In terms of image as an element of the promotional mix, reality is of relatively little consequence: it is the consumer's *perception* of reality that matters, and destination promoters should bear this in mind when seeking to develop destination images.

The last word on image in Latin America must go to one of the UK tour operators who was contacted in connection with a survey by the authors. He summed up the situation in this way:

> Little is done to promote South America as a tourist destination, presumably due to a lack of funds for most countries. There is very little press coverage – most of which is negative – such as terrorism, theft, drugs, violence, poverty etc. Although these are problems, most people are totally unaware of the great potential of the continent for a marvellous holiday.

REFERENCES

Aaker, D. A., Batra, R. and Myers, J. G. (1992) *Advertising Management*, 4th edition, Prentice-Hall, Englewood Cliffs, NJ.

Ashworth, G. and Goodall, B. (1988) 'Tourist Images: Marketing Considerations' in B. Goodall and G. Ashworth (eds), *Marketing in the Tourism Industry: The Promotion of Destination Regions* (pp. 213–38), Croom Helm, Beckenham.

Baldridge, H. D. (1976) *Shark Attack*, Everest Books, London.

Bales Tours (1995) 'Security', *The Magic of Brazil – Rio and Igassu Falls: Tour Notes 1995*, Bales Tours Ltd, Dorking.

Barham, J. (1993) 'Argentina to Probe Italian Bribes Link', *Financial Times* (19 March).

Behan, R. and Walker, G. (1999) 'Cuban Crime-busters "Go Over the Top",' *Daily Telegraph* (17 April).

Boudon, L. (1996) 'Guerrillas and the State: The Role of the State in the Colombian Peace Process', *Journal of Latin American Studies*, Vol. 28, pp. 279–97.

Box, B. (1999) 'Honduras Lures Visitors with Mitch Disaster Tours', *Daily Telegraph* (16 January).

Brodie, I. and Davies, H. (1989) 'Bush is Willing to Send Troops to Colombia', *Daily Telegraph* (6 June).

Chisnall, P. M. (1995) *Consumer Behaviour*, 3rd edition, McGraw-Hill, Maidenhead.

CNT (1994) Data supplied by Statistics Department, Corporación Nacional de Turismo, Santafé de Bogotá.

Crawford, L. (1991) 'Chile Shown Horrors of the Past', *Financial Times* (5 March).

Denton, D. (1993) 'Acapulco Renaissance', *Business Mexico*, Vol. 3(3), pp. 15–16.

The Economist (1993) 'Robin the Hood', *The Economist*, Vol. 326(7796) (30 January).

The Economist (1995) 'Life's a Beach', *The Economist*, Vol. 335(7909) (8 April).

The Economist (1998) 'The Season of "El Niño"', *The Economist*, Vol. 347(8067) (8 April).

Euromonitor (1994) *Travel and Tourism in Latin America*, Euromonitor, London.

Fraser, D. (1994) 'Poverty Leads to Peasant's Revolt', *Financial Times* (5 January).

Fraser, D. and Conger, L. (1993) 'Mexico Acts on Wrong Arm of the Law', *Financial Times* (1 July).

Gámez, C. (ed.) (1994) 'Pulso Latinoamericano – Pronóstico para 1995', *El Tiempo* (21 November).

Gartner, W. C. (1993) 'Image Formation Process' in M. Uysal and D. R. Fesenmaier (eds), *Communication and Channel Systems in Tourism Marketing* (pp. 191–215), The Haworth Press, New York.

Gilbert, D. C. and Houghton, P. (1990) 'An Investigation of the Format, Design, and Placement of Tour Operator Brochures', paper presented to the Conference: *Tourism Research into the 1990s*, Durham, 10–12 December.

Griffith, V. (1991) 'Paradise Lost', *Financial Times* (16 October).

Gyimah-Bremong, K. and Muñoz de Camacho, S. (1998) 'Political Instability, Human Capital and Economic Growth in Latin America', *The Journal of Developing Areas*, Vol. 32, pp. 449–60.

Halperin, E. (1976) 'Terrorism in Latin America', *The Washington Papers (Vol. 4, no. 33)*, Sage Publications, Beverly Hills, California.

Hargreaves, C. and Timmons, S. (1991) 'Peru's Cholera Epidemic Claims 1,000', *Daily Telegraph* (19 April).

Harlow, J. (1994) 'Holiday Firm Drops Coral Island "Hell"', *Sunday Times* (6 November).

Hart, N. A. and Stapleton, J. (1987) *Glossary of Marketing Terms*, 3rd edition, Heinemann Professional Publishing, London.

Haywood, K. M. (1990) 'Revising and Implementing the Marketing Concept as it Applies to Tourism', *Tourism Management*, Vol. 11(3), pp. 195–205.

Haywood, R. (1991) *All About Public Relations*, 2nd edition, McGraw-Hill, Maidenhead.

Jamieson, B. (1997) 'Who Tops the Sleaze League?' *Sunday Telegraph* (19 January).

Kendall, S. (1994) 'Violence Mars Road to Colombia Elections', *Financial Management* (9 March).

Laurence, C. (1994) 'Wind Shift Drives Fire Closer to Tortoises', *Daily Telegraph* (25 April).

Lea, J. (1988) *Tourism and Development in the Third World*, Routledge, London.

Lumsdon, L. M. and Swift, J. S. (1993) 'The Development of Tourism in Latin American Gateway Cities', paper presented to the 7th General Conference of EADI: *Transformation and Development: Eastern Europe and The South*, Berlin, 15–18 September.

Lumsdon, L. M. and Swift, J. S. (1998) 'Ecotourism at a Crossroads: The Case of Costa Rica', *The Journal of Sustainable Tourism*, Vol. 6(2), pp. 155–72.

McGreal, C. (1989) 'US Sends Advisers to the Medellin War', *Independent* (1 September).

Middleton, V. T. C. (1994) *Marketing in Travel and Tourism*, 2nd edition, Butterworth-Heinemann, Oxford.

Muller, T. E. (1991) 'Using Personal Values to Define Segments in an International Tourism Market', *International Marketing Review*, Vol. 8(1), pp. 55–70.

O'Shaunessy, H. (1985) 'Third Quake Shakes Mexico', *Observer* (22 September).

O'Shaunessy, H. (1988) 'Blood-streaked Bunting over the Town Hall', *Observer* (13 March).

Papadopoulos, N. (1993) 'What Product and What Country Images: Are and Are Not' in N. Papadopoulos and L. A. Helsop (eds), *Product-Country Images: Impact and Role in International Marketing* (pp. 3–38), International Business Press, New York.

Quinn, T. (1989) 'Tourism Hit as Colombia Faces Judges Strike', *Daily Telegraph* (27 September).

Rao, S. R., Thomas, E. G. and Javalgi, R. G. (1992) 'Activity Preferences and Trip-Planning Behaviour of the US Outbound Pleasure Travel Market', *Journal of Travel Research*, Vol. 30(3), pp. 30–42.

Richter, L. K. and Waugh, W. L. (1991) 'Terrorism and Tourism as Logical Companions' in S. Melik (ed.), *Managing Tourism* (pp. 318–26), Butterworth-Heinemann, Oxford.

Rushton, A. and Carson, D. J. (1985) 'The Marketing of Services: Managing the Intangibles', *European Journal of Marketing*, Vol. 19(3), pp. 19–40.

Ryan, C. (1993) 'Crime, Violence, Terrorism and Tourism: An Accidental or Intrinsic Relationship?', *Tourism Management*, Vol. 14(3), pp. 173–83.

Salter, A. (1998) 'Airtours Dumps Sun Island Hotels', *Manchester Evening News* (19 March).

Scarpaci, J. L. and Frazier, L. J. (1993) 'State Terror: Ideology, Protest and the Gendering of Landscapes', *Progress in Human Geography*, Vol. 17(1), pp. 1–21.

Seaton, A. V. (1989) 'Promotional Strategies in Tourism' in S. F. Witt and L. Moutinho (eds), *Tourism Marketing and Management Handbook* (pp. 335–441), Prentice-Hall, Hemel Hempstead.

Seaton, A. V. (1990) 'Symbolism, Structural Branding and Representation in Tourism Choices', paper presented to the Conference: *Tourism Research into the 1990s*, Durham, 10–12 December.

Sönmez, S. F. and Graefe, A. R. (1998) 'Influence of Terrorism Risk on Foreign Tourism Decisions', *Annals of Tourism Research*, Vol. 25(1), pp. 112–44.

Speer, L. J. (1993) 'Once Popular Tourist Mecca Looking to Bounce Back', *Hotel & Motel Management*, Vol. 208(10), p. 27.

Taylor, F. (1988) 'Emergency Declared Over Cocaine War', *Daily Telegraph* (18 January).

Vanvolsem, W. (1993) 'Dance with Danger in Río', *Daily Telegraph* (20 February).

Wearne, P. (1990) '50 Murders a Day as Cocaine War Explodes', *Sunday Times* (6 May).

WTO (1994) *Report of the Experts Meeting on Tourist Safety and Security*, World Tourism Organization, Madrid.

WTO (1996) Data supplied by WTO Statistics Department, WTO, Madrid.

WTO (1998) Data supplied by WTO Statistics Department, WTO, Madrid.

Ya (1986) 'Veinte mil hombres protegerán al Papa durante el viaje', *Ya* (1 July).

Yunis, E. (1994) *Prospects for Tourism in South America*, Travel & Tourism Intelligence, London.

CHAPTER 9

Impacts of Tourism

INTRODUCTION

Previous chapters have explained the tourism offerings throughout Latin America and the enormous potential for tourism development. This chapter provides an analysis of the extent to which tourism has had an impact (positive or negative) on the environment of the region as a whole and on certain destinations in particular. Despite the relatively low overall levels of visitors to Latin America (when viewed in terms of world demand patterns), certain areas have registered considerable increases generally in smaller areas, such as around capital cities, or sites of archaeological interest. In this respect, Holloway claims that: 'Countries subject to rapid growth in tourism, particularly where this is confined to small regions, will experience not just economic change but also social and environmental effects which will have both political and economic consequences' (1988, p. 252).

This 'rapid growth' is particularly the case with certain Latin American destinations, which have witnessed spectacular rates of increase in numbers of foreign visitors; for example, in the case of Colombia, incoming tourist growth increased from 79,196 in 1965 to 1,227,666 in 1980, a growth rate of some 1450 per cent. It is the subsequent impacts of such growth rates on various destinations that form the basis of this chapter – in particular, the *nature* of tourism impacts: i.e. *which* tourism activity has had an impact on a destination and *in what way*? (Holder, 1988, p. 119).

Given the nature of public and private sector involvement in tourism development, it is difficult to undertake an economic analysis without also including some form of political evaluation. Thus both criteria are evaluated together, as the 'politico-economic' environment. As legal considerations are a facet of political (and sometimes economic) decisions, any legal impacts will also be considered in this section.

Another dimension is added to this framework, one which Green and Hunter (1992, p. 32) have termed the 'natural' environment', and which comprises the flora and fauna of destinations – i.e. elements that are not made by human beings, but which may well form the focal point of a destination offering, as in the case of 'nature-based' tourism.

THE POLITICO-ECONOMIC ENVIRONMENT

Introduction

Historical assessments of the value of tourism in Latin America tended to concentrate solely on economic factors, using income multiplier models (Fletcher and Archer, 1991), and emphasizing the positive contribution of tourism to the economy (Cater, 1988, p. 55). By the 1980s a new realism had emerged: writers had begun to question not just the socio-cultural impacts of tourism, but its almost mythological status as what *The Economist* described as 'a miracle industry, able to transform any economy' (*The Economist*, 1989). The linkage between the tourism sector and economic growth in developing countries has been subject to critical evaluation in the literature. Many authors suggest that tourism does little to bridge the gap between developed and developing economies (Gormsen, 1988; Hall, 1992). Holloway, for example, has suggested that 'there is no clear link between tourism growth and economic development, owing to many other complicating factors such as inflation, the ability of an area to diversify and the willingness of the local population to work hard' (1988, p. 252).

Thus, the very basis of tourism's contribution to the economy continues to be an issue (Oppermann, 1992). However, an additional debate relates to whether the benefits it brings are greater than the dis-benefits. Most of the positive politico-economic impacts, such as increased levels of employment, increased GDP and increased inward investment, have already been examined in Chapter 2: there are clearly benefits even if they amount to marginal gains in GDP and improved employment prospects in certain regions within particular countries. Nevertheless, this needs to be evaluated in relation to negative impacts.

Negative Impacts

One area of discussion is the creation of local or regional imbalances within the economy, exacerbating further the disparities of income between rural and urban zones in particular. A case in point is that of Buenos Aires, which is one of the most expensive cities in Latin America. As the city is the focal point of tourism in Argentina (see Chapter 7, 'Urban Tourism'), and as some of the most prestigious hotel development has taken place within the city, companies inadvertently contribute to the imbalance that exists between the capital and the rest of the country, in particular the poorer northern regions. Furthermore, it could be argued that the influx of immigrants to Buenos Aires which, according to Carlevari (1993, pp. 133–4) really began between 1975 and 1980, has, in effect, contributed to the pressure on accommodation in the city, which in turn has contributed to inflation.

It is very difficult to establish a link between increased tourism and inflation as many other factors are involved in the process. The very nature of international tourism implies an increasingly greater degree of worldwide economic integration. In addition to the increased wage levels and pressures on real estate in cities, tourism can be said to have contributed to inflation and a negative balance-of-payments level through the importation of (expensive) foreign goods.

The importation of foreign goods is an area of tourism that is of particular importance for developing countries, such as those of Latin America. Encouraging high-spend European or North American visitors may be a good strategy for the development of the tourism industry in general; however, problems begin to emerge when one analyses what else, other than the core destination offerings of scenery, beaches, wildlife, etc., is demanded by the foreign visitor. Belk refers to the practicalities of tourism development and the importing of 'liquors, toiletries, and sweets, as well as capital goods such as elevators, cars, and air traffic control equipment' (1993, p. 30). Thus, tourism could also be said to contribute (if only indirectly) to a *negative* balance of payments.

Whilst it is claimed that tourism has the potential to spread investment and development throughout the country, in fact, the opposite may be true: tourist areas act as magnets, drawing in development funds and encouraging migration, usually at the expense of other areas of the country. This is most definitely the case with integrated resorts and urban tourism.

A good example of the extent to which inequalities still exist is to be found in Brazil. In the early 1990s, despite some 20 years of tourism growth, Rabahy and Ruschmann pointed to the 'imbalance in the growth of the economy' (1991, p. 140). The situation had apparently improved little towards the end of the 1990s, according to the EMBRATUR 'National Tourism Policy' document for the period 1996–9, in which the reduction of regional inequalities and the socio-economic and cultural integration of the population are given as two of the ten key strategic objectives underlying Brazilian national tourism policy (EMBRATUR, 1995, p. 9). The question of inequalities is further complicated by the fact that the very existence of a tourism resource (which has positive economic impacts for those involved) may have negative economic impacts for those who work outside tourism (Cater, 1988, p. 55). This has been of particular concern with regard to eco-tourism: Morris refers to the opposition faced by the Ecuadorian authorities from local farmers when it was decided to redesignate large tracts of productive farming land as National Reserves, with obvious losses in income (1987, p. 16). A similar point is made by Place (1991) in her study of the Tortuguero National Park in Costa Rica.

Whilst accepting that, in general economic terms, incoming tourism can be of great benefit to developing countries, there are also less desirable outcomes. Some have already been examined; others include issues such as the repatriation of profits of multinationals, legislation dealing with the levels of local versus expatriate employment, and the extent to which small domestic operators can effectively compete against multinationals, operating in a free market. As Belk points out:

> although the travel industry is made up of a series of smaller industries such as airlines, travel agencies, hotels, restaurants, and car rental agencies, in each of these industries there are multinational corporations that may overwhelm local interests. Increasing vertical integration between airlines, hotels, and Travel Agencies locks out Third World participation to an even greater degree.
>
> (1993, p. 31)

THE SOCIO-CULTURAL ENVIRONMENT

Introduction

Culture, as defined by Herskovits, is 'the instrument whereby the individual adjusts to his total setting' (1952, p. 625). Hofstede has described it as 'the collective programming of the mind which distinguishes the members of one human group from another' (1984, p. 21). Culture is the most pervasive all-embracing element of any society. It affects people and the way they live their lives – in many respects it dictates *how* they live their lives – and it influences many of the daily decisions that people make about their lives. Thus, an analysis of the impact of tourism on the socio-cultural environment of a given society is, in effect, an analysis of the effects of tourism on the very basis of that society.

Tourism presents innumerable opportunities for contact between different cultures. Despite the fact that many visitors travel with the specific intention of experiencing new cultures, many more travel in complete indifference to the local culture; some will expect the destination to which they travel to adapt to their particular cultural standards, and will feel aggrieved or alienated if this does not happen. Thus, heightened cultural contact can, unfortunately, present problems in terms of what has been described as 'culture collision' (Gee *et al.*, 1989, p. 160), or 'culture shock': 'the shock we experience when we are confronted with the unknown and the "foreign"' (Marx, 1999, p. 5).

Cultural clashes tend to be at their most severe when the psychic distance between the cultures involved is at its greatest. Psychic distance is a combination of cultural affinity, trust and experience in relation to the other party (Hallén and Wiedersheim-Paul, 1984, p. 18). A study by Swift (1999) suggested that cultural similarity ('closeness') was instrumental in engendering cultural affinity, which in turn was influential in decreasing the level of psychic distance. In terms of culture clash, therefore, the degree of cultural affinity is of great importance: the greater the degree of affinity, the lower the level of cultural misunderstandings.

In terms of Latin America, the key factor of interest is the extent to which incoming tourism has affected specific destinations, and the ways in which these destinations have responded to these differences. If by 'response' we mean 'change' or the 'consequences' of tourism, then a distinction should be made between permanent and temporary consequences. Permanent (or long-term) changes are where the foreign culture (or cultures) has had a lasting socio-cultural influence on elements of the host population: perhaps the best example of this is to be found in the area of food and drink, and the internationalization of various national food styles – such as the popularity of *pasta* and *pizza* in Argentina. A temporary (or short-term) change is where the host population has responded to the demands of outside cutural influences, but has still retained its own cultural standards: an example of this would be the wide availability of McDonald's restaurants in many of the larger cities.

The degree of impact is dependent on a number of factors; Ap and Crompton (1998) cite five: (1) the economic state of the area, (2) the degree of local involvement in tourism, (3) the spatial characteristics of tourism development, (4) the viability of the host culture and (5) other characteristics. Fox (1977) has suggested that socio-cultural impacts on the host community can be measured in terms of the level or degree of change undergone in terms of seven socio-cultural norms: (1) value systems, (2) family relations, (3) collective lifestyle, (4) community organization, (5) creative expressions, (6) traditional ceremonies and (7) moral conduct.

Lea (1988, p. 63) divides the impacts into two main groups ('social impacts' and 'cultural impacts'), with various sub-divisions for each:

1. 'Social impacts': religion, health, language, social change and moral behaviour (which includes prostitution, crime and gambling).
2. 'Cultural impacts': cultural communication, physical products and non-material customs.

Regardless of the model used, the extent or degree of impact is dependent on the degree of cultural (or psychic) distance between the cultures in contact, and the respect they hold for each other. In general terms, long haul tourism (which is predominately *from developed* countries *to developing* countries) has the potential to engender the greatest level of cultural conflict or change, as there is generally a high level of difference between the cultures involved. As Nettekoven observes:

> When mass tourism from highly industrialized societies is introduced into an economically underdeveloped country, the contrast between the two societies is apt to be stark and the consequences often great ... The difference between the consumer habits of the tourists and the living conditions of the indigenous population is thus accentuated and the differences between the two societies emphasized.
>
> (1984, p. 137)

Socio-cultural Impacts

What Lea referred to as the 'social impacts' of tourism have generally been most widely felt in terms of 'value systems' and relationships within and between families and, in the wider sense, the collective lifestyle and community organization. As indicated in previous chapters, one consequence of increased tourism in a particular area is increased migration to that area, by people looking for work. This has the effect of destroying the traditional cohesion of the extended family group, which is prevalent throughout most of the developing world. It also has a similar effect on the wider community in which people live. Despite any economic benefits that may accrue from tourism, in terms of family values and social cohesion, on balance the impacts are generally negative.

The gradual fragmentation of society brings with it other problems, including those of a social nature, what Fox (1977) refers to as 'moral conduct', such as increases in the levels of crime. This is particularly the case when combined with the social consequences of wealthy tourists from the developed world coming into close contact with very much poorer host populations. Vandepitte (1996) wrote about the economic impacts of tourism on Cuba (see Box 9.A). If the

---

Box 9.A. Social tensions in Cuba

To attract the Western tourists, the sector is performed according to Western standards of comfort and patterns of consumption. Owing to the painful local circumstances, this luxury is almost reserved for foreigners. At the very moment that the Cubans are confronted with a sharp decline of their consumption, before their eyes a pleasure-industry is being developed in which they cannot participate. Such a 'consumption-apartheid' inevitably creates social and political tensions.

(Vandepitte, 1996)

---

traditional societal checks and balances have been weakened or removed altogether, then there is a greater likelihood that certain members of the local population will become involved in crime, especially when they are in close proximity to wealthy tourists. Certainly published studies indicate a correlation between increased tourism and increased crime, even in destinations which have traditionally been virtually crime-free.

Cuba is a good example of how a sudden increase in the numbers of tourists has resulted in an increase in instances of petty crime, drugs and prostitution (Fidler, 1995). There are few accurate measures of the growth in tourism in Cuba which are strictly verifiable; furthermore, researchers are in agreement that coastal tourism has undoubtedly provided a significant boost to the Cuban economy, with tourism revenue exceeding 1 billion US dollars in 1995 (de Holan and Phillips, 1997).

It is difficult to assess, but environmental degradation through pollution of coastal waters by sewerage discharge, beach sand erosion, and destruction of coral reefs, is a cause for concern among environmental groups. As the scale of tourism development is both greater and more rapid than initially planned by the Cuban government, the environmental carrying capacity of the coastal regions has been exceeded (Hall, 1992). However, it is considered that social impacts are a far more crucial issue.

Social impacts in Cuba are similar to those experienced in other Latin American countries but are accentuated within the cultural context of the island. The drive to earn much-needed foreign exchange leads to the social exclusion of the resident population from dollar-based visitor enclaves, distorts the local wage structure and encourages an informal economy. The dual economy in Cuba of the US dollar (for the visitor) and the Cuban peso (for the resident), and the formal rationing of food and other essential products such as oil, tend to accentuate the divide. The hotel sector, therefore, is usually the province of the visitor only, as hotels tend to sell rooms *en bloc* to overseas tour operators. Domestic tourism is reliant on organized tours provided by the state and using poorer quality accommodation for residents only. The remainder of the market is VFR (visiting friends and relatives) and this is estimated to be very small scale in a country where per capita income is so low.

There are other negative aspects, primarily prostitution, particularly in La Habana, but also evident at coastal resorts. Sex tourism has always been a feature of Latin American tourism but nowhere is it more prevalent than in Cuba (Seaton, 1997, p. 316; Mawer, 1999).

There are other social impacts, which have been assessed in different tourism economies. For example, Reynoso y Valle and de Regt (1979) found in their study of the Ixtapa-Zihuatanejo region that tourism was directly responsible for the increased numbers of women in employment. Similarly, Chant cites the Mexican coastal resort of Puerto Vallarta as an example of a destination that has seen profound social changes in this respect, and claims that one of the social consequences is an increase in the number of households headed by women (1992, p. 97). She explains the changing aspects of gender, and the positive effect that tourism in Mexico has had on increasing the level of females employed in the labour force:

> The entry of women into paid jobs in Mexico is significant because traditionally women have represented a fairly low proportion of both the rural and urban labour force ... Reasons for historically low rates of female employment in Mexican cities range from discrimination by employers to restrictions operating from within the home (especially in the case of married women, who generally have exclusive responsibility for childcare and domestic labour, and whose husbands have often resisted the idea that their wives should work).
>
> (Chant, 1992, p. 96)

The other two aspects referred to by Fox (1977) are 'creative expressions' (arts and crafts, etc.) and 'traditional ceremonies' (celebrations, festivals, etc.). As both of these form the basis of many (anthropological) tourism offerings, it is not surprising that they have been greatly affected by tourism. The issue is really one of authenticity, or what MacCannell (1973 and 1984) has described as 'staged authenticity', and the extent to which a 'traditional' ceremony remains traditional. As Getz observes:

> When festivals and other special events are consciously developed and promoted as tourist attractions, there is the risk that commercialization will detract from the celebration; that entertainment or spectacle will

replace the inherent meanings of the celebrations. In other words, tourism might destroy cultural authenticity, the very thing contemporary travellers appear to be seeking.

(1994, p. 313)

To what extent a ceremony or festival remains unaffected by tourism is open to debate, although it might well be argued that the presence of tourists will engender a degree of self-consciousness that can only detract from the original focus of the ceremony or activity.

In terms of artisan industries, a study carried out by Henrici (1999) in Pisac, Peru, revealed that many local craftsmen were adapting their jewellery, pottery, etc. for the tourist market. Not only has the tourist trade influenced the artisan offerings of the region, but in some instances it has also had an effect on the lifestyle activities of the locals. Henrici claims that the poorer farmers

> would descend from the hillsides as they have for centuries on Sunday market days and feast days. However, now this effort occurs not only for the long-established objectives of selling produce, attending mass and taking care of political business but also in order to lure tourists.

(1999, p. 169)

A study by Van de Berghe (1994) in Chiapas, Mexico, advocates tourism development including ethnic commodities and folkloric productions but states that this must be controlled and involve the pro-active participation of local people, primarily the peasant sector. The conclusions tend to verify the conclusion of an earlier study of self-managed indigenous craft production based on case studies in Colombia and Ecuador:

> When communities have retained a significant land base, have experience in local and regional marketing and maintain institutions of social reproduction, they can engage in reproduction for the world market. This can result in locally controlled capital and cultural self-defence. What is important for scholars and planners alike is to note that these unique conditions cannot be imposed, they can only be inherited.

(Stephen, 1991, p. 125)

By contrast, it is argued that some communities might remain ostensibly 'fossilized' for the benefit of tourists; this is particularly the case with a number of Amazonian Indian communities of Peru and Brazil. Somewhat incongrously, tourists (travelling in motor vehicles along paved roads or in motorized boats) often gain an expectation that the Amazon Forest and indigenous communities are unaffected by the outside world, and they want to see the 'traditional' way of life of the villages, as if little had changed in the past 5000 years. For instance, a Titan Tours brochure of 1999 describes an 'authentic' encounter with *Yagua* Indians in the manner indicated in Box 9.B.

Box 9.B. The Yagua Indians, Peru

Day 10: An enchanting days excursion with lunch included as we journey by boat to the local community of Yagua Indians. Here you will see a blowpipe demonstration and have the opportunity to trade with them for some of their local crafts.

(Titan Travel Ltd, 1999)

The issue is to what extent the 'traditional' Indian community remains a developmental 'time warp' in order to seek economic gain by whetting the appetites of the tourist market. Ironically, the tribes may also have been forced to change some traditional practices, in order to present a traditionally authentic experience for tourists: whilst the production of 'crafts' may well be an authentically traditional pursuit, it is likely that the level of demand now far exceeds that which traditionally fulfilled the everyday needs of the community. In other words, production schedules, and probably the type of artifacts themselves, may have been changed to present the visitor with the appearance of a way of life that has remained 'unchanged' by outside influences.

What is becoming increasingly clear from the literature is that there is diversity across communities and households in terms of economic activities such as fishing, extraction of timber and tourism (Barham and Coomes, 1997, p. 184). In some instances, tourism appears to be becoming more important. In the case of the more isolated indigenous communities, the threat comes mainly from governments and primary industries (mining, tree-felling, forest clearance, etc.), which seek to exploit the wealth of natural resources from their lands. For example, the 70,000 *Aquarama* and *Huambisa* peoples living in Condorcanqui on the Peruvian-Ecuadorian border are concerned that roads and other development projects will seriously affect their way of life. Other authors chronicle numerous accounts of the subjugation of indigenous communities in relation to the development of local economies throughout Latin America (Polanco, 1997; del Pilar Uribe Marin, 1999; Reichel-Dolmatoff, 1999).

Another issue is to what extent the ceremonies would 'develop' or 'change' regardless of the level of tourist interest. In the Mexican *Día de los Muertos*

(Day of the Dead) ceremony, which takes place on the night of 1/2 November, gifts (including skulls made out of sugar) are taken to graveyards and people spend the night in vigil over the graves of their ancestors. Conversations with older members of the community revealed that they felt the ceremony had changed over the years; it has generally become more commercialized, as local traders have sought to satisfy the specific demands generated by the occasion. The small provincial town in which it was held was virtually unaffected by tourism, yet there existed a degree of what might be termed 'natural' change, suggesting that tourism cannot be held solely responsible for changes in local customs (Swift, 1976).

Summary

Socio-cultural change and dilution/adaptation is a likely consequence of increased tourism contact; the real debate should, therefore, be centred around the *extent* to which such change should be allowed or encouraged, and for what reason. To perform ritualistic ceremonies out of context, for the sole gratification of tourists and the financial benefit of the performers, can be criticized as being both hypocritical and exploitative; on the other hand, it could also be argued that it gives the tourist a sense of priviliged voyeurism, and brings revenue into a community which has few other economic opportunities on which to support cultural affiliations.

The debate is complex, but as has already been indicated, many socio-cultural customs and traditions are under threat, regardless of whether or not they are promoted as tourist spectacles. Ethnographic studies of indigenous communities, for example, bear witness to the continued assault on the cultural identity of different peoples through economic exploitation over the centuries (Gray, 1997). Thus, it is difficult to evaluate the extent to which, in any given circumstance, socio-cultural changes in the way of life of local communities are reflective of wider economic and socio-political influences, or whether tourism has had a significant catalytic effect on their development.

THE NATURAL ENVIRONMENT

Introduction

The natural environment is also at risk as a consequence of tourism, particularly with the growth in eco-tourism and adventure tourism. As has been explained in previous chapters, it is predominately the natural or physical

---

Box 9.C. 'Journey to the Ecuadorian Amazon'

a short walk soon reveals a huge variety of flora and fauna; a monkey just bigger than a mouse, flocks of blue and yellow macaws, a liana as thick as a man's waist, giant electric-blue morph butterflies, a dry leaf that suddenly sprouts legs and starts walking.

The Lodge owns 3,500 acres of rainforest covering a variety of different habitats, mostly in primary jungle, ranging from terra firma to swamps to rivers and lakes. Although most tours are on foot, some can be combined with river trips in a dugout canoe. The forest canopy has also been made accessible by the construction of an observation tower that climbs 135 ft into the epiphyte-laden branches of a kapok tree. The jungle stretches to the horizon in all directions.

(Voyages Jules Verne, 1999)

---

environment that gives Latin America its strongest market offering. Typical of the flora/fauna mix offered by tour operators is the package put together by 'Voyages Jules Verne', in the Ecuadorian Amazon (see Box 9.C). To what extent does the increased expectation and visitation of such sites conflict with the need to conserve the significant, yet delicate, bio-diversity in such sites?

Tourism Impacts

There is another consideration: tourism cannot be evaluated in isolation – for example, centuries before the Amazon forest became a tourist destination, it was being systematically destroyed by commercial interests, from sugar plantations in the sixteenth century to coffee plantations in the eighteenth (Hecht, 1989). The nineteenth century saw the beginning of the rubber boom, and millions of areas of virgin jungle were given over to the cultivation of rubber trees (Coomes, 1995). For example, Henry Ford had some 2.5 million acres of land turned over to rubber. These brought both the environmental devastation to vast tracts of the forest and the exploitation of indigenous communities such as the Amerindians (Stanfield, 1998).

The early twentieth century saw a concentration on agricultural produce, such as cacao, rice and various spices – the most important of which was black pepper. By the mid-1900s, the raising of Brahma cattle began to assume great importance. At the time, it appeared that everybody was pressing for the economic development of the Amazon: in 1966, the Brazilian Congress passed a law exempting investors in Amazonian development from income tax in proportion to their investment and a year later Manaus was declared a Free Port, thus heralding the beginning of significant commercial development in the Brazilian Amazon.

The dangers of such developments were only just beginning to be appreciated by the 1970s, but even then, it was blithely assumed that any problems created by human interference in the environment could be just as easily solved through human ingenuity:

> Where the Amazon supports the largest tropical rainforest in the world – including also the areas it covers in the countries contiguous to Brazil, the forest is roughly the size of continental United States – it becomes unproductive when the covering of trees is removed. The tremendous run-off of water together with exposure to the sun leaches the soil of its nutritive minerals. Through diligent work with fertilizers the Japanese are restoring much of the lost nutrition to the soil where they farm.
>
> (Ellett, 1972, p. 24)

Box 9.D. Deforestation in Latin America (1990–5)

Country	Average annual deforestation (%) % of land loss
Costa Rica	3.1
Paraguay	2.6
Nicaragua	2.5
Honduras	2.3
Panama	2.2
Guatemala	2.0
Ecuador	1.6
Bolivia	1.2
Venezuela	1.1
Mexico	0.9
Brazil	0.5
Colombia	0.5
Argentina	0.3
Peru	0.3
Argentina	3.0

(United Nations Development Programme, 1998)

However, the process of deforestation is still significant in Latin America, as is illustrated in Box 9.D. In Brazil, the degree of urbanization, especially in Manaus and Belém, has encroached on pristine tropical forest (Godfrey, 1991). As Redclift and Goodman point out, most nations in Latin America have suffered from the impact of commercial concerns on the environment for many years, if not centuries (1991, p. 11). It was in response to issues such as this, and a growing awareness of the ecological importance of the rainforest, that the first measures for preservation were taken, usually in the form of the development of National Parks, in which economic exploitation was severely limited or prohibited. In Costa Rica, for example, the Tortuguero National Park was created in 1975, according to Place:

> primarily to protect the last remaining major green turtle nesting beach in the western Caribbean. About 20,000 hectares of lowland tropical forests adjacent to the 30 km beach were also included within the park, protecting them from destruction by the rapidly moving frontier of colonisation on Costa Rica's Caribbean coastal plain.
>
> (1998, p. 110)

In Argentina the development of the Biosphere Reserves, in conjunction with the worldwide UNESCO programme, began in 1980. These reserves each have three distinct zones: a nucleus where no activity is permitted that will damage or degrade the flora or fauna, a secondary zone encompassing those areas where strictly controlled development can take place, and finally a transition zone, where any development is subjected to less rigorous controls. To date, there are seven such areas throughout the country (see Table 9.1).

Whilst in general terms the creation of National Parks, or similar protected zones, generally required government and non governmental organization influence and initiative, it has become increasingly more apparent that unless large amounts are spent on their continued protection and maintenance, there will be continual degradation in the long term. The scientific market they attracted at first could contribute relatively little in the way of finances, so other means of paying for them had to be found. Tourism was proposed as a partial

Table 9.1. Biosphere Reserves in Argentina, 1997

Reserve	Date created	Location	Size (hectares)
San Guillermo	1980	Iglesia, San Juan	850,000
Laguna Blanca	1982	Belén, Catamarca	929,270
Parque Costero del Sur	1984	Magdalena y Punta Indio, Buenos Aires	30,000
Nancuñán	1986	Santa Rosa, Mendoza	11,900
Laguna de Pozuelos	1990	Santa Catalina, Yavi y Rinconada, Jujuy	380,000
Yabotí	1995	Guaraní y San Pedro, Misiones	253,773
Parque Atlántico Mar Chiquito	1996	Mar Chiquita, Buenos Aires	26,488

Source: Navarra (1997)

Box 9.E. National Parks and conservation

South and Central America contain some of the world's largest and most pristine areas of protected natural habitats in National Parks. The income from sensible tourism on a limited scale contributes towards creating a sustainable economic benefit for local communities, this in turn helps preserve these areas of great natural history, safeguarding them from exploitation and destruction. Our lodges are specially chosen to achieve these objectives and we support the work of Conservation International in the Bolivian rainforest.

(Veloso Tours, 1999)

---

solution, as revenues could be ploughed back into the conservation areas. The introduction to the Veloso Tours brochure explains the situation (see Box 9.E). Whilst it could be argued that a certain level of tourist activity is necessary for long-term sustainability, the problem is one of capacity thresholds and demand management: the numbers of tourists and the effect they have on the environment through which they pass. In terms of sustainable development, the term used in the Veloso brochure – 'sensible' tourism – is the key: but what is sensible in terms of carrying capacity? Tourists need the infrastructure to support them (hotels, electricity, running water, etc.), the people to run the hotels and the means by which the hotel can accessed on a daily basis (roads). In their analysis of eco-tourism lodges in the Brazilian State of Amazonas, Wallace and Pierce commented that the living conditions of the lodge employees were generally better than those of the local population, but they were concerned that more infrastructural developments were needed for the area (1996, p. 854).

All of these considerations are potentially damaging to the environment if not managed properly. As Schlüter points out, it is not enough simply to protect certain species: 'It is also necessary to take other general measures to protect the environment. Such measures should include some less romantic factors as sewage treatment and noise and air pollution control' (1994, p. 259).

In 1980 the OECD (Organization of Economic Cooperation and Development) published a list of seven negative effects of tourism on the environment; these criteria will be used as indicators of the extent to which the environment has suffered as a consequence of tourism. Of the seven, the following three are, unfortunately, becoming more common throughout Latin America:

Effects of Pollution (air, water, noise, litter)

Cater comments that 'Apart from problems of erosion, environmental pollution is a frequent problem. Excessive dumping of garbage is not only unsightly but ecologically damaging, and tends to be concentrated around sites of maximum usage' (1988, p. 57). Pollution is a major concern throughout the whole of Latin

America. Reference has already been made to the destructive effects of litter in Acapulco in Mexico (Chapter 8). The study by Wallace and Pierce referred to earlier found the use of disposable drinking cups and utensils at one site in the Amazonas, and in addition, they claimed that sewage was either dumped into landfill sites with 'very basic septic systems', or perhaps worse still, dumped into rivers (1996, p. 855). In 1997, at the beautiful artificial tourist lake of 'Cabra Corral', near Salta, in the North West of Argentina, litter had become such a problem that rubbish tipped into the reservoir had begun to clog the dam outlets (*El Tribunal*, 1997). Another site to suffer from poor management is Machu Picchu, where, according to Hide (1999): 'All the rubbish collected at Machu Picchu is dumped in the river below as soon as the day-trippers leave'.

Destruction of Flora and Fauna

In addition to the problems caused by litter, Machu Picchu has suffered from a growing denudation of the local vegetation: 'Indian porters are forced to collect firewood to cook and keep warm because cut-rate tour operators refuse to provide shelter or cooking fuel. As the vegetation disappears, so do rare birds, orchids and the endangered Andean spectacled bear' (Hide, 1999).

Effects of Congestion (including overcrowding)

In his study of Costa Rica, Brüggemann comments on the problems of overcrowding in the Monteverde Reserve:

> where occasional visits by nature-interested tourists rapidly turned into a crush. The reserve protects a cloud forest which is the habitat of the colourful Quetzal bird. Annual visits to the reserve jumped from 3,100 in 1980 to 26,000 in 1990 and more than 30,000 during the first half of 1991.
>
> (1995, pp. 260–1)

Other problems include the loss of natural landscape, including agricultural and pastoral lands, through commercially based tourism activity, such as the construction of lodges, hotels, access roads, etc. Even tourist trails, along which regions are accessed by foot only, can be detrimental to the environment and disturb the wildlife (Cater, 1988, p. 57).

Conclusion

Accepting the need to limit demand for tourism in ecologically sensitive areas is an important first step; the second step has been how to restrict these numbers so as not to exceed carrying capacity limits. Cater points out that, whilst tourism enclaves may be useful in concentrating development into certain defined areas, in terms of 'prime ecotourism sites, however, concentrated visitation may well result in an unacceptable level of degradation' (1994, p. 76). The key is through appropriate management, either by restricting numbers on a quota basis (as is done in some of the parks in Costa Rica), by only issuing tour companies with a certain number of licences per year (as in the Galapagos Islands), or by pricing some tourists out of the area. Either option is divisive.

SUMMARY

Unless governments and the private sector combine to halt the deterioration, the point will soon be reached at which the wealth of natural beauty, cultural diversity and differences in Latin America is no longer sufficiently unique, different or unspoiled to attract long haul tourists. Greed, ignorance and indifference, on the part of national governments and both national and foreign tour operators/travel agents, will indeed have 'killed the goose that laid the golden egg'.

A survey of National Tourism Planning documents undertaken by the authors in 1999 revealed that, despite what most governments may say about sustainability, the major focus of their projected strategies is on financial and promotional issues, with sustainability being afforded a lower priority.

On a more optimistic note, however, there are some measures that are already being taken to halt the environmental degradation. Guatemala, for example, has produced a policy document entitled 'Sustainable Tourism Development Up To The Year 2005', in which it outlined seven objectives that would ensure the sustainable development of tourism within Guatemala (see Box 9.F). Other

---

Box 9.F. Sustainable Tourism Development in Guatemala

- To increase and diversify the tourism offering.
- To increase and refocus investment, as much towards infrastructure developments, as to the tourism sector.
- To strengthen promotion and marketing operations.
- To make destination communities more aware of both the work involved and the potential benefits to be had, from a more sustained involvement in tourism.
- To aim for an increase in quality in terms of services, and to increase the numbers employed in this sector.
- To force the preservation of cultures and ecosystems.
- To increase cooperation for regional development projects.

(INGUAT, 1995, p. 3)

---

authorities mention sustainability in their overall strategies, but appear to have done little in practice; there is a major gap between policy frameworks and implementation.

It has been argued that the private sector is, in reality, responsible for self-regulation and the education of its customers. For example, there are some companies that approach the problem in an enlightened and informed manner: in the UK, 'Dragoman' (eco-adventure overland holidays) produce an 'Environmental Guidelines' booklet, which refers to minimizing cultural conflict through respecting local customs, helping local economies, the environmentally friendly disposal of waste and protecting local flora and fauna. The leaflet also informs customers of the activities of organizations such as 'Survival International' ('a worldwide movement to support tribal peoples'), CERT (the 'Centre for Environmentally Responsible Tourism'), and Green Globe, 'a worldwide environmental management programme for travel and tourism companies and tourist destinations' (Dragoman, 1999).

There are also long-standing groups of destination-based tour operators which practise sustainable tourism: 'Horizontes' is an example of a Costa Rican operator that also takes the issue of conservation seriously. In addition to their commercial business, the company is very much involved in educational programmes for youth groups and universities, attending bio-diversity conferences and hosting other sustainability initiatives (Horizontes, 1995). Nevertheless, there is concern that such companies represent a minority and that the majority of operators appear willing to compromise such principles for short-term gain.

REFERENCES

Ap, J. and Crompton, J. L. (1998) 'Developing and Testing a Tourism Impact Scale', *Journal of Travel Research*, Vol. 37(2), pp. 120–30.

Barham, B. L. and Coomes, O. T. (1997) 'Rain Forest Extraction and Conservation in Amazonia', *The Geographical Journal*, Vol. 163(2), pp. 180–8.

Belk, R. W. (1993) 'Third World Tourism: Panacea or Poison? The Case of Nepal', *Journal of International Consumer Marketing*, Vol. 5(1), pp. 27–68.

Brüggemann, J. (1995) 'In Search of the Green Paradise: Tourism and Conservation in Costa Rica' in N. Häusler, C. Kemp, P. Müller-Rockstroh, W. Scholz and B. E. Schulz (eds), *Retracing the Track of Tourism: Studies on Travels, Tourists and Development* (pp. 253–76), Verlag für Entwicklungspolitik Breitenbach GmbH, Saarbrücken.

Carlevari, I. (1993) *La Argentina 1993: Estructura Económica (10 a. Edición)*, Ediciones Macchi, Buenos Aires.

Cater, E. (1988) 'The Development of Tourism in the Least Developed Countries' in B.

Goodall and G. Ashworth (eds), *Marketing in the Tourism Industry: The Promotion of Destination Regions* (pp. 39–66), Croom Helm, Beckenham.

Cater, E. (1994) 'Ecotourism in the Third World: Problems and Prospects for Sustainability' in E. Cater and G. Lowman (eds), *Ecotourism: A Sustainable Option?* (pp. 69–86), John Wiley, Chichester.

Chant, S. (1992) 'Tourism in Latin America: Perspectives from Mexico and Costa Rica' in D. Harrison (ed.), *Tourism and the Less Developed Countries* (pp. 85–101), Belhaven Press, London.

Coomes, O. T. (1995) 'A Century of Rain Forest Use in Western Amazonia: Lessons for Extraction-Based Conservation of Tropical Forest Resources', *Forest Conservation History*, Vol. 39(1), pp. 108–20.

de Holan, P. and Phillips, N. (1997) 'Sun, Sand and Hard Currency: Tourism in Cuba', *Annals of Tourism Research*, Vol. 24(4), pp. 777–95.

del Pilar Uribe Marin, M. (1999) 'Where Development Will Lead to Mass Suicide', *The Ecologist*, Vol. 29(1), pp. 42–6.

Dragoman (1999) *Environmental Guidelines For Overland Travellers*, Dragoman Overseas Travel Ltd, Stowmarket.

The Economist (1989) 'Third World Tourism: Visitors are Good for You', *The Economist*, Vol. 310(7593), 11 March.

El Tribunal (1997) 'Cabra Corral, Tierra de Nadie?', *El Tribunal (Salta)* (23 March).

Ellett, W. H. (1972) 'Pioneering the Amazon', *Américas*, Vol. 24(10), pp. 20–4.

EMBRATUR (1995) *Política Nacional de Turismo, 1996–1999: Principais Diretizes, Estratégias e Programas*, Instituto Brasileiro de Turismo-EMBRATUR, Ministério da Indústria, do Comércio e do Turismo, Brasília.

Fidler, S. (1995) 'Ambitions Lie Upmarket', *Financial Times Survey: Cuba* (26 September).

Fletcher, J. E. and Archer, B. H. (1991) 'The Development and Application of Multiplier Analysis' in C. P. Cooper (ed.), *Progress in Tourism, Recreation and Hospitality Management (Vol. 3)* (pp. 28–47), Belhaven Press, London.

Fox, M. (1977) 'The Social Impact of Tourism: A Challenge to Researchers and Planners' in B. Finney and B. Watson (eds), *A New Kind of Sugar: Tourism in the Pacific* (pp. 27–48), Santa Cruz Centre for South Pacific Studies, University of California, Santa Cruz.

Gee, C. Y., Makens, J. C. and Choy, D. J. L. (1989) *The Travel Industry*, 2nd edition, Van Nostrand Reinhold, New York.

Getz, D. (1994) 'Event Tourism and the Authenticity Dilemma' in W. Theobald (ed.) *Global Tourism: The Next Decade* (pp. 313–29), Butterworth-Heinemann, Oxford.

Godfrey, B. V. (1991) 'Modernizing the Brazilian City', *Geographical Review*, Vol. 18, pp. 18–35.

Gormsen, E. (1988) 'Tourism in Latin America: Spatial Distribution and Impact on Regional Change', *Applied Geographical Development*, Vol. 32, pp. 65–80.

Gray, A. (1997) *The Last Shaman: Change in an Amazonian Community*, Berghahn Books, Oxford.

Green, H. and Hunter, C. (1992) 'The Environmental Impact Assessment of Tourism Development' in P. Johanson and B. Thomas (eds), *Perspectives on Tourism Policy* (pp. 29–47), Mansell, London.

Hall, D. R. (1992) 'Tourism Development in Cuba' in D. Harrison (ed.), *Tourism and the Less Developed Countries* (pp. 102–20), Belhaven Press, London.

Hallén, L. and Wiedersheim-Paul, F. (1984) 'The Evolution of Psychic Distance in International Business Relationships' in I. Hagg and F. Wiedersheim-Paul (eds), *Between Market and Hierarchy* (pp. 15–27), University of Uppsala, Department of Business Administration, Uppsala.

Hecht, S. B. (1989) *The Fate of The Forest: Developers, Destroyers, and Defenders of the Amazon*, Verso, New York.

Henrici, J. (1999) 'Trading Culture: Tourism and Tourist Art in Pisac, Peru' in M. Robinson and P. Boniface (eds), *Tourism and Cultural Conflicts* (pp. 161–80), CAB International, Oxford.

Herskovits, M. J. (1952) *Man and His Works*, Alfred A. Knopf, New York.

Hide, S. (1999) 'Inca City "In Danger"', *Daily Telegraph* (13 March).

Hofstede, G. (1984) *Culture's Consequences*, Sage Publications, Newbury Park, Ca.

Holder, J. S. (1988) 'Pattern and Impact of Tourism on the Environment', *Tourism Management*, Vol. 9(2), pp. 119–27.

Holloway, J. C. (1988) *The Business of Tourism*, 2nd edition, Pitman Publishing, London.

Horizontes (1995) *Costa Rica*, Agencia de Viajes Horizontes de Costa Rica S.A., San José.

INGUAT (1995) *Guatemala: Desarrollo Turistico Sustenable Hacía El Año 2005*, Instituto Guatemalteco de Turismo (INGUAT), Guatemala, C.A.

Lea, J. (1988) *Tourism and Development in the Third World*, Routledge, London.

MacCannell, D. (1973) 'Staged Authenticity: Arrangements of Social Space in Tourist Settings', *American Journal of Sociology*, Vol. 79, pp. 589–603.

MacCannell, D. (1984) 'Reconstructed Ethnicity: Tourism and Cultural Identity in Third World Communities', *Annals of Tourism Research*, Vol. 11(3), pp. 375–91.

Marx, E. (1999) *Breaking Through Culture Shock: What You Need to Succeed in International Business*, Nicholas Brearley, London.

Mawer, F. (1999) 'Cuba', *Daily Telegraph* (19 June).

Middleton, V. T. C. (1998) *Sustainable Tourism: A Marketing Perspective*, Butterworth-Heinemann, Oxford.

Morris, A. (1987) *South America*, 3rd edition, Hodder and Stoughton, London.

Navarra, G. (1997) 'El Patrimonio Natural y Cultural del País, Bajo la Lupa de la UBA', *La Nación* (29 March).

Nettekoven, L. (1984) 'Mechanisms of Intercultural Interaction' in E. de Kadt (ed.), *Tourism: Passport to Development? Perspectives on the Social and Cultural Effects of Tourism on Developing Countries* (pp. 135–45), Oxford University Press, New York.

Oppermann, M. (1992) 'Intranational Tourism Flows in Malaysia', *Annals of Tourism Research*, Vol. 19, pp. 482–500.

Place, S. E. (1991) 'Nature Tourism and Rural Development in Tortuguero', *Annals of Tourism Research*, Vol. 16(2), pp. 186–201.

Place, S. E. (1998) 'How Sustainable is Ecotourism in Costa Rica?' in C. M. Hall and A. A. Lew (eds), *Sustainable Tourism: A Geographical Perspective* (pp. 107–18), Addison Wesley Longman, Harlow.

Polanco, H. D. (1997) *Indigenous Peoples in Latin America: The Quest For Self-Determination*, Western Press, Boulder, Colo.

Rabahy, W. A. and Ruschmann, D. (1991) 'Tourism and the Brazilian Economy' in C. P. Cooper (ed.), *Progress in Tourism, Recreation and Hospitality Management (Vol. 3)* (pp. 140–53), Belhaven Press, London.

Redclift, M. and Goodman, D. (1991) 'Introduction' in D. Goodman and M. Redclift (eds), *Environment and Development in Latin America* (pp. 1–23), Manchester University Press, Manchester.

Reichel-Dolmatoff, G. (1999) 'A View from the Headquarters', *The Ecologist*, Vol. 29(4), pp. 276–80.

Reynoso y Valle, A. and de Regt, J. P. (1979) 'Growing Pains: Planned Tourism Development in Ixtapa-Zihuatanejo' in E. de Kadt (ed.), *Tourism: Passport to Development?* (pp. 111–34), Oxford University Press, Oxford.

Seaton, A. V. (1997) 'Demonstration Effects or Relative Deprivation? The Counter-Revolutionary Pressures of Tourism in Cuba', *Progress in Tourism and Hospitality Research*, Vol. 3(4), pp. 307–20.

Schlüter, R. G. (1994) 'Tourism Development: A Latin American Perspective' in W. Theobald (ed.), *Global Tourism: The Next Decade* (pp. 246–60), Butterworth-Heinemann, Oxford.

Stanfield, M. E. (1998) *Red Rubber, Bleeding Trees: Violence, Slavery and Empire in Northwest Amazonica, 1850–1933*, The University of New Mexico Press, Albuquerque.

Stephen, L. (1991) 'Culture as a Resource: Four Cases of Self-Managed Indigenous Craft Production in Latin America', *Economic Development and Cultural Change*, Vol. 40(1), pp. 101–31.

Swift, J. S. (1976) Unpublished study: Xalapa, Veracruz, Mexico.

Swift, J. S. (1999) 'Cultural Closeness as a Facet of Cultural Affinity: A Contribution to the Theory of Psychic Distance', *International Marketing Review*, Vol. 16(2/3), pp. 182–201.

Titan Travel Ltd (1999) *Titan HiTours: Quality Escorted Tours Worldwide*, Titan Travel Ltd, Redhill.

Van de Berghe, P. L. (1994) *The Quest for the Other: Ethnic Tourism in San Cristobal, Mexico*, University of Washington Press, Seattle.

Vandepitte, M. (1996) 'A Sudden Entrance into the World System. The Case of Cuba', paper presented to the 8th General Conference of EADI (European Association of Development Research and Training Institutes): *Globalisation, Competitiveness and Human Security: Challenges for Development Policy and Institutional Change*, Vienna, 11–14 September.

Veloso Tours (1999) *Veloso Tours: Life in Latin America*, Veloso Tours Ltd, London.

Voyages Jules Verne (1999) *Latin America: A Selection of Journeys in Central & South America Including Expedition Cruising to the Arctic & Antarctic, May 1999–October 2000*, Voyages Jules Verne, London.

Wallace, G. N. and Pierce, S. M. (1996) 'An Evaluation of Ecotourism in Amazonas, Brazil', *Annals of Tourism Research*, Vol. 23(4), pp. 843–73.

CHAPTER 10

The Future of Tourism in Latin America

INTRODUCTION

Lumsdon and Swift (1994) have argued that tourism development in Latin America is likely to be minimal during the early part of the twenty-first century. They considered that the processes of transition, both economic and political, would continue at a slow pace, and hence the barriers to development in the past would continue to retard tourism growth in the next decade. However, the pace of change during the past five years is driving tourism development much faster than previously anticipated. The reasons are explained partly by the international tourism market, and partly by transnational tourism operators seeking new global opportunities.

There are signs, however, that the sustained worldwide growth witnessed in the last three decades will not be continued at a similar rate in the future. The tourism sector has in many respects matured and therefore the expansion rate could well be set to slow; this is reflected in recent tourism data. Nevertheless, the level of international visitor arrivals is expected to double between 1990 and 2010. Table 10.1 illustrates the global and regional trends.

Table 10.1. Forecasts: International visitor arrivals

Region	Visitor arrivals (millions)		Average % growth p.a.
	Arrivals (1996)	Forecast (2020)	
The Americas	116.10	285.00	3.8
Mexico	21.40	49.00	3.6
Central America	2.65	7.00	4.2
South America	14.00	43.00	4.7
The World	594.80	1,600.00	4.3

Source: adapted from Bar On (1998)

These prognostications are verified by a number of other forecasts, for example, by the World Travel and Tourism Council and those produced by the major manufacturers of aeroplanes. They range from an annual growth rate of between 3.8 and 5.7 per cent (World Travel and Tourism Council, 1996). However, the growth is not uniform across all tourism regions. There are distinct regional patterns. While the average growth rate per annum between the year 2000 and the year 2010 is expected to be 3.55 per cent, this is expected to be far higher in Latin America (Bar On, 1998, pp. 85–9). How might these figures be explained and what are the driving forces underpinning the changes to tourism in Latin America?

CHANGES IN THE MARKETING ENVIRONMENT

The rapid growth of tourism throughout the past 50 years is well documented (Cooper *et al.*, 1998). The degree to which the pace of change, the diffusion of the holiday-taking by the population of generating countries, and how shifting patterns of consumer motivation have shaped patterns of tourism in the early years of the twenty-first century is also well researched (Ryan, 1991). The rapid growth has been fuelled by a number of interrelated factors, as summarized by Baum (1995):

- Economic prosperity in the developed world as well as the rapidly developing countries of Asia.
- Lifestyle and work-related changes, giving greater free time for travel and leisure.
- Technological change (especially in aviation and communications).
- Changes in the demographic structure of most affluent societies, especially improved health among those retired.
- Reduced international tensions and the elimination of much of the bureaucracy of travel to and from many countries.
- A growing awareness of and interest in other cultures and ways of living, a sense of belonging to 'one world'.

While the trends reported by Baum are of a general nature, there is a growing consensus in the literature about their importance, although several specific matters have been questioned, for example, the degree of leisure time available in developed markets such as the USA (Schor, 1991). Secondly, the Asian economic crisis of the 1990s has slowed tourism growth, but this could well be a temporary phenomenon and these economies may now begin to revive.

Lumsdon (1997) refers to the major structural shifts in the mature markets of northern Europe and North America, and feels that in many respects these will have several consequences for developing markets such as Latin America. The key characteristics of the marketing environment are set out below.

Environment

- Fragmentation of the market: for example, in the demand for adventure/ nature tourism in Costa Rica.
- Increasingly discerning visitors: seeking authenticity and close proximity to local communities.
- Dissatisfaction with despoiled destinations, such as tropical rainforest reserves, 'worn-out' coastal resorts etc.
- More short break-taking: this is particularly apparent in the Mexican market.
- Travel for pleasure becoming an integral part of life: particularly in urban sectors of the community across Latin America.
- Travel for business becoming a less attractive option than the use of new technology: for example there is an increasing use of video conferencing between the USA and Latin America; there is also rapid growth in electronic mail.
- Rapidly emerging pocket markets in lesser developed countries: Argentina and Chile being prime examples of this.

Supply

- Increased competition: for example, between airlines.
- Growth of new destinations: such as the development of resorts in the North East of Brazil, and eco-adventure destinations.
- Rejuvenation of old destinations: the reconstruction and repositioning of resorts such as Cartagena de las Indias, Colombia.
- Sharpening focus on quality and environment: the all-inclusive resorts of Mexico.
- Winners and losers in use of distribution systems: for example, the changing relationship between tour operators and travel agents in Latin America.

Government

- Developing a role as enabler in the face of continued privatization: such as in the provision of improved transport systems, but increasingly relying on private sector finance.
- Increasing regulation to meet the demands on local communities and pressure groups in favour of conservation: for example, the protection of reserves in the Amazon Basin.

- Renewed interest in regional agreements on tourism development and promotion to fit new trading alliances: such as Mercosur, Pacto Andino and the North American Free Trade Agreement (NAFTA).

TOURISM DEVELOPMENT FACTORS

Introduction

Of all of the global trends affecting the development of markets and the supply of tourism summarized there are two principal factors which are identified by Lumsdon (1997) as being particularly significant in determining the nature and the increasing pace of tourism development in Latin America: (1) globalization and (2) political and economic reform.

Globalization

Globalization refers to the way in which organizations trade or operate within a world context, integrating research, finance, technology and production on a scale hitherto unknown. The process respects neither geographic nor nation state boundaries and has been rapidly diffused in recent decades (Kotler *et al.*, 1996).

Globalization has been one of the key driving forces of international trade, but it is very much conditioned by a change in the framework in which international trade is conducted:

> The most important driver of globalisation, though, is the widespread change in ideology – from state socialism to market capitalism – it has unleashed much internal deregulation and liberalisation from France to the former Soviet Union. The embrace of openness that took hold during the late 1980s and early 1990s trailed a half century of growth and global peace.
>
> (Rangan, 1999)

It has been argued that the process of globalization will continue to change the economic structure of business sectors throughout the world (Tse and West, 1992). At least one study concluded that the technological speed and diffusion of communications suggests a new stage of trade dominance, referred to as 'transperialism' (Bray and Bray, 1998); others refer to an 'epochal shift' (Waters, 1995; Robinson, 1998, p. 468). It will eventually erode, so it is claimed, the differential between developed economies and the emergent economies of Latin America. This point is often made in connection with the successes of East Asia in the last decade, and it is suggested that the lessons learnt from countries such as Korea and Taiwan could be repeated elsewhere (Wolf, 1999). In terms of manufacturing and technology, where labour costs are lower, Brazil has been advancing rapidly, and Argentina, Chile and Mexico are becoming increasingly important. Integration into a global economy, it is argued, will bring a more even pattern of development, including throughout Latin America:

> A powerful force drives the world toward a converging commonality, and that force is technology. It has proletarianized communication, transport and travel. IT has made isolated places and impoverished people eager for modernity's allurements. Almost everyone, everywhere wants all things they've heard about, seen, or experienced via the new technologies.
>
> (Levitt, 1983, p. 92)

However, Mowforth and Munt are more critical in terms of the winners and losers in the process: globalization represents the ascendancy of Western, capitalist forms of modernization which is both complex and uneven (1998, p. 21). Bray reinforces the point when discussing free trade as an instrument of dominance:

> the current international economic climate, the neoliberal model, which calls for open economies is the dominant paradigm even in many nations of the Third World. Under the guise of 'free trade', a new structure of domination, the World Trade Organization (WTO), has been created that will make economic policy even less responsive to the interests of the smaller, weaker nations in the international system.
>
> (1999, p. 55)

In many respects world tourism reflects the emerging tri-polarity of the world economy, namely an enlarged and growing Europe, North America (which includes Mexico as the country is a member of the North American Free Trade Agreement and is considered in the World Tourism Organization's statistical analysis as an integral part of North America) and East Asia – in particular Japan. Europe remains the most important tourism economy followed by the Americas. The USA forms the prime market for tourism. In contrast to this, Shaw and Williams point to gains made by semi-peripheral economies (1994, p. 33); in Latin American terms, these are represented by countries such as Costa Rica, Panama and the Dominican Republic.

Nevertheless, investment in tourism development has occurred mainly in the three poles, and transport and communication networks have reinforced the linkages between them. Until recently, investment in Latin American economies by international tourism organizations such as transnational hotel groups and transport operators has been small by comparison. Following the crises of East Asia in the 1990s global suppliers have returned belatedly to look more favourably on Latin America; it is currently a major focus of renewed interest. The extent to which resources are allocated to the development of new infrastructure and the opening of marketing channels are both clear indicators of the market power of transnational companies. During the debt crises of the 1980s, there was little interest in developing the Latin American portfolio; now it is more buoyant, but still represents a significant percentage in terms of overall global investment patterns.

In terms of the level of support afforded by government, tourism is becoming more important, but it is not a major concern for most countries. The traditional approach of supporting industrial sectors far exceeds the commitment to service sector development throughout Latin America. Most governments, in reality, have not invested heavily in tourism. The exceptions are Brazil and Mexico, but elsewhere commitment to tourism development at a governmental level has been somewhat mixed. As a WTO forecast concluded:

> Those countries which invest in infrastructure and tourist facilities ..., manpower education and training, and well-targeted and sufficiently extensive marketing campaigns will fare better than those which do not. It is up to the individual country or tourism operator: those who take proper account of the changes in the patterns of tourism and undertake effective planning and marketing will be the 'winners' in the coming decades.
>
> (WTO, 1994, p. 68)

In summary, the traditional tourism supply sectors of Latin American countries are being overlaid by a pattern of globalization. Large-scale global companies continue to enter the market through investment in accommodation projects, specifically integrated or all-inclusive resorts, or up-market city hotels. Transport operators, particularly airlines, seek to forge alliances in order to open up world markets (Hanlon, 1996, pp. 100–10). Latin American tour operators are increasingly forging stronger ties with the European and North American long haul operators. They seek to raise standards in order to meet the expectations of their world partners and the experienced travellers these companies target. The process of transformation is increasingly one which is characterized with global concerns. In tourism, as in other sectors, this is evidenced by discontinuities and a range of costs and benefits, which affect destinations in different ways.

While these trends are discernible, and the impacts on tourism in Latin America are beginning to take effect, a parallel track featuring intra-regional development continues; this tends to be at a lower scale and in future it is likely to be focused on trading zones. By contrast, it is important to note that currently the majority of tourism providers in Latin America are small scale, and lack investment or aptitude to upgrade their offerings. They are unlikely to yield higher revenues from a world market but they might gain in the short term from intra-regional development. In the long term their prospects are far less promising. Unless they change, many will withdraw from the tourism sector as competition from more progressive Latin American suppliers and acquisitive trans-national companies will squeeze all but local markets.

Political and Economic Reform

The second major factor which is pertinent to the Latin American market is the process of democratization, albeit one which infrequently embraces pluralism and popular participation (Valverde, 1999, p. 401). The structural changes evidenced in many Latin American economies during the last quarter of the twentieth century have been more widespread and sustained than commentators might have previously expected. As noted in Chapter 1, during this period most Latin American countries have transformed from authoritarian military dictatorships to a form of neo-liberal republics. The neo-liberal approach is symbolized by:

- less government control over the economy,
- privatization of key utilities such as the energy and transport sectors,
- the de-regulation of market supply,
- and to a lesser extent, the degree of protectionism.

Within this context, several political systems have allied themselves more closely to the USA model of political-economy, especially Mexico, Argentina, Chile and Costa Rica (Swift and Dueñas, 1995, pp. 24–5). Researchers have referred to this approach to development as the Modernisation Theory (Harrison, 1992, p. 9).

While many factors can be identified which offer an explanation for this transformation in Latin America, the impetus came initially from a series of major debt crises in the 1980s. These related economic crises brought many economies to the point of collapse, a position similar to the severity of the World Depression of the 1930s (Peeler, 1998). Major banks and financiers called in their loans to recover debts and refused any extension of credit. In these circumstances, Latin American governments had no choice but to approach the world's international economic forums, especially the International Monetary Fund and the World Bank. They in turn sought to influence the developing economies in Latin America. More significantly, they used the tools of economic support packages as a way to exact changes in the political as well as economic structure of Latin American countries (Gwynne and Kay, 1999, p. 9).

Despite advances in the extent of the democratization, the level of citizen participation is still limited by the standards of the generating countries of the North. However, the fledgling neo-liberal regimes of the late 1980s have remained intact, despite mounting internal tensions brought about by periodic economic austerity measures (Green, 1991). Only Cuba has maintained a divergent role, adhering to a centralized, communist economy (Alfonso, 1994). Tourism can only thrive in conditions of political stability, and this has been a crucial factor for the development of many Latin American countries during the latter part of the twentieth century. Market perception of personal security and risk are fundamental prerequisites of travel. Despite the decades of negative imagery, confidence is now returning, albeit slowly.

The new regimes, however, exhibit their inability to alleviate poverty, which is acutely visible to the visitor, where, in most cities, there are children working the streets (Morley, 1995; Jones, 1997, p. 39). Regardless of the rhetoric, results have as yet been limited, as governments have not been able to overcome all of the major structural problems (Lloyd-Sherlock, 1997, p. 23). Some have exacerbated economic instability: for example, Peru and Venezuela. Nor have they removed the vast inequalities of wealth and uneven development (Smith *et al.*, 1994; Scott, 1996).

There is an associated argument. Tourism also offers a valuable alternative to the traditional approach of heavy industrialization and import substitition policies. Tourism is a form of development, it is argued, which can disperse wealth throughout local economies, without bringing the major impacts of large-scale industrial plant. The work of O'Hare and Bennett (1999, p. 47) in Peru illustrates that dispersion is not as widespread as has been suggested. Furthermore, given neo-liberal policies, or more precisely an unwillingness to intervene in the market, there is unlikely to be a greater diffusion of tourism spend.

Others are critical of the role ascribed to tourism. They point to the inexorable process of globalization, suggesting that the theory of dependency can aptly be applied in tourism. The world tourism system, they argue, continues to be dominated by the developed generating markets of Europe and North America. Latin America is not central to this axis of market development; the relationship is asymmetrical (Shaw and Williams, 1994, p. 42). This inequality leads to dependency and inequality, a model of development often referred to as Underdevelopment or Dependency Theory (Harrison, 1988). In this context, the developing economies of Latin America are, for the most part, reliant on the North American and/or European markets for any significant growth in tourism.

Furthermore, global tour companies, transport operators and international accommodation consortia control both the level of investment at any given destination and the supply of a high spending visitor market. In addition, the level of economic contribution to local tourism economies often tends to be overstated as much of the visitor spending leaks back into the developed economies rather than remaining in the host countries concerned (Lundberg *et al.*, 1995, p. 139).

There is an additional factor to consider: Latin American tourism investment has undoubtedly gained as a consequence of the weakening of many Far Eastern economies: in the mid-1990s this had led to a partial collapse of tourism development in that region. Had these Far Eastern countries not failed to sustain the level of expected market development, Latin America would have remained a lower priority for external investment and the development of long haul tourism. As Asia regains its economic stamina, Latin America may once more lose favour. This argument remains to be proven. At this stage of tourism development, it is difficult to predict at what point interest will recede, if at all, assuming that political stability remains.

The most important factor in terms of the political economy is that the overall trend towards political reform, and the economic liberal reform witnessed in the past two decades, has not brought about a significant change in the plight of the urban and rural poor throughout Latin American. The converse is true: the standard of living is getting worse for many Latin American citizens. An analysis of World Bank data undertaken by Gwynne and Kay suggests that there has been and continues to be an increased divergence between the economies of the developed world and those of Latin America:

> Already in 1978, the per capita income enjoyed by inhabitants of the center countries of the world economy was virtually 5 times that of the highest income economies and 12 times the lowest income economies in Latin America; however, by 1995 the ratio had increased to virtually 7 and 30, respectively.
>
> (1999, p. 5)

Within this overall context, tourism is not likely to bring about improved conditions for a large majority of the population in Latin America. The move towards more inclusive grassroots participation in relation to the sustainable development of rural economies might gain acceptance in wider policy formation (Schmink and Wood, 1992), but participation in tourism development *per se* is less likely in the wider canvas of economic progress. The trend towards 'enclave' tourism will, for the most part, work against policies to disperse benefits to local tourism economies and it is a trend that is set to continue in the coming decades (Ortiz, 1990).

Other Major Factors

The final decade of the twentieth century brought a number of authoritative reports seeking to analyse and predict the changing nature of the market for tourism, three of which are summarized by McIntosh *et al.* (1995). Ritchie (1991) reports the findings of one of these expert panels, the International Tourism Policy Forum, which identified 19 important forces which tourism decision-makers and suppliers should address. These included the growing recognition of the importance of the physical environment and the limitations of tourism development. The Forum also pointed to a decreasing level of government resources for tourism, the rise of global transnational firms and an overwhelming trend towards market-driven economies and political integration. A third set of forces related to the widening gap between the North and South, including intra-regional conflicts and consumer concerns over health and personal security. Finally, the list included issues such as a lack of government recognition of tourism, the potential growing dissatisfaction with governing systems, and other processes which may lead to a new framework for tourism.

McIntosh *et al.* (1995) codify the main issues raised by these reports into 12 main categories, and discuss the implications of the major findings regarding the changes in tourism being brought about by emerging global forces. They refer to each factor as a *new horizon*, and then suggest *new realities*, or outcomes which might follow. The work provides useful insight into tourism development and the framework is adapted here in relation to a discussion of Latin American tourism. It is likely that Latin America could well be expected to gain from these forces or trends, but not all are applicable or would fit the Latin American scenario of development.

1 *The pivotal position of the environment*
   Most tourism will be constrained by the requirement to adhere to more sophisticated development models, which evaluate or more precisely

quantify environmental dis-benefits, especially in relation to environmentally sensitive sites. In terms of theoretical outcomes, this presents an opportunity for Latin American countries to safeguard and manage the conservation of its rich cultural and natural diversity. The model presented is one of providing higher quality experience for lower numbers of visitors, at a premium price, with potential outcome of lower impacts at specific destinations.

In reality, those countries that have planned visitation, or have inadvertently allowed it in relation to sensitive heritage and natural sites, are under pressure from higher levels of demand than expected. The private sector, albeit with some notable exceptions, has failed to provide self-regulation, and visitor demand invariably exceeds the government resources necessary to protect natural assets. International pressure groups have campaigned for the introduction of more regulatory conservation mechanisms, but their efforts have only been partially successful at certain destinations, mainly in Brazil or Costa Rica. As new markets develop such as cruise liner business, or eco-adventure holidays, the principles of sustainability will continually be compromised to meet demand, as the neo-liberal economic approach adopted by many Latin American governments means that it will be difficult to embrace an effective sustainable strategy, which safeguards encroachment by developers and poor people seeking survival (Macdonald *et al.*, 1997).

Therefore, the issue will continue to remain pivotal in academic discussion and among specialist international scientific organizations or conservation groups. Beyond this arena of discussion it is likely that rhetoric will be more in evidence than real measures to regulate demand. The reverse position is more likely where pressures will continue to increase visitor numbers. Given this scenario, the physical and social carrying capacities of many unique habitats of Latin America will be exceeding or already have exceeded acceptable limits. The situation is likely to worsen in the short term.

2 *The spread of democracy*

It is argued that tourism development processes will become increasingly democratic. A wider public debate and consultation will both slow down tourism and ensure that there are fewer inappropriate developments. Furthermore, a resident input or vision of tourism in local economies will lead to a commitment to a more balanced approach to the level and type of development.

In the Latin American context, the diffusion of this process is likely to be a long-term one. Large-scale tourism projects rarely feature participation by local communities (Mader, 1999). While tourism issues are reported in the media, and potentially at national forums, the political systems of many Latin American countries are not finely tuned to respond to public opinion; the transformation of democratic institutions has at best been marginal. While fundamental issues such as the abuse of human rights, the attrition of the culture of minority groups, and widespread corruption remain, there is little scope for widening democracy to embrace host community feedback in relation to tourism development. In this respect, there has been a resurgence of grassroots groups, but not always enjoying success. Evidence concerning the development of *El Mundo Maya*, for example, indicates that the consultation process failed to absorb the tensions or dissent of host communities in relation to the prospect of economic gain by promoting the route (Gunson, 1996). The marginalization of Mayan communities in Mexico and Guatemala is the subject of considerable discussion.

3 *Demographic shifts*

The ageing populations of generating countries, in relation to the diverse lifestyles of these people and their increased discretionary income and time, is expected to continue to prime the demand for tourism. It is also envisaged that there will be a shift in motivation for different vacation experiences. Standardized offerings will be more difficult to sustain. This is borne out by the proliferation of 'customized' packages offered by many tour operators. Ironically, the increasingly ageing population of Latin America will not enjoy similar benefits; the poorest sectors of society are likely to become the most isolated.

Poon (1993), for example, refers to a new consumer base for tourism. She argues that the degree of fragmentation of markets reflects a fundamental shift of tourism from an old framework of packaged, destination-based holidays signified by mass tourism to a new form of tourism. The latter refers to non-standardized offerings that are tailored to meet the requirements of many smaller micro-markets, each with its own particular wants and desires. Poon argues that the new customer base will become more sophisticated, environmentally conscious, and seek new experiences which enhance the quality of life in comparison to homogenized packages offered to mass tourism markets. Box 10.A shows the promotional literature for the 'Tailor Made Holidays' segment, offered by the UK operator 'Distant Dreams'.

Box 10.A. 'Tailor Made Holidays'

Experience the Choice: A Distant Dreams holiday is all about choice. The freedom to select not just where you travel, but also when and how. There's a virtually limitless range of appealing à la carte options, offering you total flexibility to 'tailor' our brochure holidays to your own style – and to enjoy independent travel at package holiday prices.
1. Choose your airport
2. Choose your airline
3. Choose the day you wish to travel
4. Choose your accommodation
5. Choose your extras
6. Choose your meal plan
7. Choose your duration

(Distant Dreams, 1999)

The prospect for Latin American countries is therefore potentially promising in that it possesses exactly what the new market for tourism desires, a very diverse supply of touristic experiences. However, while Poon is right in diagnosing the bi-polarity of the market for tourism, she may well have under-estimated the continuing momentum of the old tourism or mass market, one in which most Latin American countries are currently investing. The rapid growth of intregrated and inclusive seaside resorts in Latin America supports the view that old tourism still dominates. This is where tourism demand is currently at its strongest, a supposition based on the recent experience of market growth to Cuba, Costa Rica, the Dominican Republic and Mexico. Both intra-regional and long haul 'sun, sea, sand and sex' markets are expected to increase to these countries.

The demand for nature, eco- and cultural tourism is also expected to expand but in comparison to the beach tourism market, the new tourism flow will be far less significant for most countries. However, the accumulative impacts, the nature and sensitivity of sites, are currently a major issue of concern, and the debate regarding the extent to which they can be exploited will become the subject of intense discussion. Furthermore, if new tourism becomes far more important, then much of the investment of the 1990s will be rendered obsolete.

There is an additional point. Wheeller (1991), in discussing the concept of sustainability, is not entirely convinced that this will be how the market will develop. He suggests that new-to-the-market vacationers from emerging countries will be similar to those from developed countries in previous decades, which now form the core of a mature market. The new cohorts will be price conscious, and be given over to escapism and entertainment, rather than being responsible tourists adhering strictly to codes of sustainable tourism.

4 *Shifts to the market economy*

The fourth *new horizon* relates to the funding of tourism infrastructure, and facilities which have traditionally been provided by the public sector, including large-scale mega-projects. There will be shifts towards private sector funding of tourism development as governments will not have sufficient funds to take forward major projects.

The approach to tourism development throughout Latin America fits the market economy model. During the past two decades the restructuring of economies in order to meet the requirements of debt reduction has brought substantive cuts in government expenditure; therefore tourism is very reliant on private sector provision. Regardless of the integration of many Latin American countries into the global economy in terms of investment, flows of capital and technological know-how, tourism is being given due consideration now, and there are limitations to the extent of this investment. The experience of Mexico in the 1990s illustrates that the private sector is only willing to risk capital development if there is planning gain, or government incentive to allay the risk attached to large-scale projects. This is set against the backcloth of the debt crisis, a decade in which the international banks would not extend loans to Latin American countries, especially in tourism. The lack of confidence of the international finance corporations and the concentration of debt for equity swaps advanced under the Brady Plan of 1989 (a plan to reduce international debt of Latin American countries) affected the availability of funds for tourism projects.

The subsequent reduction of debt, trade liberalization measures, and a more market-oriented approach of governments is restoring the confidence of international investors, but not necessarily in terms of investing in tourism projects other than those that are best described as 'enclavic'. This neo-liberal model of tourism development in Latin America in the twenty-first century is likely to be continued in line with other less developed countries, but Cuba's position remains equivocal and development of its socialist economy is dependent on the dictates of President Fidel Castro, and the future foreign policy of the USA (Parker, 1998).

5 *Cultural diversity in a homogeneous world*

The increasing acceptance of world brand leaders by visitors will place pressure on specialist tour operators and providers. Equally, the uniqueness of cultural events and attractions may diminish through the commoditization of tourism offerings. The implication is that cultural diversity will be lost in the face of modernity, a modernity that has a distinct European or North American identity. There is an additional strand to the argument. Some argue that tourism is one of the ways in which cultural attributes can be preserved whilst others dismiss tourism as a potential destroyer of culture (de Kadt, 1979; Smith, 1989).

Latin America has a very strong and diverse cultural offering which is recognized in the literature, as was discussed in Chapter 6. It presents an evolutionary world of identity and modernity which need not necessarily be mutually exclusive (Larraín, 1996). However, critics have pointed to the dilution or loss of identity through the commercialization of cultural events, or the removal of traditional ways of doing things, often described as 'commoditization'. It is important to note, therefore, that the attrition of cultural diversity in Latin America is not entirely attributable to tourism encroachment but is a complex mix of economic and social factors that are constantly changing, especially the internationalization of Latin American economies. This has prompted some authors to describe such tourism development, tailored to the needs of a Northern market, as neocolonization.

6 *The technology–human resource dilemma*

The human resource base of the tourism sector is recognized as the core factor of tourism delivery. Of equal weight are the rapid advances in information technology (IT) and its growing importance in the design and distribution elements of the tourism system.

Levels of adoption of IT in Latin America are low, and the lack of staff training is evident across many tourism sectors in many countries. There is a need for a sustained investment in human resources, especially the training of employees in IT-based processes. However, it is unlikely that Latin America will reach the level of penetration of the major generating countries from which it receives visitors, and the gaps in distribution systems might well retard development in the short term. The stronger economies of Argentina, Brazil, Chile and Mexico are embracing the communications revolution more readily, but elsewhere the pace of adoption is far slower. There is also a considerable gap between the capital and other major cities and the poorer rural regions of many Latin American countries.

7 *Addressing the 'North–South gap'*

McIntosh *et al.* (1995) point to the inadequacies of the tourism infrastructure in the South, which is often lacking, primarily because the resource base is vastly underfunded in comparison to that of the North.

There is also often a mis-match in terms of the visitor and the host community expectations from the tourism process and this inevitably leads to tensions that are represented, for example, in the form of petty crime, begging and gain through the informal economy.

The fundamental issue is whether tourism development in Latin America can help to bridge the gap between the wealthy nations and developing countries. The forms of tourism development most prevalent suggest not, for 'enclave' tourism is growing faster than other types of tourism in many countries. Furthermore, an evaluation of indicators of standards of living in Latin American signal that the poor are getting relatively poorer in relation to developed countries (Gwynne and Kay, 1999, p. 24). Tourism currently plays a small part in the overall economic process of Latin American economies, with the exception of Mexico, and therefore it is unlikely to meet the role ascribed to it by practitioners and academics.

8 *Shifting value systems*

Tourism could be viewed as a societal extravagance in relation to the core issues of sustainable development, global warming and the control of pollution. This type of value system could lead to a resistance to travel by some market segments. Furthermore, the propensity for people to spend a greater amount of time at home for leisure purposes might lead to a reduction of demand for travel (Cushman *et al.*, 1994). Given the nature of the global economy, and the transmission of such values by way of the media and internet, there could be a shift away from the current dominant value system which projects tourism as a good phenomenon to one which emphasizes the negative effects of travel.

While the explosion of leisure at home is a global trend, it has not yet retarded the growth of tourism. On the contrary, the potential for travel within Latin America as a region could be significant, possibly at a time when long haul tourism is fast reaching maturity. It is possible that more specialist forms of tourism such as eco- and adventure tourism will flourish but there is also no current evidence to support the view that beach tourism is in decline. Latin America is well positioned to gain from this if the natural and cultural assets, which are currently under threat, are managed with a view to a long-term horizon.

9 *Quest of stability and security*

The ninth *new horizon* relates to the way in which increases in crime, exposure to disease and sickness are of increasing concern to potential travellers. This also relates to ageing populations, and the consequent strains placed on medical systems, which in some cases can barely cope with demand.

As mentioned in the discussion of *new horizon 7*, the response in several Latin American countries has been to invest in 'enclave' tourism in order to meet the expectations of long haul visitors. This does not support the argument that tourism enables visitors and the host community to learn more about each other or to share common values. It is a divisive form of tourism development which reinforces the divide between the North and South. Adventure tourism is also packaged in a similar fashion, to the extent to which guides and other local staff have been increasingly equipped to avoid unwelcome aspects of petty crime and misdemeanour that might impinge on the enjoyment of their visitors.

10 *The knowledge-based society*

IT processes and knowledge-based environments might have two consequences. First, new media such as teleconferencing could have the effect of reducing travel. Secondly, knowledge-based employees might decide that travel brings too many risks.

The move towards technology-based production and a growth in the services sector during the latter part of the twentieth century has paralleled the rapid growth of tourism. The appeal to travel is strong within our cultures, and there is a desire to escape the world of work and urban living (Krippendorf, 1987). As yet, there is little evidence to suggest that there is a resistance to travel. People working in knowledge-based sectors might also wish to understand in more detail the nature of the destination being visited. The growth of mass tourism in Latin America indicates that for most visitors a holiday is no more than a temporal break from home life.

11 *Rise of the city state*

The rise of the city state refers to destination areas with high profiles. They will gain ascendancy in comparison to smaller destinations, especially those which do not exhibit strong appeal. The promotion of countries will in future be more selective, concentrating on destinations rather than on generalized country images. There could well be strategic alliances between city states if circumstances are appropriate, and where their tourism offerings are complementary.

This type of tourism destination promotion is very common in Latin America as governments and tourist associations have limited resources. Key destinations are featured, and invariably these are promoted in relation to major gateway cities. Alliances have been forged between several cities in offering multi-stage long haul holidays such as between Rio de Janeiro, Lima and Santiago de Chile.

One of the major problems in Latin American is that the gateway cities are very congested. Rural–urban migration between 1970 and 1990 brought increasing pressures to capitals or other major cities. The migrants brought strains to the overloaded infrastructure, and have for the most part been absorbed into the informal economy of begging, selling goods on the street and other activities. Many have joined the dispossessed of the peripheral shanty towns, such as the *favelas* of Rio de Janeiro, the *pueblos jovenes* of Lima. Greater tourist numbers have simply added to the problems faced by the cities.

12 *Pressures for population migration*

Nation states or single economic communities will become increasingly strict in terms of visitor entry in order to avoid illicit immigration. Conversely, migrants from previous generations will seek vacations that take them to their 'roots', to see relatives and to understand the ways of life of their parents' home country.

In Latin America, there was a considerable inward flow of migrants from other continents until the 1920s. Since then the pattern of international migration has been primarily intra-regional or to and from the USA (Chant, 1999). With regard to the latter this involves the neighbouring countries of Mexico and near islands of Cuba and the Dominican Republic. Illegal immigration across the border and by sea to Florida remains a fundamental issue of concern, although with the advent of the NAFTA, migrant issues between the USA and Mexico are increasingly less of an issue. Elsewhere, the main flows have been to Argentina and to a lesser extent Colombians migrating to Venezuela. In Central America Costa Rica has received cross-border migrants from El Salvador, Nicaragua and Panama. Chant notes that migration is determined mainly by economic reasons.

In several Latin American countries, border disputes over land have also been a major cause of illegal immigration, such as in Peru and Ecuador, Colombia and Venezuela. Countries are concerned about the smuggling of goods, especially narcotics across borders. In contrast the establishment of trading zones has brought a much more positive attitude towards cross-border tourism and this could be of benefit in future years.

SUMMARY

Pizam refers to a vision for the future of 2050 in which the tourist sector is 'vibrant, economically successful and innovative' (1999, p. 343). The future of tourism in Latin America will be determined by the extent to which suppliers and governmental organizations can respond to many of these new horizons envisaged by McIntosh, some of which are very pertinent to Latin America, others less so. However, there are a number of challenges which will not easily be overcome. They relate to the continued external forces of globalization which will impact more intensively and in a similar way on the indigenous tourism sector of each particular country. Those employed in the new internationally driven tourism ventures will be better trained, and enjoy an improved standard of living than their counterparts elsewhere. In other tourism sectors the lack of investment in both infrastructure and people will lead to a continued spiral of decline.

Other factors will affect the sector, namely the lack of infrastructure in Latin America's premier resorts and cities, and the spread of the informal economy, crime and poverty within these urban conglomerations. The WTO forecast previously referred to highlighted the lack of investment in infrastructure development as a major constraint on the growth of tourism in the Americas, concluding that there is 'Less-than-full provision of funding from capital markets for all the infrastructure and tourist facilities required to realise the total tourist potential of the region in the time period under review' (WTO, 1994, p. ix). The report highlighted air transport as being a particular problem:

> Transport infrastructure (especially airport capacity) limitations in several of the countries of the region and limited international and intraregional air services ... both of which may serve either to redirect tourist flows (possibly to destinations outside the region) or to prevent the full realisation of the region's tourist demand potential.
>
> (WTO, 1994, p. ix)

It is also the vast disparity of resources and skills between the wealthy and poor, and the unwillingness of governments to devote more resources to social care and education, that continues to increase regional and urban disparities despite patterns of growth (Batley, 1997). Within this overall context, it is difficult to predict how tourism can develop as a major sector, given demographic trends and labour market deficiencies in many Latin American countries. The development will therefore be erratic, and with an imbalance between countries. Argentina, Brazil, Chile and Mexico will advance more rapidly than other countries, where the gains are likely to be relatively partial.

The other major challenge will be sustainability. Latin American tourism destinations will continue to encourage greater numbers of visitors over the coming decades. If this can be achieved, by combining private sector innovation within a governmental planning framework, then tourism growth can be managed within the physical and social capacities of the location:

> the challenge is to pursue tourism growth in a manner resilient enough to respond positively to a changing global environment and social structure, while remaining compatible with the principles and practice of ecologically sustainable development.
>
> (Wahab and Pigram, 1997, p. 3)

The challenge is whether this can be achieved without compromising the rich diversity of sensitive cultures and landscapes which form the core appeal of this exceptional collection of tourism offerings.

REFERENCES

Alfonso, H. D. (1994) 'Cuba Between Utopia and the World Market: Notes For a Socialist Debate', *Latin American Perspectives*, Vol. 21(4), pp. 46–59.

Bar On, R. (1998) 'The Americas', *Tourism Economics*, Vol. 4(1), pp. 85–96.

Batley, R. (1997) 'Social Agency Versus Global Determination in Latin America', *Third World Planning Review*, Vol. 19(4), pp. 333–46.

Baum, T. (1995) 'Trends in International Tourism', *Insights*, 6 (March), pp. A117–20.

Bray, D. W. and Bray, M. W. (1998) 'Scholarship in the Age of Transperialism', *Latin American Perspectives*, Vol. 25 (November), pp. 32–7.

Bray, M. W. (1999) 'Trade as an Instrument of Dominance', *The Latin American Experience*, Vol. 26(5), pp. 55–74.

Chant, S. (1999) 'Population, Migration, Gender and Employment' in R. N. Gwynne and C. Kay (eds), *Latin America Transformed: Globalization and Modernity* (pp. 124–35), Edward Arnold, London.

Cooper, C., Fletcher, J., Gilbert, D. and Wanhill, S. (1998) *Tourism Principles and Practice*, Longman, London.

Cushman, G., Veal, A. J. and Zuzanek, J. (eds) (1996) *World Leisure Participation: Free Time in the Global Village*, CABI Publishing, Wallingford.

de Kadt, E. (ed.) (1979) *Tourism: Passport to Development?*, Oxford University Press, Oxford.

Distant Dreams (1999) *Distant Dreams: Worldwide Holidays, October 1999–December 2000*, Distant Dreams Ltd, Bromley.

Green, D. (1991) *Faces of Latin America*, Latin American Bureau, London.

Gunson, P. (1996) 'Marketing Men Put Curse of Tourism Industry on Mayas', *Guardian* (28 September).

Gwynne, R. N. and Kay, C. (1999) 'Latin America Transformed: Changing Paradigms, Debates and Alternatives' in R. N. Gwynne and C. Kay (eds), *Latin America Transformed: Globalization and Modernity* (pp. 2–29), Edward Arnold, London.

Hanlon. P. (1996) *Global Airlines: Competition in a Transnational Industry*, Butterworth-Heinemann, Oxford.

Harrison, D. (1988) *The Sociology of Modernization and Development*, Unwin Hyman, London.

Harrison, D. (ed.) (1992) *Tourism and the Less Developed Countries*, John Wiley, Chichester.

Jones, G. A. (1997) 'Junto Con Los Niños: Street Children in Mexico', *Development and Practice*, Vol. 1(1), pp. 39–49.

Kotler, P., Bowen, J. and Makens, J. (1996) *Marketing for Hospitality and Tourism*, Prentice Hall, Englewood Cliffs, NJ.

Krippendorf, J. (1987) *The Holiday Makers: Understanding the Impact of Leisure and Travel*, Butterworth-Heinemann, Oxford.

Larraín, J. (1996) *Modernidad, Razón e Identidad en América Latina*, Andrés Bello, Santiago de Chile.

Levitt, T. (1983) 'The Globalization of Markets', *Harvard Business Review*, Vol. 61(3), pp. 92–102.

Lloyd-Sherlock, P. (1997) 'Policy, Distribution and Poverty in Argentina since Redemocratisation', *Latin American Perspectives*, Vol. 24(6), pp. 22–55.

Lumsdon, L. M. (1997) *Tourism Marketing*, International Thompson Business Press, London.

Lumsdon, L. M. and Swift, J. S. (1994) 'Latin American Tourism: The Dilemmas of the 21st Century' in A. V. Seaton (ed.), *Tourism: The State of the Art* (pp. 359–65), John Wiley, Chichester.

Lundberg, D. E., Stavenga, M. H. and Krishnamoorthy, M. (1995) *Tourism Economics*, John Wiley, New York.

Macdonald, G. J., Nielson, D. L. and Stern, M. N. (eds) (1997) *Latin American Environmental Policy in International Perspective*, Westview, Boulder, Colo.

McIntosh, R. W., Goeldner, C. R. and Ritchie, J. R. B. (1995) *Tourism, Principles, Practices, Philosophies*, John Wiley, New York.

Mader, R. (1999) 'Ecotourism Research and Promotion on the Web: Experiences and Insights', *International Journal of Contemporary Hospitality Management*, Vol. 11(2/3), pp. 164–81.

Morley, S. (1995) *Poverty and Inequality in Latin America*, Johns Hopkins University Press, Washington.

Mowforth, M. and Munt, I. (1998) *Tourism and Sustainability*, Routledge, London.

O'Hare, G. and Barrett, H. (1999) 'Regional Inequalities in the Peruvian Tourist Industry', *The Geographical Journal*, Vol. 165(1), pp. 47–61.

Ortiz, M. F. (1990) 'A Global Perspective and Case Studies of Sustainable Development in Latin America', *RSA Journal*, Vol. CXXXXVIII(5405), pp. 154–62.

Parker, D. (1998) 'The Cuban Crisis and the Future of the Revolution: A Latin American Perspective', *Latin American Research Review*, Vol. 33(1), pp. 239–56.

Peeler, J. (1998) *Building Democracy in Latin America*, Lynne Reinner, London.

Pizam, A. (1999) 'Life and Tourism in the Year 2050', *Hospitality Management*, Vol. 18, pp. 331–43.

Poon, A. (1993) *Tourism, Technology and Competitive Strategies*, CAB International, Wallingford.

Rangan, S. (1999) 'Seven Myths to Ponder Before Going Global', *Financial Times* (29 November).

Ritchie, J. R. B. (1991) 'Global Tourism Policy Issues: An Agenda for the 1990s', *World Travel and Tourism Review*, Vol. 1, pp. 8–17.

Robinson, W. I. (1998) '(Mal)Development in Central America: Globalisation and Social Change', *Development and Change*, Vol. 29, pp. 467–97.

Ryan, C. (1991) *Recreational Tourism: A Social Science Perspective*, Routledge, London.

Schmink, M. and Wood, C. (1992) *Contested Frontiers in Amazonia*, Columbia University Press, New York.

Schor, J. B. (1991) *The Overworked American: The Unexpected Decline of Leisure*, Basic Books, New York.

Scott, C. (1996) 'The Distributive Impact of the New Economic Model in Chile' in V. Bulmer-Thomas (ed.), *The New Economic Model in Latin America and Its Impact on Income Distribution and Poverty* (pp. 346–62), Macmillan, London.

Shaw, G. and Williams, A. M. (1994) *Critical Issues in Tourism: A Geographical Perspective,* Basil Blackwell, Oxford.

Smith, V. (ed.) (1989) *Hosts and Guests: The Anthropology of Tourism,* University of Pennsylvania Press, Philadelphia.

Smith, W. C., Acuña, C. H. and Gamarra, E. A. (1994) *Latin American Political Economy in the Age of Neoliberal Reform: Theoretical and Comparative Perspectives for the 1990s,* New Brunswick, NJ.

Swift, J. S. and Dueñas, A. (1995) 'Amenazas y Oportuinidades en el Entorno Comercial a Fines del Siglo Veinte: El Papel de Marketing', *Mercadeo & Desarrollo (Bogota),* Año 10(18), pp. 20–7.

Tse, E. and West, J. (1992) 'Development Strategies for International Tourism Hospitality Markets' in R. Teare and M. Olsen (eds), *International Hospitality Management: Corporate Strategy in Practice* (pp. 20–33), Pitman, London.

Valverde, G. A. (1999) 'Democracy, Human Rights and Development Assistance for Education: The USAID and World Bank in Latin America and the Caribbean', *Economic Development and Cultural Change,* Vol. 147(2), pp. 401–7.

Wahab, S. and Pigram, J. J. (1997) 'Sustainable Tourism in a Changing World' in S. Wahab and J. J. Pigram (eds), *Tourism Development and Growth,* Routledge, London.

Waters, M. (1995) *Globalisation,* Routledge, London.

Wheeller, B. (1991) 'Tourism's Troubled Times: Responsible Tourism is Not the Answer', *Tourism Management,* June, pp. 91–6.

Wolf, M. (1999) 'Of Tuna, Turtles and Red Herrings', *Financial Times* (17 November).

World Travel and Tourism Council (1996) Personal communication with authors.

WTO (1994) Data supplied by Division of Economics & Market Research, World Tourism Organization, Madrid.

Name Index

Subject Index

Page references followed by t refer to tables and page references followed by f refer to figures.